-

HIGHLANDERS

A History of Heathwood Hall
Episcopal School
1951–2021

TREY POPP

First Edition
For information, address Heathwood Hall Episcopal School,
3000 South Beltline Blvd., Columbia, SC 29201

The text of this book is composed in Caslon
Manufacturing by Ingram Spark
Book design by William Sulit

Library of Congress Cataloging-in-Publication Data

Names: Popp, Trey, author.
Title: Highlanders : A History of Heathwood Hall Episcopal School,
1951–2021 / Trey Popp; with commentary by Walter Edgar.
Description: First edition. Includes bibliographical references.
Identifiers: Library of Congress Control Number: 2021924700 |
ISBN 978-0-578-33959-7 (hardcover)

Subjects: 1. Education—History—United States. | 2. Private schools—South
Carolina—Columbia—History—20th century and 21st century. | 3. School
integration—United States—History—20th century. | 4. School integration—South
Carolina—Columbia—History—20th century. | 5. Episcopalian church—South
Carolina—History.

Cover illustration by Mary Bentz Gilkerson

To my teachers—you know who you are.

CONTENTS

FORWARD
by Walter Edgar

In the United States in 2021, it is considered proper that individuals follow the practice of full disclosure. Therefore, I freely admit that for more than 40 years I have had almost a continuous personal connection with Heathwood Hall Episcopal School. Daughter Eliza Edgar '92 entered K-5 in 1979 and grandson Stuart Williams graduated in 2018. In between, like other parents and grandparents, I became an involved member of the Heathwood community as a volunteer and as a trustee. That said, I read *Highlanders: A History of Heathwood Hall, 1951-2021* as I would read any other work of local history.

In 1783, French historian and philosopher the Abbé de Mably wrote to John Adams, one of our nation's Founding Fathers, asking for his guidance on doing research on the American Revolution and the creation of the new United States. In his reply, Adams noted that in order to pursue the subject, de Mably needed to understand the "History of the Colonies" from their beginnings. Furthermore, when the Frenchman began looking at the colonies, he needed to focus on four principal institutions: towns, churches, schools, and the militia. Two centuries later, noted American historian Michael Kammen gave the same advice to a gathering at the National Archives.

For more than a half-century as a student of South Carolina history, I have found this advice to be particularly useful. For in order to understand our state, you have to examine its institutions. However, there is a caveat when using institutional histories. Are they isolated stories? Or do the authors place their institutions in context?

History matters. And it should matter. What a community is in 2021 didn't just drop out of the sky. Its population, its attitudes, its governance are sometimes the result of actions and decisions made by others during the course of its existence—be that three years or 300 years. The Columbia of 2021 is a different place from the Columbia of 1790 or the Columbia of 1963.

The same historic framework applies to institutions. The Heathwood Hall of 2021 is a different school from the Heathwood Hall of 1951 and the Heathwood Hall of 1974. Yet there is a continuity—a linkage—connecting the iterations of Heathwood Hall over the 70 years of its existence. And the decisions that shaped the school were influenced by events occurring outside the classroom and boardroom.

In this splendidly researched history of Heathwood Hall, Trey Popp '93 has woven the development of the school within the context of the larger history of Columbia and South Carolina. Through the skillful use of traditional historical sources enlivened by interviews with former students, parents, and teachers, he has compiled a lively narrative. More importantly, he has been willing to tell the whole story—not a varnished version. The school has had challenges, some from within and some from without. However, because of the sense of community—the *esprit de corps*—that has been a touchstone of the Heathwood family since its founding, Heathwood Hall has been able to surmount those challenges and move on.

Walter Edgar
Author of *South Carolina: A History*

PREFACE
Cast of Characters

Norrie Nicholson Cooper would remember learning to read through the heart-thump rhythms of Henry Wadsworth Longfellow, whose verse she encountered in a pearl white manor where the bathrooms featured claw-foot tubs. These were the earliest days of school at Heathwood Hall, when neighborhood children could almost still smell the burros that had lately traipsed over the Manning family's grounds at the old Heath Mansion, to be ridden by guests who cared or dared to. Gayle Boineau Darby would recall the camellia blossoms and mid-1950s Easter egg hunts, and singing "Day by Day" in the chapel that had been fashioned out of a spacious second-floor hall. Susan Milliken Umbach would remember sealing friendships in the colossal concrete tubes turned upon their sides out beyond the sandbox—"you would go in there to tell a secret"—and the sweet smile of Coles Cathcart, whose religion classes dispensed with rote recitals in favor of art projects that made it fun no matter how much or little of the Bible a particular pupil craved. "She loved every child who came through there."

So did Page Steinert—Ms. Page—who was cherished in turn by far too many kindergartners to list even the barest fraction here, for she saw that of God in every one of them, and would have recoiled from the thought of a roster containing any fewer than all of their names.

Clinch Belser would remember asking if there might be a way he and his classmates could play basketball at recess—and marveling at the power of his question to cause the erection of a hoop over a flat patch of grass.

Kickball would stand out most vividly in Michael Perry's memory—in fact a single kick, which sent the ball into the backyard of a singularly daunting neighbor. "Now there's a fellow over there, very famous, and he's a big segregationist," Perry had been warned by his father—who was famous in his own right as a legal pioneer in the civil rights movement. So as young boys do, Michael made it his goal to kick a ball over the wall belonging to former South Carolina governor Jimmy Byrnes. "So that I would be able to climb up it and see if I could see anything," he would explain many years later. And he did. He saw Jimmy Byrnes in a wheelchair, attended by an "elderly, stately looking Black man"—that being Willie Byrd, Byrnes' longtime chauffeur. And there transpired a moment at once banal and unforgettable to a Black child born into the final throes of the Jim Crow South. The governor and the gradeschool boy locked eyes from across the walled divide. "I saw him and he saw me," Perry would recall. "And he told the man, 'Well, go ahead and get him his ball.'"

Kevin Dickey—a son of another famous man, the poet and novelist James Dickey—remembered taking Latin in sixth grade: "a great thing," he would come to think, for a young person bound for a career in medicine. A survey of his memories would also surface the wooden paddle that hung in Mrs. Nuckols' math classroom, branded with stern letters reading BOARD OF EDUCATION. "As if it was going to be used for some kind of corporal punishment," Dickey later laughed, noting that to his knowledge its deployment was limited to the purpose of deadpan humor.

Deep into his adulthood, Steven Larkin would carry Mrs. Nuckols' mathematical admonition that no matter what else happens in life, "the numbers do not change." This lesson he would learn well enough, coupled with his reputation as a straight shooter, to be elected treasurer of the student council. And that victory carried special significance for a boy who most afternoons took the city bus back to his home in Waverly. "I got almost 100 percent of the white vote!" he would cackle with delight decades down the line.

His supporters surely would have included Will Prioleau, who has never forgotten the culmination of an unsanctioned boxing tournament the boys organized one fateful lunch hour. "Steven and I were the two best athletes at Heathwood Hall," Prioleau would recall, and so it was perhaps inevitable that they would be the last pair standing. As the championship bout loomed, their classmate Richard Allen Green asked Steven the question on every last boy's mind. "So: you and Prioleau. Who's going to win?" A quaver jellied Prioleau's spine. "Steven looked at me and I was scared," he would recount. "He was tough. The fact was, I was the second-best athlete at Heathwood. He was the best. And Steven paused, and then he said, 'Me and Prioleau don't fight.' And I knew then: that dude's my friend for life."

Everyone in those days would remember the regal bearing and fierce protectiveness of headmistress Elsie Lamar. Just as everyone would reminisce about Janie Green—Ms. Janie—selling chocolate milk and Lance crackers to go along with the children's brown bag lunches. And everyone would retain melodies and lyrics beyond counting from the music lessons of Nell Mellichamp.

Later, Leslie Haynsworth would remember learning to read in the mansion's pre-fab classroom annex, and then practicing in the afternoons on gas-station billboards as her mother waited in line during the Oil Shock of 1973. Then it would suddenly be February 5, 1974, and Leslie found herself riding with Chalmers Poston in a car driven by headmaster Earl Devanny—"a distant figure but not a scary one"—out to the east bank of the Congaree River, where they plunged a shovel into a soybean field to break ground on a new campus.

Thus Claudia Barton went from gazing at the ornamental plaster in the mansion's old dining room to a 133-acre blank slate where she would become one of the first girls to don a Heathwood basketball jersey in an actual indoor gym. "Periodically disguised as our chapel, assembly hall, theatre, 'workshop,' and auditorium"—as the editors of the 1975 yearbook described it—the gym was "equipped with a roll-away altar, and bleachers that double as pews."

Landing on the new campus in a windfall of bow-tied plaid, Jim Gasque toiled in the gardens of high-school prose, prodding his pupils to replace mere daffodils with stargazer lilies and ballerina orchids, while yanking out adverbs like vile weeds.

In those days "the farmland came right up to the back of the swing set," Wade Mullins would recollect, and parents hung their hopes for mosquito control in the form of bird boxes to shelter purple martins—

whose initial population, bug-hounded Highlanders would later jest, may possibly have eaten itself to death.

But bird boxes were just the beginning. Tuition-paying volunteers pushed wheelbarrows while their children sowed the barren clay with loblolly pine seedlings—barely imagining the possibility that these would one day conceal the entire campus from the ribbon of highway that would soon extend Interstate 77 a scant mile from the school's southern flank. What the board members and parents did during that era was crystal clear to young Anna Ponder: "They carved the school out of almost nothing."

The flood of 1976 swamped their good work but not their resolve. They weren't always sure what they were making, but creation was an unending process, not a single act.

"Everything was so new, nobody completely knew what they were doing," August Krickel would reflect. The question was not what they wanted, but how to bring it about. So they asked themselves: "If we were a great school, what would we do?" And answered with experiments. "Well, maybe we would have something beyond geometry—maybe we would let kids take trigonometry and calculus if they wanted to. Maybe we could let them take a second year of chemistry, if they wanted to. Maybe some random kid wants to take a fourth year of Latin—well, if some teacher's crazy enough to teach him, why not let him?

"There were an awful lot of things like that," Krickel recounted: "Let's just try for a first time and see if it works. And miraculously, it did."

Just who was crazy enough to quadruple down on Latin, the documentary record does not reveal. But soon Robert Shirley became headmaster, and the experimentation accelerated. "We kept children moving," recalled Lower School principal Margaret Adams. "So if you knew your math, we moved you to the next grade level ... You didn't have to sit and wait for everybody. So you had fifth graders who went to sixth grade for math. We had a second grader who went up to fourth grade for math." (But woe to the student sent to "Dr A." for disrupting class, to be handed a dreaded trash bag and charged with cleaning up messes rather than making them.)

As in academics, so in extracurriculars. Thus when Ryan Waldron failed to make the varsity on the strength of basketball obsession alone, he pitched the powers-that-be on commandeering the public-address system to call the games like a Carolina Coliseum announcer. And just like that, the gym rafters began to reverberate with an inimitable voice: "Good evening, ladies and gentlemen," he would begin, before dramatically sliding up and down an octave: "and … welcome to the Carpet Dome!"

A revitalized progressive rigor spread through the classrooms, while who could guess what might crop out outside of them. Eric Sribnick lip-synched to a faux children's song titled "Let's Talk Dirty to the Animals" at the Mr. Highlander Pageant. W.D. Morris nailed a buzzer-beating jumper from the elbow to clinch a state championship. Josh Lieb, long before he would write for *The Simpsons* and cart home a bucketful of Emmy Awards behind the scenes of *The Daily Show with Jon Stewart*, delivered a diaphragm-rupturing campaign speech for student council that would remain unsurpassed until his 2009 book *I Am a Genius of Unspeakable Evil and I Want to Be Your Class President*.

Having turned the page on its original incarnation as a K-4 elementary school where tiny classes met in former bedrooms, Heathwood became a K-12 institution distinguished by cross-class camaraderie. One Lower School cohort lived for the surprise appearances of Chip Duffie—whose high school break schedule, one suspects in retrospect, must have been short on attended study halls. A decade later, a steady stream of second graders with loose lower incisors would find their way to Michael Popp, a Middle Schooler whose magical tooth-pulling prowess rivaled that of Ms. Page. By twists and turns the spirit animating the all-school Highlander Games would morph into traditions like Book Buddies, which found seventh graders reading aloud to first graders who hung on every word. Stan Wood trained high-schoolers to belay smaller children across the obstacles of the PEAK ropes course. Rites of passage knit the classes together in other ways: "Lessons and Carols" at Trinity Cathedral; the annual seventh-grade camping trip; the senior-class service trip to Johns Island; re-enactments of the 1914 Christmas Truce during World War I, centered on a student-built trench modeled after the Western Front.

Yet despite the tendency of school memories to grow more vivid with every step away from an actual blackboard—or marker board, or overhead projector, or digital smart board—plenty of Heathwood students would also take their first steps toward fulfilling careers.

"I wasn't a doctor's child, or a lawyer's child, and I didn't live in Heathwood or Spring Valley, so that was a little imposing for me," recalled Sarah Sturtevant, whose father was an Episcopal priest. "But I believe it was because of Heathwood that I was able to get into Clemson—and get out of Clemson in four years," and go on to a lifelong vocation as a nurse. Duncan Belser would undertake a senior-year "exhibition of mastery" applying cutting-edge computing techniques to his own original translation of the third book of Virgil's *Aeneid*—leading to a job offer from an audience member that would become the first step in a long career in digital technology. Nate Terracio would pivot from laboratory-grade science fair projects to drama productions on the stage and behind it—cultivating the taste and technical chops that would lead him to Jazz at Lincoln Center on his way to the directorship of Columbia's Koger Center for the Arts. A'ja Wilson would break her arm but insist on running suicide sprints alongside her basketball teammates, cast swinging, honing leadership qualities that would one day be honored with the WNBA's Most Valuable Player award.

Sometimes the through-line was more complicated. Sometimes the journey was fraught. Charlice Hurst would seethe at her mother for sending her to Heathwood, where she felt cut off from Black intellectual culture and alienated by her lack of wealth in a place that overflowed with it. But even a student who felt out of place could find the space to grow, and to become. "I got to try on a lot of different identities," she would recall. Meanwhile Lark Palma would emerge as a formative faculty influence, Jim Gasque would champion her writing, and she would deliver a self-guided senior capstone project on the teaching of African American history and literature that would alter the way Bob Shirley approached the subject for the remainder of his career in education.

And here we arrive at the fundamental truth about any school. "The buildings are important," as Noble Cooper would put it. "The curriculum is very important. But at the end of the day, it's the students you interact with each day that really transform you."

Seventy years after its founding, multiple generations have passed through Heathwood Hall. In one sense, the school is a common touchstone that binds them all. Yet in another and perhaps truer sense, the experience of every single cohort is particular to it alone. The Heath Mansion, felled by the wrecking ball in 1975, had all the solidity of hearsay to the Class of 1990. Who among the Class of 1995 could have dreamed up the existence—just a few years before—of a Smokers' Table available to high-schoolers whose parents had signed a cigarette-burning permission slip? It would have been no more believable than the outlandish claim that high-schoolers had once driven Heathwood's buses. Did anyone in the Class of 2005 know of Coach Cy Szakacsi, whose 800-plus victories on the hardwood and the baseball diamond were surpassed only by his legendarily unprintable huddle harangues? (Ask Bob Haarlow, who was sent by Margaret Adams to spy on him.) Who among the Class of 2010 could envision the novelty that lived in the 5.25-inch floppy disks that Bill Cherry taught their forebears how to slip into the humming drive of an Apple II? (Oregon Trail, 1848. One of the oxen is injured. Juliet has cholera. Inadequate grass. Press #8 to hunt for food!) When the Class of 2016 celebrated Rip Blackstone's selection as SCISA Teacher of the Year, did any of them know how the 25-year fixture of Heathwood's mathematics program first appeared to the freshmen of 1989—as a lawyer attacking career doldrums with maniacal full-court pressure in some of the most joyously coached junior-varsity basketball ever played?

Heathwood Hall's 21st-century alumni could scarcely imagine the decade when their school first took shape, hemmed in by the stark inequities of Jim Crow segregation. Nor could any student from Heathwood's first 69 years conjure up what their successors would confront in the 70th as pandemic respiratory disease overwhelmed morgues across the globe.

So a history of Heathwood Hall must be many things at once: a reacquaintance with careworn memories that doubles as a journey of discovery and revelation; an account of teachers and curricula that recognizes that every school's inner life resides ultimately in its students; a tapestry of satisfactions and shortfalls, continuities and disruptions, pain and achievement. It must take stock of the societal dynamics that have influenced the school's evolution, and ways the school in turn has contributed to the city's growth. Members of Heathwood Hall's extended family may see themselves reflected in its story, but must also be given a second chance to recognize perspectives that may have eluded them the first time around. And for any educational institution worth its salt, a history must challenge and reward its readers with opportunities to learn.

INTRODUCTION
Ninety Candles

It was the first Saturday of May, 1969, and the students of Heathwood Hall wore spotless Sunday clothes. Gathered alongside their teachers a short walk west of the Greek Revival school mansion where they spent their weekdays, boys and girls in knee socks, button-up shirts, and summer dresses waited to witness a spectacle without precedent in Columbia's Heathwood neighborhood. One of the school's next-door neighbors was celebrating his birthday and wedding anniversary, which fell on the same day, and President Richard M. Nixon was scheduled to join the Heathwood students for singing and cake.

The neighbor was former South Carolina Governor James F. "Jimmy" Byrnes, a man of unmatched political achievements in the state's 20th-century history, and rivaled only by John C. Calhoun on a longer timescale. After serving in both the US House of Representatives and the Senate between 1910 and 1941, Byrnes won an appointment to the US Supreme Court—only to step down at the conclusion of a single term after the United States entered World War II. Shifting to the executive branch as the inaugural Director of Economic Stabilization and then head of War Mobilization under Franklin D. Roosevelt, Byrnes exercised such sweeping authority over domestic affairs that he became known as the "assistant president"—which Roosevelt acknowledged "comes close to the truth." The Charleston native then became Harry S. Truman's Secretary of State, whereupon he played an instrumental role in the decision to detonate atomic bombs over the Japanese cities of Hiroshima and Nagasaki without warning. When Byrnes was sworn in as South Carolina's governor in 1951, he thus became one of only three individuals in American history to have served in the top tier of all three branches of US government and also as chief executive of a state.[1]

On this day Byrnes was accomplishing the more idiosyncratic feat of celebrating his 90th birthday on the 87th anniversary of his birth. As a young man he had claimed his older sister Leonore's birth date as his own in order to obtain his first government job as a court stenographer. The alteration, which added exactly three years to his age, would persist in public records for the rest of his life. His marriage to Maude Busch Byrnes, however, was the real thing: they had wed on the bridegroom's birthday 63 years before, in 1906.[2]

If Jimmy Byrnes was more familiar to Heathwood's students as the dog-loving retiree whose back wall formed a boundary for their kick-ball games, they doubtless regarded Richard Nixon with that special mixture of mystery and veneration that sitting presidents have traditionally inspired in American schoolchildren. So it was for the president that the children waited.

And waited. And waited.

"I just hated to wait," recalled second grader Karen Ibach in a thank-you note later sent to the Byrneses. "I was burning up a storm." She went on, deploying age-appropriate syntax and spelling: "When I heard it was about 11:30 I said 'Hurry up Nixon! If I new that I would have to wait this long I would not of come here.'"[3]

Although the *Columbia Record* would later deem the weather to have been "perfect,"[4] Karen was not alone in complaining about the heat. "It was so hot my friend Anne almost fainted," wrote Penelope Jones, another pupil in Mrs. L. W. Heriot's second-grade section. "When I got home, I slept until 6. Now isn't that something?"

Anne Witten, for her part, graciously elided her purported near-fainting spell in her own letter. "Thank you for letting us come to your house to see President Nixon," she wrote. "It is the first tine [sic] I have ever seen Nixon. It was a special day for me. Thank you for the cake. I loved the cake."

All three girls had better luck than their classmate Frank McCrory. "Thank you for asking Heathwood Hall to come and see Nixon," he wrote to the former governor. "But one thing, 'I didn't see him'! I didn't see him because there was too much of a crowd. Also somebody soct me in the

Page Steinert and students greet Richard and Pat Nixon in 1969.

'stomach'! So I kept trying to get through the croud, but I never made it." Nevertheless, he signed his letter "Love, Frankie."

And even Karen, despite all that waiting, gushed, "When I saw Nixon I just bursst! ... I hated waiting but I loved to see Nixon. I really enjoyed it, Gov. Byrnes! And I loved the cake you sent us," she added—echoing another common theme—"Thank you!"

Richard Nixon left a minimal record about the occasion. The White House official daily diary noted that between 11:35 and 11:40 a.m., "Before entering the Byrnes' residence, the President shook hands with children from Heathrow Hall [sic]."[5] But as the owner of a politician's heart, he presumably would have been cheered by the poster held aloft by several pupils[6] scrummed around Ms. Page Steinert within arm's reach of the President and First Lady as they engaged with the crowd. It read in full: OUR 1ST GRADE VOTED 17 TO 3 IN FAVOR OF NIXON.

First graders, of course, only vote in mock elections. And first graders anticipating a presidential visit are liable to take that audience into account when memorializing their votes on a poster, particularly if they have been well-trained in Southern politesse. Nevertheless this placard merits scrutiny, for like much else about the occasion where it was displayed—and the late-1960s tumult that surrounded Nixon's election—it reveals more than first meets the eye.

To a student of US history, one remarkable thing about the first grade's 17-3 vote tally would be its lack of a third column. The 1968 presidential election was a three-way race: Nixon was the Republican nominee, Hubert Humphrey the Democrat, and George Wallace won five Southern states as a third-party candidate who campaigned against racial integration. To a student of South Carolina history, a further question might occur: Which candidate had attracted the three losing votes in this strikingly lopsided contest? In 1968 Nixon became the first Republican since the end of Reconstruction in 1877 to secure South Carolina's electoral votes while winning the White House—but he did so by collecting just 38 percent of the state's popular vote, and Wallace was the runner-up with 32 percent.

Insofar as elementary-school mock elections tend to reflect the political preferences of pupils' parents, Nixon's margin of victory among Heathwood's first graders is less surprising. In Columbia's Ward 16, where the school was located and many of its families lived, Nixon won nearly 80 percent of the vote.[7] Wallace suffered a definitive rejection in this part of the city, where he trailed Humphrey by a large margin.

Nixon owed his strength in such wards—and his victory in South Carolina—in no small part to Jimmy Byrnes. Indeed, that was why the president had planned this two-and-a-half-hour stop in Columbia on his way to attend the Kentucky Derby: to honor a promise he had made to Byrnes for his help during the campaign.

Jimmy Byrnes had actually been a source of aid since Nixon's first presidential run in 1960. In September of that year, the man who had risen to political distinction as a New Deal Democrat became one of the first prominent Southern politicians—and the first South Carolina governor since the withdrawal of federal troops at the end of Reconstruction—to publicly endorse a Republican for president.[8] That was not enough to propel Nixon past John F. Kennedy in a very close election—a loss that Byrnes attributed, in a letter to Nixon, to a public pledge made by the Republican vice presidential candidate Henry Cabot Lodge in North Carolina that a Nixon administration would reserve a cabinet position for a Black[9] appointee. Byrnes judged that promise to have been fatal to the GOP's performance among white voters below the Mason-Dixon Line.[10] In 1968 Nixon took care not to make the same mistake—and Byrnes and his Palmetto State allies would leverage the intense passions surrounding school desegregation to turn the tide.

This is a discomfiting history, but the story of Heathwood Hall is impossible to understand without examining the social and political context in which the school took shape.

The Democratic Party's 88-year dominance of the South had begun to fray in 1964, when GOP candidate Barry Goldwater won five states in Dixie (and only one other, his home state of Arizona). But the challenge Nixon faced in 1968 was to limit the defection of white Southerners to Wallace, whose strength in the South was augmented by blue-collar support in the industrial Midwest. Through the summer of that year Wallace steadily gained ground in Gallup's national polls,[11] consistently leading outright in the 13-state region of the South.[12] By the second half of September, the Nixon campaign projected that Wallace would win seven Southern states including both Carolinas.[13] That would have been enough, when combined with razor-thin margins in several other states, to potentially prevent any candidate from achieving an Electoral College majority.[14]

This was precisely the kind of needle Byrnes had threaded throughout his career. In the hotly contested white-only primary elections of South Carolina's Democratic Party in the early 20th century—where triumph effectively guaranteed victory in the general election—Byrnes had mastered the art of letting his opponents joust for recognition as the fiercest racial demagogue, while presenting himself as a reliable segregationist who preferred to focus on kitchen-table issues.[15]

In September and October of 1968, Nixon borrowed a page from this "sage political wizard,"[16] as Byrnes was dubbed by campaign strategist Harry S. Dent, a fellow South Carolinian who became known as the architect of the GOP's Southern strategy. The issue he chose was schooling.

Despite the Supreme Court's integration order in *Brown v. Board of Education II* (1955),[17] public schools remained segregated across vast swaths of the South into the 1960s. No state resisted integrating public educational institutions longer than South Carolina—where the litigation leading to *Brown* had begun, in Clarendon County, as *Briggs v. Elliott*.[18] As governor, Byrnes retained one of the country's top lawyers to defend school segregation in *Brown*,[19] lobbied former colleagues on the Court to rule against the plaintiffs,[20] and threatened to "abandon the public school system"[21] rather than submit to integration.[22]

South Carolina's dam of resistance broke in 1963, when a series of legal challenges led to the admission of Harvey Gantt to Clemson College.[23] Later that year civil rights litigation forced Charleston County's school board to admit 11 African American students to what had been white-only public schools.[24] Yet as other counties gradually followed suit, a common template emerged across the South: so-called "freedom-of-choice" plans that permitted students to transfer to other schools within their district, but did not require districts to fully racially integrate their schools, or to replace the dual system of racially based schools with a unitary system for children of all colors. Since virtually no white parents opted their children into Black schools, and social intimidation severely limited the number of Black parents willing to thrust their children into white ones, the result was barely any integration at all. In the 1965-66 school year, 98.5 percent of the African American students in South Carolina still attended schools containing no white students.[25]

Yet even that was more than a growing number of white Southern families could bear. So as public school desegregation inched forward, private schools proliferated as a means to keep Black children out of white classrooms. Between 1964 and 1967, 32 private schools opened in South Carolina—all of them racially segregated.[26] The trend would continue. By 1977, nearly 200 new private or church-related schools would begin operation in South Carolina,[27] the overwhelming majority for white students. The most prominent example in Columbia was Hammond Academy, named after the 19th-century planter, politician, and outspoken slavery advocate James Henry Hammond. It was founded in 1966 and experienced a sharp surge in enrollment in 1968 after the Columbia Public School Board announced plans to geographically zone the city's elementary schools as a means to desegregate them.[28]

Resistance to school integration by white citizens, in other words, was both strong and effective. In response, the US Department of Health, Education and Welfare (HEW) under President Lyndon Johnson had begun using Title VI of the Civil Rights Act of 1964 to withhold federal funds from Southern school districts that refused to issue comprehensive plans for integration.[29] Hubert Humphrey backed that approach—which gave Nixon an opening. In a TV interview in Charlotte in mid-September of 1968, Nixon came out firmly against HEW's stance, and added that he had no timetable for nationwide school integration[30]—which the Supreme Court had unanimously ordered to be carried out with "all deliberate speed" 13 years before.[31]

Nixon's stance, cloaked in the language of government overreach, soothed white Southern anxieties without shocking the conscience in the manner of George Wallace's notorious "Stand in the Schoolhouse Door." (Promising "segregation now, segregation tomorrow, segregation forever" as Alabama's governor, Wallace had tried to physically block the entry of two African American students into the University of Alabama in 1963.) Nixon's victory in the general election, combined with Wallace's extraordinary performance in the South, testified to the apprehension felt by many Americans about changes to the status quo.[32]

Those changes and the apprehension they caused were hardly limited to the realm of election-campaign machinations. The same day the *Columbia Record* published a photograph of the Nixons mingling with Heathwood students at Byrnes' birthday party, the newspaper's lead local news story concerned the not-guilty plea entered by nine state patrolmen charged with violating the civil rights of Black demonstrators shot in the "Orangeburg Massacre." In early February of 1968, a series of protests that had begun with a peaceful attempt to desegregate a bowling alley culminated in a rowdier demonstration on the campus of South Carolina State College in Orangeburg, where police opened fire on a crowd of unarmed students, killing three teenagers and wounding 27—many of whom were shot in the back while attempting to flee. Two months later the Rev. Martin Luther King Jr. was assassinated in Memphis, Tennessee. And although South Carolina would largely avoid confrontations on the scale of the 1957 armed standoff in Little Rock, Arkansas, or Wallace's 1963 stand against the National Guard in Alabama, tensions surrounding school integration would occasionally boil over in violence. In the spring of 1970, two buses carrying African American elementary and high school students to newly desegregated schools in Lamar, South Carolina, were stormed by roughly 175 white parents wielding ax handles, bricks, baseball bats, and lengths of heavy chain. The mob smashed the windows, shattering glass that injured some of the children trapped inside, and overturned the vehicles before a small army of police drove them away with tear gas.[33]

So as Heathwood's elementary-grade students stood upon Jimmy Byrnes' lawn in church attire that spring Saturday in 1969, the country around them roiled with racial unrest and retrenchment. Which made another fact about their school all the more remarkable, particularly given the dominant trajectory of private education in the state: Heathwood Hall had definitively embraced integration four years before.

Heathwood Hall Episcopal School was established in 1951 as an independent school under the aegis of the Episcopal Diocese of Upper South Carolina. It began by enrolling boys and girls in kindergarten through fourth grade. At its founding, the school framed its mission in explicitly religious terms. "The first value of a church school is the thoroughness of instruction which young people will receive," explained Col. Wyndam Manning, vice president of Heathwood's inaugural executive committee. "The religious training received is important because that which they receive only on Sunday is not enough."[34]

But by 1969, the school had become a qualitatively different institution of learning. It now educated children through sixth grade and was considering further expansion. Though it remained in the Heath Mansion, the school's trustees were increasingly focused on acquiring property capable of supporting a far more ambitious campus.[35] The character of Heathwood's religious orientation had also evolved. The Rev. Richard Nevius, who became headmaster in 1969 and projected

A page from the 1969 yearbook.

a distinctly intellectual (and liberal) brand of Episcopalianism, articulated the change in a speech given that year. "Part of our self-image at Heathwood Hall has always been, in a sense, that we are 'a public school annex where prayers can be said.' Such an image is useful if it serves to keep us aware of what is going on in the main stream of American education. But if such an image means that we are content to 'tag along' behind public schools, then it is time we remind ourselves that we are really part of the great tradition of independent schools, and it is to the beat of that drum that we should be marching." Noting that Heathwood belonged to the National Association of Episcopal Schools, Nevius advocated joining the National Association of Independent Schools.[36]

The most momentous change, however, was Heathwood's decision in 1965 to admit children without regard to racial identification. In its first 14 years, the school had exclusively enrolled white children. The reversal of that policy, and the embrace of integration, distinguished Heathwood from its peer institutions in the South Carolina Midlands,[37] many of which would remain segregated into the 1980s. By the time of the Nixons' visit, approximately ten African American boys and girls, along with a smaller number of students of Asian descent, were part of Heathwood's student body.[38]

Michael Perry was one of the first. The son of pioneering civil-rights attorney Matthew J. Perry Jr.—who played an instrumental role in the desegregation of Clemson[39] and the University of South Carolina[40]—Michael began kindergarten in 1965. His recollection of that experience testifies both to the characteristics of Heathwood's community at that time and the complexity of racial relations as integration progressed through subsequent stages in the years to come.

"I never felt that I integrated Heathwood," Perry would later reflect. "I just, kind of in my own way, meshed in with the friends that I made. My experience there is not the story of Heathwood integrating. I really think that probably happened with the kids that came along five or 10 years after me."

Although two other African Americans enrolled at Heathwood the same year, Perry was the only Black student in his kindergarten section and would largely feel like a "one-off" presence among his classmates as he advanced through his early years at the mansion and then on the new campus by the Congaree River. "My experience at Heathwood was never really confrontational—though it was sometimes awkward to be in situations where I wasn't familiar with some things that were taken for granted by my classmates," he recalled. Like the time he won third-place in an essay competition sponsored by the Daughters of the American Revolution, and "surprised" his hosts by his dark-skinned presence at a celebratory luncheon they hosted. Or, as he grew older, instances when opposing sports teams refused to take the court against Heathwood if Perry participated.

Yet even such occasions frequently had a way of underlining the extent to which his peers at Heathwood embraced his belonging—his classmate Elizabeth Moore telling him "you stay next to me" at the DAR luncheon, or a basketball teammate declaring, "If Mike ain't playing, we ain't playing," in response to another team's racist animosity.

"There's no doubt that I had solidarity and support from my classmates and my schoolmates," Perry recalled. "I did hear conversation from people there about things that happened in the years after I was there. But when I was there, if there were any people that had a problem with my being there, they didn't voice it—for whatever reason, maybe because when they came in I had been there, and kind of had some tenure. The things I remember about Heathwood largely have to do with friends that I had, and stood by me."

This culture of inclusivity was established so thoroughly—and so quickly—that Noble Cooper, who came in 1966 as the only African American in that year's four-year-old kindergarten, would progress through Heathwood believing that it had been a racially integrated school from the very beginning. "We were a church-affiliated Episcopal School, so Heathwood was never segregated at all," the Class of 1980 graduate said many years later. "It was always an open school."

Yet the evidentiary record tells a different—and more interesting—story. The exclusionary nature of Heathwood's enrollment policies prior to 1965 is unmistakably demonstrated by documents and meeting minutes recording decisions by the school's trustees, administrators, and affiliated

Heathwood's student fire marshals in 1969.

church officials. The men and women who occupied these roles in the mid-1960s did not inherit a fully "open" institution—they created one. They did so in response to civil-rights advocacy by Black citizens in South Carolina and across the country. They were guided also by the early—but incompletely realized—vision of Heathwood Hall's founders. The resulting changes provoked some countercurrents in reaction to the unsettling of old norms, but these lacked the strength to reverse the tidal flow toward greater equity, inclusion, and excellence.

In helping to turn the tide in that direction, Heathwood's leadership set a momentous process in motion. They effectively transformed a small private school in a secluded neighborhood into an educational institution that would quietly help to bend the trajectory of Columbia's social history. In this they were assisted by a larger school community—parents, pupils, teachers, church figures, and the very families newly welcomed into that fold—in a collective effort that may be even more remarkable: fostering a culture of openness and inclusivity authentic enough to convince Heathwood's first Black K-12 graduate that this spirit had animated the school from the first day it opened its doors to the first five grade cohorts of white children.

So although Heathwood Hall was founded in 1951—and traces its origins a full century further back in time, to a seed laid in the last will and testament of the 19th-century planter Francis Marion Weston—the school has a history that is rich in new beginnings. The year 1969, when President Nixon paid his visit, found Heathwood in the midst of its first major transition. The process set in motion in 1965 would reach a full flowering in 1973, when the first African American joined a board of trustees that was purposefully reconstituted to model the diversity it hoped to cultivate across the institution.[41] "It was different from other schools," remembered mid-1970s Board of Trustees chairman Robert V. Royall half a century later. "You have to think in terms of 50 years ago. The board was made up of Christians, Jews, men, women, Blacks, and whites. And I don't know of any other school that could claim that."[42]

Heathwood Hall's pursuit of racial inclusivity in the mid-1960s is only one element of a history whose full dimensions embrace matters of pedagogical philosophy, spiritual life, scholarship, service to others, personal development, and varied approaches to leadership. But the quest to expand the school's community amid one of the most divisive decades in US history—at a time when most private schools in the state were moving in the opposite direction—exemplifies the way Heathwood's culture has continually been forged under the pressure of social dynamics that are often in tension with one another. The tension Heathwood navigated in the 1960s juxtaposed two of the most fundamental forces in American life. On one side were the passions aroused by electoral politics, which at times are intensified by appeals to fear and prejudice, but nevertheless reflect the civic reality of a society distinguished by the latitude it affords people to espouse widely contrasting ways of living and being. On the other side was a commitment to universal values rooted in the Episcopal Church's insistence on the inherent value and dignity of every human being. In the course of contending with that tension, Heathwood Hall emerged as an institution whose mission was refreshed and reinvigorated by the struggle.

The school would continue to initiate new chapters as it met fresh challenges and opportunities. The story of each one has played out on many fronts: new buildings, new administrative and faculty leaders, new approaches to the art and technology of teaching and learning. The most important factor has always been the one that ultimately defines every school: the teachers, students, and families who come together to create a community of learning. In the end, the story of a school is made up of the stories of its people. The people comprising Heathwood Hall have long been a diverse mix, with perspectives as varied as their personalities, and priorities that have shifted from one era to another. Each of these periods is reflected in a chapter of this book, which aims to represent the evolution of Heathwood Hall in all its dimensions: as a physical campus, as a community of learners, and as an institution that has by turns reflected and helped to shape the civic life of the state's capital city.

chapter one

THE MANSION AND
THE MATRIARCHS

❧

*Mansion school at $15/month—the Heath daughters—an antebellum
will—"a female school in Columbia"—Susan Gibbes Robinson—
Deweyan progressivism—ecumenical Episcopalianism—the Little
Red Schoolhouse—Ms. Page—"a French granddaddy"—Nell
Mellichamp—Trinity Parish Easter Egg Hunt—PrinciPAL Elsie
Lamar and the thinking chair—the Kindness Club*

[1951-1963]

In the spring of 1951, an advertisement was circulated in Columbia announcing the formation of a new school enrolling students that fall.

Tuition would be $15 per month, which in annual terms represented roughly 3.5 percent of the national median income in 1951;[1] adjusted for inflation, it equates to about $1,350 in present-day dollars.[2] Classes were to be held in a mansion built in 1914 by the South Carolina cotton and real estate broker M.C. Heath. The school's physical location was made possible by Heath's two daughters—Elizabeth Heath Coleman and Mrs. Burwell Deas Manning. But the school itself owed its establishment to the fact that a certain 19th-century gentleman fathered no children of his own.

HEATHWOOD HALL

EPISCOPAL CHURCH SCHOOL
FOR BOYS AND GIRLS
Kindergarten through Fourth Grade
OPEN SEPTEMBER 1951

TUITION: Kindergarten .... $12.50 **per month**

Grades .... $15.00 **per month**

(Plus Registration and Material Fees)

REGISTER NOW!

Mrs. Henry Woodward   1724 Enoree Ave.

Phone 4-5791 After 3:00 P. M.

Newspaper ad for Heathwood Hall, circa 1951.

In 1854 a Georgetown County, South Carolina, planter named Francis Marion Weston died, leaving a last will and testament that would take nearly a century to play out. Weston bequeathed his estate to his only son, Plowden Charles J. Weston.[3] Any assets that remained upon the younger Weston's death were to be equally divided between his own children and grandchildren. Yet in the absence of such heirs, the will directed that the remaining assets be sold and be distributed in six directions: to a $30 annual allowance for the maintenance of four family slaves "in case of sickness or infirmity" (approximately 220 others were to be sold off);[4] and the establishment of four charitable trusts. These were to be given variously to the College of Charleston and the Protestant Episcopal Churches of South Carolina, Georgia, and Tennessee. Weston directed the South Carolina church to use the funds to establish "a female school in Columbia" that would instruct "young females in the appropriate branches of education and particularly in the truths of the Christian religion."[5]

So when Plowden Charles J. Weston died childless in 1867, the Episcopal Diocese of South Carolina received $7,000[6] for that purpose. Precisely why it would take more than eight decades to carry out Weston's wishes is difficult to say, though the aftermath of the Civil War may have discouraged efforts to focus on the educational needs of young women. That might especially have been the case in Columbia, one-third of which had been destroyed by fire in February of 1865, leaving roughly 1,000 people homeless.[7] Yet this assumption runs into the countervailing fact that the state actually experienced a postbellum boom in the formation of private academies, including many for females. At least seven schools for girls and young women opened in Columbia in the three years immediately following the Civil War.[8]

The initial delay in putting Weston's funds to use may have derived from the postwar state of the South Carolina Episcopal Diocese itself. Ten of its churches were burned during the conflict. Upwards of a dozen more suffered substantial damage, ranging from artillery bombardment to the stripping of wood and other materials to build bridges.[9] The Diocese may have prioritized the revitalization of its parishes over the launch of a new school. Poor investment decisions and bad luck may also have intervened; by 1894 the Weston fund's value was $3,788.16 and in 1910 it stood at $6,126.92.[10] (Repeated recessions marked this period, in which the Panics of 1873, 1893, and 1907 each caused economic contractions on the order of 30 percent. Considered in light of those shocks and the Great Depression, the most remarkable thing may be that Weston's bequeathal lasted as long as it did.) When in 1935 the fund was deemed insufficient to start a school, a court granted permission for the bishop to use some of it to sponsor scholarships at existing girls' schools in South and North Carolina.[11] Yet by this time it was growing at an impressive clip. In 1950, when Upper South Carolina Episcopal Bishop John Gravatt called a diocesan convention to discuss the school's establishment, Weston's bequest stood at $42,608.27—equivalent to about $425,000 in 2020 dollars.[12]

This enabled the purchase of the mansion and its 4.78-acre grounds from the Heath daughters, who conveyed it to the school for $58,000[13]— a fraction of its appraised value of $240,000,[14] or the $165,000 asking price specified by a real estate listing in 1949.[15] (In a further act of generosity, the bulk of the purchase was accepted in the form of a long-term, low-interest mortgage, permitting the new school to conserve cash.) The school adopted its name in honor of the Heaths. In order to free the church from financial responsibility, the diocesan convention determined that an independent board of trustees be formed, comprising four clergymen and four laymen, to run the school as an independent eleemosynary corporation in accordance with the Weston will.

One of the board's first actions was to obtain a court order permitting a deviation from Weston's wishes. Arguing that "the only feasible way to accomplish the primary intent of the donor" was "to admit boys on the same term[s] as girls," the trustees paved the way for Heathwood Hall Episcopal School to begin operation as a co-educational intuition that was affiliated with but substantially independent from the Episcopal Church.[16]

※

The Heath Mansion.

The 98 children who arrived in September 1951 entered a setting of rare magnificence, especially for what was essentially a neighborhood elementary school. On the southern end of a landscape perfumed by magnolia blossoms and dotted with camellias, a double row of boxwoods formed a sightline running from Devine Street to the white-brick mansion's front facade. Fourteen towering Corinthian columns framed the entrance, creating a deep portico from which double-level porches extended on either side. The upper porch, carried by smaller columns crowned with Ionic capitals, wrapped all the way around the building's 16,000-square-foot interior. The rooms within bore mahogany paneling, crown molding, and other ornamental details that had previously served as a backdrop to the property's rich history of hospitality. The Heath family had made the house a frequent hosting ground for social functions. During World War I they threw parties for soldiers stationed at Fort Jackson. A decade later the Columbia Junior League was founded in the mansion, which also became a meeting place for a variety of other social clubs. And in what has been described as the largest gathering ever assembled in a private home in Columbia, some 2,500 guests attended a 1948 reception on the mansion's grounds in honor of the French ambassador to the United States.[17] Several sessions of the South Carolina legislature considered the Heath property as a possible governor's mansion.[18]

Now it was an elementary school.

Adapting the Heath Mansion for that purpose involved some alterations: upgrading the boiler, modernizing the electrical wiring, and installing exterior fire escape stairways.[19] A certain number of silver doorknobs and other fancy fixtures were also removed during the renovations, along with the Manning family's prodigious collection of snakes in the basement.[20] A central hall on the second floor was converted into a chapel, headed by an altar. Due to these changes, "you didn't think of it as a mansion, it was just a school," recalled Norrie Nicholson Cooper, who was among the first students to enroll as a first grader. "But the bathrooms were funny—they had tubs," she added, "so it was homey in that respect."

In terms of the people, Heathwood Hall did not start completely from scratch. A number of its students and faculty came from the Good

Shepherd Parish School, a 78-student elementary school which the diocese decided to merge with Heathwood. Three classroom teachers made
the move to the mansion, along with Good Shepherd's teacher-principal,
Susan Gibbes Woodward.[21] (She later assumed the last name Robinson,
upon her 1955 marriage to David Wallace Robinson.)

Woodward furnished the ambitious vision that would guide
Heathwood's early development. "We are aiming for the progressive
and for the highest academic standards," she told *The State* newspaper
upon Heathwood's opening.[22] Her use of the term *progressive* signaled
an alignment with ideas articulated in the early 20th century by the
American philosopher John Dewey, who advocated for the education
of the "whole child," with an emphasis on experiential learning and so-
cial-emotional development, as opposed to the traditional pedagogical
focus on book learning and rote memorization. Dewey envisioned education as a fundamentally civic enterprise: a process by which individuals
could realize their fullest potential while gaining the skills and habits of
democratic citizenship by which they could advance the greater good. "I
believe it is the business of every one interested in education to insist
upon the school as the primary and most effective instrument of social
progress and reform," he declared. "I believe, finally, that the teacher is
engaged, not simply in the training of individuals, but in the formation
of the proper social life."[23]

Woodward was in some ways a curious choice as the inaugural
head of a church-affiliated school. For one thing, she was not a regular
churchgoer. In this she took after her father. James Heyward Gibbes, a
medical doctor who also served as head of the Columbia School Board
in the 1940s, had become "disenchanted" with Trinity Church and so
the family had largely ceased attending when Susan was young.[24] Dr.
Gibbes enjoyed rich social connections that reached into the most pres-
tigious ranks of South Carolina society, yet also had a reputation as
something of a freethinker. In a portrait that now hangs in the Medical
University of South Carolina, he insisted upon being depicted holding
his favorite book, turned to expose its title: Laurence Sterne's bawdy
and proto-modern 18th-century novel *The Life and Opinions of Tristram*

Founding headmistress Susan Gibbes Woodward Robinson.

Shandy, Gentleman. Sterne's irreverent wit found reflection in Gibbes, whose independent cast of mind was a trait that many would come to recognize in Susan as well.

Woodward was educated at Converse College and began her teaching career outside of Columbia in Olympia Mill village, where she was given a cohort of students who had repeatedly failed and were considered difficult to reach. She got through to them partly by means of a school garden project, which appears to have been an epiphany about the effectiveness of thinking beyond the blackboard. After tragedy ended her first marriage to Henry Woodward, who died early in World War II, she proceeded to St. Catherine's School in Richmond, Virginia.[25] It would become an important influence.

Founded in the 1890s by Virginia Randolph Ellett (whose name the school carried until it was sold to the Episcopal Church in 1920), St. Catherine's had built a formidable reputation as a girls school that rejected that era's reigning expectations about the role of women in society. Combining intellectual rigor with experiential learning and physical exercise—at a time when all three were frequently deemed inappropriate for, or even detrimental to, women of what was then called "good breeding"—Ellett built an institution that elevated not only its pupils but Richmond itself, which became one of only eight cities in the world where college entrance board exams were administered annually to women.[26]

As Woodward's daughter Susan "Susu" Ravenel would later reflect, "I think she found at St. Catherine's that girls were empowered to do more than just be housewives—and that wasn't the norm in Columbia." Another profound influence was the Teacher's College of Columbia University in New York, where Woodward pursued graduate study in the late 1940s—attending classes mostly during the summers. "That gave her a different perspective," Ravenel said. Along with her master's degree in education from the University of South Carolina, her time at Columbia University also may have deepened Woodward's interest in the use of IQ and aptitude tests to help guide instruction for individual students. Woodward's interest in the burgeoning field of educational-aptitude testing was apparent from Heathwood Hall's opening, when she stipulated that "reading-readiness" tests rather than "arbitrary dates" and "birthday deadlines" would be used to place children in grades.[27]

Woodward was not drawn to the public spotlight, nor did she seek the kind of attention that comes from claims of credit. She established her legacy through the curriculum she implemented and the people she charged with carrying it out. At the outset of 1951, that team was comprised of a teacher for each grade, two kindergarten leaders, and three faculty members whose subject areas testified to Robinson's progressive ambitions. These were music teacher Nell Mellichamp; religion instructor Peggy Belser; and Maurice Stephan, a University of South Carolina professor of 20 years' standing who oversaw a program in French language instruction. The equipoise between Episcopalian values and the substantially secular bent of Woodward's scholastic orientation formed the first in a series of productive tensions that would shape Heathwood Hall in the years to come.

The school opened on September 10, 1951, with a chapel service conducted by Bishop John J. Gravatt in the mansion's spacious second-floor hall.

Heathwood Hall's charter mandated that the school's religious education be directed by a confirmed member of the Episcopal Church, and based upon the Book of Common Prayer. In addition to chapel, which was held several times a week, students received Bible instruction (using the Episcopal Church's favored King James version). Yet from the very beginning, Heathwood sought to attract and welcome families of all faiths. As the school's leaders took care to emphasize in multiple newspaper announcements in the months leading up to opening day, "Children of all denominations will be welcome to attend."[28]

Their success in this effort may be measured by the very first item presented in Susan Woodward's first annual report in 1952: a religious census of the student body, which came before any discussion of curriculum or faculty issues. It reported that among the 101 children enrolled at the end of the first academic year, there were 60 Episcopalians, 14 Presbyterians, 10 Methodists, 6 Baptists, 3 Lutherans, and smaller numbers marked variously as Roman Catholic, Greek Orthodox, Congregationalist, or "no church affiliation."[29] The 1953 annual report, which began in the same fashion, counted 6 Jewish students.[30]

Chapel in the Heath Mansion.

The collection of this information attests to two realities: the social significance of religious affiliations in 1950s South Carolina, and the determination of Heathwood Hall's leaders to foster a degree of religious toleration exceeding that which was to be found in some other realms of Columbia society. They seem to have accomplished that in large part by projecting a studied indifference in the presence of the school's children. Susan Milliken Umbach, who numbered among Heathwood's Presbyterian students in the school's opening decade, was one of many alumni to retain "no memory" of any conversation about religious identities. "There was never any discussion of who was Jewish or this or that," she recalled. "There was an educational attitude of inclusive excellence."

The school's administrators sought to advance their goal of denominational diversity, in other words, by downplaying its significance—at least within earshot of the children. Yet it would remain an abiding concern during Heathwood's first decade—as evidenced by the appearance of similar denominational censuses in annual reports as late as 1961. And there is reason to believe that the institutionalization of that value would later buttress the school's approach to racial integration.

In the judgment of Bernie Dunlap, who counted Susan Woodward as a "very attentive godmother" who recruited his own mother to teach Bible stories and world mythology at the mansion in the early years, this emphasis on religious diversity reflected a guiding principle of the ethos Woodward aimed to instill. "The school was to be progressive—not just as a matter of general educational philosophy, but pointed toward a more liberal attitude," the cultural historian and longtime president of Wofford College would later reflect. "When Heathwood Hall began, South Carolina was deeply entrenched in resisting integration," he added. "The very fact that Heathwood embraced as wide an initial diversity of white students as it did seemed significant in many ways. South Carolina in the 1950s was a very, very conservative place, and Columbia was no exception … But within the Episcopal Church in those days, some were also of a more liberal disposition on racial matters."

In the beginning, Heathwood Hall's enrollment was driven primarily by demand for kindergarten—which was not offered by South Carolina public schools on a statewide basis until the 1970s. This dynamic was apparent by the second academic year, when kindergarten was split into 4-year-old and 5-year-old groups, and a second section of first grade was added. The skew toward younger children helped to drive propulsive growth, doubling the size of the student body by the third year. (During the mid-1950s there were relatively few independent schools in South Carolina; an annual report from the state superintendent of education during this period listed only 16 "private and denominational schools" in the state, four of which were in Columbia.)[31] This growth in turn occasioned the first campus expansion. It arrived in 1954—the same year Heathwood added 6th grade—in the form of an old carriage house that had been used as a kindergarten for nearly half a century already.

This was donated by Ms. Louly Shand, who had been teaching young children there since the early 1900s in the backyard of her College Street house.[32] Transported to Heathwood's grounds, it was repainted and christened the Little Red Schoolhouse. That year's annual report also detailed an early instance of financial aid: a full scholarship sponsored by Bishop Clarence A. Cole to cover the annual tuition—which had risen to $235—of one (already enrolled) student to be selected by Heathwood' teachers.[33]

A school that prioritized the character development of very young children could have found few teachers who nurtured boys and girls with greater care than Page Steinert. Ms. Page, as she was universally known, functioned as a spiritual pillar of Heathwood's early-childhood program from the mid-1950s into the 1990s.[34] Good will flowed from her in waves of gentle affection, and spread among children as readily as chickenpox. "Everyone who touched Heathwood in those days remembers Ms. Page," recalled Class of 1986 alumnus Wade Mullins, echoing a sentiment commonly voiced by students one generation removed from him on either

Nap time with Ms. Page.

side—the older of whom often also treasured memories of her colleague Ann Gilpin. "They were just loving, and just so encouraging," remembered Noble Cooper, who would go on to distinguish himself as a dentist in adulthood. "I think each kid, at that time, we don't know what our gifts are. But they could see the potential, and taught each one of us in a different manner: They treated each child differently, in positive way. They looked at our skills and gifts, and then would encourage us—I would use the word transform us—to be the best that we could be."

By means of small class sizes and a "whole child" educational approach that mixed Episcopalian values with progressive pedagogy, this was what Heathwood aimed to do at every grade level. Its effectiveness is perhaps best judged by a student who was uniquely equipped to notice the ways Heathwood differed from the public elementary schools of that era. Gayle Boineau Darby came to the mansion in 1954 in the third grade—after running away from McMaster Elementary School.

Darby had attended McMaster since she was six years old. She had been happily surrounded by family members and friends there. But for reasons she never quite pinned down, she soured on school in the third grade. And one day, after walking two blocks to school with her sister and cousin, she entered her class's cloakroom only to sneak out through a side door. "I don't know what was going on in my life—my sister says nothing," Darby later recalled. "We had a wonderful family life, lots of cousins and people around us ... But I would walk to school with them, and walk into the cloakroom ... pretend like I was hanging up my coat—and then I would walk out into the hall and walk home."

She never hid. And her mother didn't get upset or angry, at least not visibly. But as the pattern continued it became clear that something needed to change. Partly on account of her parents' acquaintance with Susan Woodward, Darby was sent to Heathwood.

She took to it right away. "They had set up a beautiful hallway for chapel, which we had every day," she recalled. "They had chairs, and somebody played the piano, and we would sing. And then we would go off into different bedrooms where the desks were set up, and learn."

The chapel services soothed her—especially the singing. She "adored" her third-grade teacher, Mrs. Sanders. And Maurice Stephan seemed like a "French granddaddy … and thinking back on it, it was extremely innovative for Heathwood to have him." McMaster hadn't offered foreign-language instruction. (And Heathwood would soon experiment with Latin as well.) By the time she started diagramming sentences in Ms. Belle Dunbar's fifth-grade class, Darby's erstwhile classmates were probably doing the same—but it all felt different to her.

"I wonder if the size of the school maybe had an effect on me. I'm an introvert," she would later reflect. "I remember enjoying McMaster, but I think maybe it was too big. Heathwood was just my speed. We had maybe eight or nine students in the third grade. We were all in the mansion, up in different bedrooms.

"The school was comforting," she concluded. "And I must have needed comfort." As Darby reached the end of her time at Heathwood—which did not yet offer middle-school grades—her parents worried about the coming transition back to public school. "But after Heathwood, I just felt more confident," she recalled. "It did for me what needed to be done."

Clinch Belser also entered Heathwood as a third grader in the early 1950s. "We got a very solid grounding in the courses we took, and also in the importance of studying," he recalled, emphasizing the latter. He was one of many students to be offered a place in Hand Middle School's accelerated program after finishing sixth grade at Heathwood. "I remember the teachers were very attentive. The small size of the classes was very important. I always felt that the good education I got at Heathwood carried me through Hand and Dreher and college and law school," said the Princeton alumnus and editor-in-chief of the *University of South Carolina Law Review*, "because I developed good study habits."

The mansion's first-floor hall became a library—whose books were supplied on a rotating basis by the Richland County Public Library.[35] Parent volunteers would often staff the stacks and read aloud to the children. To build its own collection, Heathwood Hall adopted a custom that elegantly combined a philanthropic ethos with student-driven decision making via "birthday books." Part of the way Heathwood students celebrated their birthdays was by donating a book of their choosing to the school library.[36]

Heathwood's religious curriculum in the mid 1950s was intricate-ly planned, as evidenced by an archival document outlining the specific sermon topics, Bible stories, psalms, and hymns taught in each grade.[37] Chapel talks for kindergartners ranged from the biblical account of Creation, to the story of Samuel and Eli, to the meaning of the Epiphany, to a sermon about "modern helpers of Jesus." Kindergartners were also taught upwards of two dozen hymns. As children progressed through the grades, they studied a curated set of psalms—beginning with Psalms 23, 100, and 150 in the first and second grades, and then adding more while learning songs such as "Venite Adoremus" and "Nunc Dimittis." (Children in the upper grades, this document boasted, "sang over 80 hymns" in a single year. It is little surprise, then, that Nell Mellichamp would loom large in the memories of mansion-era students, some of whom also took piano lessons from her.) Older students also supple-mented Bible reading with Pilgrim Press titles like *How the Bible Came to Us* and *How the News of Jesus Traveled*, as well as *Chapters in Church History* from Seabury Press. Puppetry projects, plays, papier-mâché, di-oramas, and other activities rounded out the singing and reading.

Less information survives about Heathwood's academic curric-ulum in the mansion era, but many former students shared Norrie Nicholson Cooper's recollection: "We did lots of reading." Cooper cited E.B. White's *Charlotte's Web* as an example. "And we would memorize a lot of poems—that was part of the way we learned to read," she add-ed. The iambic cadence of Henry Wadsworth Longfellow's "The Village Blacksmith" stood out in her memory, along with similar verse. Students also wrote poetry, spurred along by what was surely a rare prospect for children of that or any other era: from time to time, Nell Mellichamp would compose music for a student's verse, transforming it into song.[38]

In the classroom, Beverley Dunlap's approach to Bible instruction also exemplified a fertile balance between traditional church-based instruction and the progressive embrace of a broader spectrum of the humanities. "As far as I can tell, my mother taught mythology," recalled Bernie Dunlap. "Both Christian stories—literature, in one sense, but really storytelling for the most part—along with various myths from around the world. And I've

Nell Mellichamp at the piano.

met many people only slightly younger than I who vividly recall what they were learning from her ... They would have learned the Bible stories anyway, but what they remembered most vividly was mostly pagan!"

Heathwood Hall's cloistered, close-knit atmosphere was a defining characteristic throughout its tenancy at the mansion. "Classes were small, like family," recalled Will Prioleau, who attended in the 1960s. "My first-grade teacher was my cousin!" But the school also tried to contribute to the civic life of the city. One of the first and best-loved ways it did so was by reviving the Trinity Parish Easter Egg Hunt. Trinity had established this as an annual event in 1935, but suspended it during World War II.

In 1952, Heathwood resurrected the tradition on the mansion grounds.[39] To say that the school welcomed more than just its own families would be an understatement. The 1952 revival—which doubled as a fundraiser with tickets priced at 25 cents—set a tone that would reverberate in the memories of children all over Columbia. Some 7,000 people attended, searching for 20,000 eggs—including three silver ones and a Golden Goose Egg.[40]

Heathwood Hall's first leadership transition came in 1956, when Mary Anderson assumed the position of headmistress after Susan Woodward's 1955 marriage to David Robinson. Robinson, according to Susan's daughter Susu Ravenel, was eager for his bride to step away from professional life so that they might raise a child of their own. "She had kind of expected to do that with my father," Ravenel reflected, before his death in World War II rendered her a single mother with a young child to support. "So I think it was time."

"Plus," Ravenel recalled, "there were a couple people who wanted her job."

One had been Elsie Lamar—a fixture at Trinity Cathedral's Sunday School who was familiar to many Heathwood families—to whom the job was offered first. But a prior commitment to the public school system (where she taught for more than 20 years)[41] prevented her from accepting it. Mary Anderson, who was hired instead, proved to be a transitional leader. Her 1960 acceptance of a part-time teaching job at Dreher High School, which she intended to carry out while shuttling back and forth from Heathwood on a daily basis, led to her dismissal by the Board of Trustees.[42] By the end of the same week Lamar had applied to replace her.[43] After a brief spell during which Virginia DuPre served as acting principal, Lamar became headmistress—and Heathwood Hall had its second inspirational leader.

"Elsie was bigger than life," recalled Gayle Darby, who had known her from Trinity. "She just ran the show." Stately, refined, lovely, and tall, Lamar was not a woman easily missed. "She would wear these big, beautiful hats," Darby said, "and just make an entrance into a room."

"She was a regal lady," recalled Betty Gasque, whose husband Jim always escorted Lamar to prime seating at Commencement in later years. "She was the grande dame of Heathwood Hall Episcopal School."

In the memories of many students, Lamar was much more than that. And if her effect on the school's culture could be summed up by a relationship with a single student, that student would be Will Prioleau.

Prioleau started Heathwood as kindergartner in 1962. "It had a lot do with Susan Robinson," he would later recall, noting that his own mother had graduated from Radcliffe College, the female institution affiliated with Harvard. "We didn't have a lot of women like her around. That was part of why she liked Mrs. Robinson so much."

But it would be Elsie Lamar, an independent woman cut from a somewhat different cloth, who would most profoundly impact Prioleau's life. "She was a tremendously protective and nurturing person," he said. "I get emotional talking about it. I remember her being much larger and taller than she was, broader-shouldered than she was. I realized as I got older that she was not this almost-Amazonian protector of us that I had pictured." That's because as he grew older, he did not grow more distant from his former headmistress. "I stayed in touch with her for the rest of her life."

Prioleau's loyalty to Lamar sprang from the love she showed his family during his mother's four-year bout with what would probably be diagnosed today as postpartum depression—albeit a case intensified by a spate of additional tragedies. Having suffered the deaths of her mother and father in quick succession, and lost her first husband to a lightning strike, Roberta Prioleau carried a pregnancy to full term only to watch her baby die within hours of delivery. "The male OB/GYNs of that era thought the best answer was to have another baby right away and get to being a housewife," Will later reflected. "That didn't work for my mother."

She wound up at the renowned Menninger Institute in Kansas, spending "six or eight months two or three times" as a psychiatric inpatient when Will and his siblings were small. And her difficulties frequently followed her home.

"Mrs. Lamar knew that, and became my second mother," he said. "There's the whole idea of how it takes a village to raise a child; well, she organized the village. My father was trying to practice law and juggle three children. Somehow, without making it obvious, Mrs. Lamar kept us all together." When his mother would sleep through afternoon pickup, Lamar would see that he and his siblings got home safely. When his mother was absent for long stretches, she would see that the children got the support they needed in school.

Lamar was not the sort of headmistress to shape children's behavior through harsh punishment. Her office door bore the lighthearted sign

Headmistress Elsie Lamar.

PrinciPAL, and when teachers sent students through it in the wake of some mischief, Lamar would seat them in a "thinking chair" and bid them to consider what they had done—and how they might feel if they were similarly treated.[44] Neither was she inclined to stratify students according to academic achievement. No honor rolls were kept during her tenure. Education, in her view, was not a competitive enterprise. She sought to foster an atmosphere conducive to the development of individual minds with spiritual depth, informed by an ethic of care for others. A devotee of handwritten notes, she perennially prefaced her signature with the phrase "Love a'plenty."[45]

Prioleau remembered Lamar as a nurturing protector of all children—a woman with no tolerance for bullying and no fear of grown men who stepped out of line in children's presence. "We were to be Christian soldiers," he said. "Mrs. Lamar was all about being who you are. She tried to make us independent. When you get older, you realize there might have been more to it than you realized at the time."

Many students recollected her in similar terms—likewise remembering her as "regal" and standing even taller than her mark on the measuring stick. "*Formidable* is the world that keeps coming to mind," said Susan Milliken Umbach, another student whose relationship with Lamar carried deep into adulthood. "She had a delightful sense of humor, but meant business … It wasn't that you didn't want to get in trouble—but you didn't want to disappoint her."

But for Prioleau, who would become one of Lamar's most regular visitors in old age at Still Hopes Retirement Community, as well as one of her last—and who would pursue a career devoted substantially to the health insurance needs of senior citizens—she was a figure without parallel.

"People have genuinely loved my mother," Prioleau reflected. "She became a person who used her experience to help a lot of other people. We had an inn at Pawleys Island, and a lot of wounded people came. Much later I discovered that many of them never paid for staying weeks at a time. My mother just had an influence on people." Yet in the years before Roberta Prioleau found the strength and insight to help others, her children depended on Elsie Lamar to help them.

"We got out of school at 1:30," Will recalled, "and my mother might show up wearing a slip with a fur coat on top at 2:03. We were known as feral children. The neighborhood raised us—and more than anything, Mrs. Lamar raised us. It's not a story you normally hear about the head-mistress of a private school."[46]

※

Though Lamar promised the trustees that she would pursue "gradual" change as Heathwood's head administrator,[47] she moved quickly to implement a number of innovations. By the spring of 1961, Heathwood Hall had organized its first student council, mounted its first science and social-studies fair, and printed its first student newspaper. The 1961 annual report showed a student body of 243 pupils, of whom "100 1/2" were clas-sified as Episcopalian.[48] A staff of 19 full-time and 2 part-time teachers conducted small-sized classes "within the framework of Christian princi-ples" while adhering to "the highest academic calibre." Annual tuition and fees came to $315—representing 5.5 percent of the national median fami-ly income, or 6.3 percent of the median family income for white families in the Southern region. (The Census Bureau now reported these figures with greater geographic and racial specificity. Heathwood's 1961 tuition would have represented 14.8 percent of the median income of non-white families in the South—a burden that would soon become germane as the school moved toward a non-discriminatory enrollment policy.)[49]

Heathwood's students, naturally, had their minds on other things. Recycling drives covered a side porch of the mansion in great heaps of bundled newspapers. The Kindness Club's code of conduct extended to the gentle treatment of honey bees that would fly in through the man-sion windows—entering the protective custody of Nell Mellichamp, who forbade her pupils from squashing them. Ms. Janie sold snacks at lunch hour: milk and a moon pie cost 15 cents, and Mrs. Lamar kept a change jar on her desk for the benefit of children who had forgotten their nickel and dime at home.[50] There was a jungle gym by now, and monkey bars that seemed to produce at least one broken arm per academic year.

The grass beneath the basketball hoop young Clinch Belser had lobbied for was eventually paved over with asphalt. None of those accoutrements put a dent in the kickball craze, which would persist deep into the decade. There were trees and hedges and a path through a stand of bamboo, and elsewhere giant cylinders of cast concrete: sewer infrastructure repurposed as hideouts where boys could holler into their own echoes and girls could whisper in confidence. The children progressed through the early 1960s much the same way as their older siblings had done before them: reading poems and stories, counting in French, singing chapel hymns, and cementing the bonds of friendship.

And as the decade approached its midpoint, the breadth of those friendships was about to expand.

The 1963-64 faculty. Front row: Bowen, Lamar, Gilpin, Going, Steinert. Back row: Nuckols, Farr, Bradford, Heriot, Long, Hill, McCrady, Dallis, Aldrich, Parker, Mellichamp, Butler, Moore, Clawson.

chapter two

AN OPEN SCHOOL

*Racial barriers "apparently" dropped—Brown v. Board—Massive
Resistance—"amalgamation" fearmongers and picture-book censors—
"released time" religious instruction—the Foundation faction—Hallie
and Matthew Perry—Bishop Pinckney—"Heathwood Hall School
stands at a crossroads"—a "protected" place—schoolyard friendship and
slumber parties*

[1963-1969]

O n February 23, 1965, a short item appeared on an inside page of the *Columbia Record*. "Racial barriers at a fashionable Episcopal day school in Columbia's Heathwood section apparently have been dropped," began the single-column article from the Associated Press. In a marvel of wire-service brevity verging on the cryptic, the report merely noted that Heathwood Hall abutted the back yard of former South Carolina Gov. James Byrnes, and that according to the Rev. John A. Pinckney, Episcopal Bishop of the Upper Diocese of South Carolina, it would henceforth be operated under "the principles of the Protestant Episcopal Church."[1]

No further details were offered. The article raised more questions than it answered. Had racial barriers been "dropped" in the form of a particular student or students? Or only in the abstract, as a matter of future policy? Hadn't Heathwood operated under "the principles of the Protestant Episcopal Church" since its founding 14 years before? Had those principles changed? And why, for that matter, was Bishop Pinckney making this announcement—rather than the school's head-mistress or one of its trustees?

The Heathwood Hall teachers, administrators, and parents who read this article would have known some of the answers—for all of them had participated in one way or another in bringing this momentous change about. But the full story was known only to a precious few, and many of the particulars would remain shrouded even from intimate participants until the present day.

Told one way, the story of integration at Heathwood Hall began in the fall of 1963, when Hallie Perry made an appointment with Elsie Lamar to discuss the possibility of enrolling her son Michael, who was then just three years old, in the next kindergarten class. But making sense of that meeting—or the circumstances surrounding it—requires going back further. In particular it requires a clear-eyed understanding of the prevailing law, customs, and attitudes in South Carolina at the time of Heathwood's founding.

When Heathwood Hall was established in 1951, there was not a racially integrated educational institution in all of South Carolina. As Clinch Belser would later reflect about his own high school education after being a student at Heathwood, "I finished Dreher in 1963, and there were no Black students in my class, or at the school ... Through 1963, integration in South Carolina was just a *word*. It wasn't a *fact*. At all."

The state's commitment to segregation was exemplified by Article XI, Section 7 of its constitution, whose language remained identical to the 1895 version that had supplanted the Reconstruction-era Constitution of 1868 (which had mandated equal access to public schools for all races). "Separate schools shall be provided for children of the white and colored races," it stipulated, "and no child of either race shall ever be permitted to attend a school provided for children of the other race."[2] (The South Carolina constitution defined a colored person as anyone with "one-eighth or more of negro blood.")[3]

As attorneys like Thurgood Marshall challenged this doctrine in court, South Carolina politicians maneuvered to maintain segregation by any means. "Whatever is necessary to continue the separation of the races in the schools of South Carolina is going to be done by the white people of the state," declared Jimmy Byrnes during his gubernatorial campaign in 1950. "That is my ticket as a private citizen. It will be my ticket as governor."[4]

Upon taking office, Byrnes wasted no time. In March 1951 he threatened to abandon the public school system rather than submit to integration.[5] At his request, the state legislature approved a ballot referendum to permit the abolishment of the state's constitutional requirement to provide a system of public education. Voters approved the measure, by a 68 percent to 32 percent margin, in 1952.[6] Meanwhile Byrnes and the legislature met the specter of court-ordered integration by passing several "preparedness measures," including paving the way for church-run private schools to function as an alternative to public ones.[7] Shortly after the Supreme Court's 1954 decision in *Brown v. Board of Education*, the state legislature repealed the law requiring mandatory school attendance.[8]

Segregationist energy was also evident in Washington, DC. Beginning with Sen. Strom Thurmond's historic 24-hour filibuster against the Civil Rights Act of 1957, South Carolina's congressional delegation opposed every civil rights bill proposed in Congress through 1965. Thurmond had laid down his marker during his own tenure as South Carolina governor: "There's not enough troops in the Army," he thundered during his 1948 third-party campaign for the presidency, "to force the Southern people to break down segregation and admit the Negro race into our theaters, into our swimming pools, into our homes, and into our churches."[9]

Children were a special concern of South Carolina segregationists in the 1950s. The 1956 revelation that Jerrold Beim's picture book *Swimming Hole* had entered South Carolina public libraries, for instance, caused a furor. For the State Library Board, this sweet story about Black and white children overcoming a racial divide to enjoy splash-filled summer afternoons aimed to show that "human values are not to be judged by physical differences."[10] But a state senator deemed it "a monstrosity and an affront,"[11] and a Richland County representative introduced legislation to remove it and similar books from libraries. Such books were "antagonistic and inimical to the traditions and customs of our state," the resolution declared, and "serve no constructive educational purpose but rather tend to confuse and warp the thinking of our young children."[12]

The following year, *The Citizens Council*, the official newspaper of the White Citizens Council groups that proliferated in the wake of *Brown*, published a special supplement designed for public school pupils. "Do you know that some people in our country want the Negroes to live with the white people?" read the portion designed for third and fourth graders. "These people want us to be unhappy … They want to make our country weak." It went on: "God put the white people off by themselves. He put the yellow, red and black people by themselves. God wanted the white people to live alone … Did you know our country will grow weak if we mix our races? It will."[13]

Just how far these attitudes extended beyond frantic would-be picture-book censors was exemplified by a November 1956 article in *The Atlantic Monthly* by the South Carolina writer Herbert Ravenel Sass. "[A]lthough it is a nearly universal instinct, race preference is not active in the very young," Sass declared. It was for this very reason that he judged school segregation to be so important—and warned that abandoning it would have the tragic consequence of the "destruction" of the white race through "amalgamation."

"Race preference," Sass wrote, "is one of those instincts which develop gradually as the mind develops and which, if taken in hand early enough, can be prevented from developing at all."[14] By Sass's reckoning—and that of many of his compatriots—it was children's very susceptibility to interracial friendship and fellow-feeling that made it so crucial to keep white and Black children apart, in schools no less than swimming holes.

So, given the realities of midcentury life in South Carolina, it was no surprise that Heathwood Hall opened in 1951 with an all-white student body. Segregation was so deeply ingrained in Columbia that the school wouldn't have found any reason to state this as a policy—which there is no record of it having done in 1951.

Is this to imply that Heathwood Hall was akin to a "segregation academy" *avant la lettre*—that it was founded before *Brown* with the same exclusionary intent as the wave of private schools established after *Brown*? There are compelling reasons to reject such a reading. The first is that South Carolinians in 1951 had every reason to expect the continuation of segregated public schooling. Based partly on his personal lobbying of his old Supreme Court colleagues, Gov. Byrnes was confident that the justices would uphold the "separate but equal" doctrine articulated in *Plessy v.*

Ferguson (1896).[15] And the legislature had taken steps to bolster the state's ability to maintain segregated schools even in the face of a contrary ruling. Put bluntly, South Carolina was an apartheid state and showed little sign of changing. Had white parents been anxious that public schools would soon be integrated, there likely would have been a boom in the formation of private schools. Yet few private schools were established in the state during the 1940s and 1950s—a period one historian has dubbed "the decline of independent education" in South Carolina.[16]

The second reason is the one articulated repeatedly by the school's founders: the primary motivation for Heathwood Hall's establishment was to provide more religious education than could be offered in public schools.

The Constitutional litigation that preoccupied Heathwood's founders appears to have been not the antecedents to *Brown*, but rather the Supreme Court's 1948 decision in *McCollum v. Board of Education*.[17] That case involved an educational practice known as "released time," by which public schools released students on a voluntary basis to receive religious instruction from church (and in some cases synagogue) officials during school hours. Pioneered in 1913 in Gary, Indiana, released-time programs mushroomed across the US in the 1940s as a way to meet parental demand for religious instruction without directly involving public schools in its delivery.[18] But when an Illinois parent sued the Champaign County Board of Education over a released-time program conducted on school grounds, the Supreme Court ruled, in an 8-1 decision, that it violated the First Amendment's establishment clause.

Although *McCollum* still left leeway for released-time programs conducted off school property, advocates of weekday religious education feared that further restrictions would follow. "It is safe to say that no decision by the highest court in the land has ever caused greater consternation than this one," declared the Illinois Rev. W. T. Smith after it was handed down, echoing widespread anxiety in the ruling's wake.[19] And in one of the first newspaper articles to announce Heathwood Hall's planned opening, trustee R. Hoke Robinson zeroed in on *McCollum*.

"The traditional concept of separation of church and state, upon which this county is founded, necessarily limits our public schools in the amount or kind of religious training they can furnish a child," he stated. "Three years ago the Supreme Court ordered the Champaign, Ill., schools to cease operating their program of 'released time' religious instruction during school hours; and there is presently before the court an effort by two New Jersey parents to force the public schools of that state to discontinue the daily reading of five verses of the Old Testament in the schools. The private school has no such constitutional or historical limitation on its teaching of the Christian way of life.

"We all know that the religious training which a child received for 40 to 60 minutes on Sundays is insufficient," he continued. "[W]e believe that attendance at a school such as Heathwood Hall for the kindergarten and early elementary grades will complete the job of providing the fundamentals of Christian education which we desire our boys and girls to have." (Robinson immediately added that attendance would "by no means be limited to children of Episcopal families," and that parents of other denominations would have "no cause for concern over what is taught at the school.")[20]

Whatever the case, there is no record that Heathwood had a written policy precluding the admission of non-white children during the first years of the school's operation. Yet by the time Hallie Perry contacted Elsie Lamar in 1963, that had changed.

The story of this change revolves around the most fundamental challenge faced by any private school: money.

When the Board of Trustees met in August 1958, the first item on their agenda concerned a financial shortfall caused by a drop in enrollment, which had necessitated a withdrawal from the school's reserve fund.[21] The next month's meeting revealed the availability of just $350 in the bank that could be used for building purposes, and $819.16 in the school's "Birthday Offering Fund." The trustees broached approaching local parishes for fundraising support, and/or to foot scholarships for their congregants.[22] (Like many such proposals over the years to lean on local churches for support, this was fated to remain wishful thinking.) Meanwhile sentiment was growing that Heathwood Hall's future depended on its ability to expand. An October 1958 meeting open to school parents focused on the best way to facilitate expansion. After some discussion about seeking land elsewhere for a bigger campus, the Board resolved instead to purchase two adjacent lots from the Manning family at an expected price of $25,000. The trustees estimated that this would permit the erection of additional classrooms—at a construction cost of $20,000—to support a student enrollment of 300, and possibly more thereafter.[23]

The Board's December meeting featured a special guest: Dr. Tucker Weston, who proposed the establishment of an independent foundation for the purpose of raising funds as well as purchasing property for the school. Board chair Mrs. W. Bedford Moore Jr. endorsed this proposal, which the trustees passed.[24] Ten days later, pressured by the feeling that these neighboring lots (which were already being used as play areas) would soon attract competing buyers, the Board passed a motion to turn certain funds over to Weston's proposed foundation and to charge the foundation with contracting to buy the two lots in question.[25]

Events progressed quickly and fatefully. The Heathwood Hall Foundation obtained a legal charter in February 1959.[26] By the next month it had contracted to purchase the two lots.[27] By 1960 a new reality was plain. "The Heathwood Hall Foundation recognizes the dire need of Heathwood Hall for the raising of funds for the development and building of a modern and adequate school," wrote the Foundation's leadership in an April 5 letter to the school's trustees. The Foundation "stands ready," they added, "to assume this responsibility, raise the necessary funds and develop the building program needed to adequately serve the school."

But there was a catch: the Foundation conditioned its support on a promise that the school would enroll no Black students. And now that

Detail of minutes from an Oct. 31, 1960, meeting between the Board of Trustees and members of the Heathwood Foundation.

it controlled title to the pivotal real estate, the Foundation was a force to be reckoned with.

Exactly when, and how widely, this became known is difficult to pinpoint. The Heathwood Hall Foundation's leadership included Hoke Robinson and Mrs. W. Bedford Moore Jr., both of whom had served as school trustees. But it was apparently not until October 31, 1960, that written documentation of this racial decree would surface in Board meeting minutes.[28] That Halloween meeting between the Board and the Foundation would make two things clear: "Those present representing the Foundation were very firm in stating they did not want H. H. integrated. Would withdraw their support if such were to happen." And the Foundation's stance provoked consternation among some Board members. "It appeared the H. H. School did not want to be bound by the Foundation in any way," the minutes state.[29]

Handwritten notes bearing the same date, penned in blue ink upon a copy of the Foundation's April 5, 1960, letter, register a sense of heightened concern. "T. Weston says segregation must be promised by Foundation!" reads the first of three notes marked with exclamation points. "Our school buildings will not be used for integrated school (B. Herbert!)," says the second, referring to Foundation member R. Beverly Herbert Jr. "To work with Foundation must sign legal agreement that there will be no integration!"

The Halloween meeting of 1960 created shock waves. Two Foundation members appear to have stormed out of it after "heated discussion." At the next meeting for which minutes survive, on Dec. 20, 1960, the Board resolved to solicit an "Anonymous Foundation" for help raising money—and to delay responding to the Heathwood Hall Foundation's proposal. A letter was sent to Tucker Weston the following day requesting more time to respond. Meanwhile, the trustees also resolved to request a legal opinion on five questions, including: "Can the school legally under the Weston Will admit other than white children[?]"

In February 1961, the Columbia law firm of Roberts, Jennings, Thomas & Lumpkin conveyed an opinion that "to admit other than white children" would be "repugnant to his [Francis Marion Weston's] intent. The school must, as a consequence, be limited to white children."[30]

This opinion is perhaps most remarkable as an instance of the malleability of common law. Nothing in the language of Weston's will imposed any racial qualifiers on admission to the school. It only mandated that the school be for girls—a stipulation the trustees had already overridden. The opinion is also difficult to square with the actual history of Weston's fund, because when the Upper South Carolina Bishop obtained court permission to use some of it to sponsor tuition scholarships in 1935, some of those scholarships were awarded to African American girls attending the Voorhees School in Denmark, South Carolina.[31] Yet it is plainly doubtful that Francis Marion Weston sought to fund a racially integrated school. He lived and died in a society that treated Black people as property, and in his will he appeared to envision the indefinite continuation of slavery.

No surviving documentation attests to the precise manner in which Bishop Alfred Cole solicited this opinion on the school's behalf. But as a general rule of legal practice, clients seek legal opinions to provide legal defense for an action they are contemplating. Legal opinions may also be useful to clients who wish to shed personal responsibility for a controversial course of action. Whatever the case, in March 1961 Board chairman James Morris presented this legal opinion at a meeting attended by Foundation representatives. "On the basis of this ruling," the meeting minutes record, "he presented the Foundation the Board's request that they join with the Board in the raising of necessary funds for the expansion of the school."[32]

Yet trepidation continued to stir the Board. At an April 1961 meeting, the trustees resolved to approach a "professional fund raising organization" in an apparent attempt to diminish the Foundation's influence.[33] In May, the Board chairman read aloud a letter he had written to Tucker Weston that "stated the Board's desire to move on with the Fund Raising Drive without committing itself to the Foundation one way or another, although inviting the Foundation to support this drive for the good of the school."[34]

In October 1961 the trustees solicited fundraising help from a New York firm called Marts & Lundy, which responded with a quote of $3,000 for preliminary services. That ended the correspondence.[35]

Finally, in November 1962 the Board appeared to see no alternative. It unanimously approved new bylaws to govern the school. They contained a stipulation that now had the force of written policy: "Students admitted to the school shall be only those who can fulfill the intention of the Weston Will, as amended by the Court."[36] The Board also drafted a letter to the Heathwood Hall Foundation representing that "in conformity with" the legal opinion it had obtained, "there is at this time no plan or expectation for integration of the white and Negro races at Heathwood School." The school, this letter promised, "will exhaust all possible procedures and efforts to prevent the said integration," and would permit the Foundation to "resist such integration in its own name or in the name of Heathwood School." Finally, "It is further understood and agreed that if the decision to integrate the school is ever made, Heathwood Hall Foundation will then and there cease to support the school in any manner whatsoever."[37]

The culmination of that process set the stage for a dramatic shift. From that point on, the story would become a chronicle of how the Heathwood Hall community changed course—in the face of considerable financial and social peril—to achieve an inclusive vision that exemplified the secular and religious values upon which the school had been founded.

Throughout 1962, the Board of Trustees wrestled with money trouble. Their inability to find a chairman for the expansion fundraising drive that spring[38] led to the declaration of the drive's "apparent failure" in the fall.[39] Meanwhile enrollment recovered—but produced overcrowding in the upper grades, putting pressure on Elsie Lamar's commitment to a 20-person limit on class sizes.[40] By 1963 the stress appeared to diminish. The school's finances were in the black, the capital campaign was on surer footing, and the school received title to the two lots from the Heathwood Hall Foundation.[41]

In the fall of 1963, Mrs. Matthew Perry reached out to Heathwood Hall to discuss enrolling her three-year-old son, Michael, in kindergarten. She was referred by the Rev. William O'Neil, rector of St. Luke's Episcopal Church in Columbia's Waverly neighborhood, a center of African American life. Sometime after Perry's November 1 appointment[42] Heathwood accepted a deposit and placed Michael on a waiting list. This fact is attested by a letter sent by Elsie Lamar to Hallie Perry the following October, returning her check. "We have held the check in case a vacancy occurred," Lamar wrote on October 6, 1964. "To date, such has not happened, and we felt that we should no longer delay in letting you make other arrangements for your son."[43] This letter, which was dictated by Board of Trustees chairman Joseph Faulk,[44] is unique in the Heathwood Hall Archive, which contains no other correspondence concerning the return of deposits (or, for that matter, the taking of deposits).

One way to gain perspective on this episode is by comparison to another Black family seeking admission to a different Southern private school with Episcopal ties the same year. In 1963, Martin Luther and Coretta Scott King applied to enroll their son Martin Luther King III in Atlanta's Lovett School. They did so with the encouragement of the Episcopal Rev. John Morris, a school parent who believed that the school was open to all children. The school's trustees, however, determined otherwise, and rejected King outright. At least one board member resigned in protest. Lovett's board also severed the school's relationship with the Episcopal Church,[45] which at the national level had officially called for the integration of its institutions.[46]

The deliberations of Heathwood Hall's Board during this period are, regrettably, difficult to parse. Meeting minutes from 1963 and 1964 contain minimal records of discussion, and the 1965 records consist of only a single meeting, on January 27—whose first order of business was to nullify the actions of a meeting held five days before.[47] The documentary trail gives the impression of conflicting voices or factions within the Board.[48] But the apparent loss or destruction of key meeting minutes before and after the January 27 meeting makes even that meeting itself— which advanced an ambiguous resolution pertaining to applications by "noncaucasians" and contemplated dissolving Heathwood Hall's connection to the Episcopal Church—impossible to interpret in the absence of information about precisely what was nullified and what happened during subsequent meetings.

Yet there is reason to believe that the school's affiliation with the Episcopal Church played an important role at this juncture.

In his 1965 statement to the press about Heathwood Hall's integration, Bishop John A. Pinckney declared that the school would abide by the "principles of the Protestant Episcopal Church." Left unsaid was a fact well known to many parishioners: there had for some time been a gap between the principles articulated by the national Protestant Episcopal Church and those espoused by its South Carolina dioceses. The closure of that gap would prove relevant to Heathwood Hall's integration.

In 1956, a South Carolina diocesan convention passed a resolution that blamed the Supreme Court for causing an "integration problem" with its *Brown* decision, and maintained that it was "unnatural and unwise to insist upon bringing those of another race into a specific congregation just because they are of a different race."[49] This provoked a scathing response from *The Living Church*, the official publication of the national Episcopal Protestant Church. Calling the resolution "heresy," an editorial in that journal explicitly compared it to actions taken by Adolph Hitler regarding racial protocols in German churches.[50] When, at the Church's 1958 national General Convention, a resolution was submitted mandating that "every race will have the freedom to enjoy, without discrimination and without separation, all opportunities in education, housing, employment, public accommodation and all other aspects of church and civic life,"[51] a member of the South Carolina delegation proposed an amendment. It stated that "a sincere belief in some degree of segregation is compatible with a belief in the dignity of all men and their equality before God,"[52] and was definitively rejected.

But the 1961 General Convention produced no such pro-segregation resolutions from South Carolina. Neither did the 1964 General Convention, which adopted a resolution that "[i]nter-racial worship, inter-racial meeting both formal and informal, freedom of all races to enter and use educational, social and health facilities, must be seen within the pattern of the Church's life and witness without compromise, self-consciousness, or apology."[53] Also in 1964, presiding over his first South Carolina convention as the bishop of the state's upper diocese, John A. Pinckney applauded moves within the diocese ending segregation in church activities.[54] "The mission program of this Diocese," he said in remarks explicitly addressing "racial tensions," was for all people to worship "together and not separated."[55]

The Rev. James Stirling, a Heathwood Hall trustee from Trinity Church, also had a reputation for advocating that worshippers of all races drink from the common cup, at a time when not all congregants agreed.[56]

Meanwhile, Pinckney appears to have been in communication with Hallie Perry about the prospect of Michael enrolling at Heathwood Hall. As Michael would recall years later, after his parents had passed away: "Both my mom and dad tell the story of how she was talking to the bishop of the South Carolina diocese. And one year they decided that it wasn't the right time—I don't think my mom decided, I think the bishop and others decided." The question of when *would* be the right time was put off once or twice, at which point Hallie Perry—an active Episcopalian who had attended the Episcopal-affiliated Voorhees School and Junior College—was ready for a decisive answer. In Michael's retelling of the family story, "Mom said to the bishop: 'Look, if we're not going to do it this year, we're going to send him to Cardinal Newman.'[57] And that's when they decided, apparently, to go ahead."

> To the Parents of Heathwood Hall School
>
> This is to remind you of the meeting of all parents of Heathwood Hall to be held on Monday, Jan.11th at 8:00 P.M. in the Chapel of St.Martin's-in-the-Fields, 4424 Winthrop Ave. This is a very important meeting and we hope that both parents will find it possible to be there. However, if that is impossible, we do most urgently ask that one, at least, be with us.
>
> P.S. THIS MEETING HAS NOTHING TO DO WITH SOLICITATION OF FUNDS !
>
> Jan 8-1965

Reminder for community-wide meeting on Jan. 11, 1965, to discuss integration.

It was against that backdrop that Pinckney addressed a letter to the entire Heathwood Hall community on January 6, 1965. "Heathwood Hall School stands at a crossroads," he wrote. "The Trustees, seeking to fulfill their responsibilities, need at this time to know the mind and will of the patrons of the School before they can proceed with plans for the future." He urged at least one member of every family to attend a "very important meeting" on January 11 at St. Martin's-in-the-Fields.[58] This urgency was underlined two days later, in a reminder to parents imploring universal attendance and promising, in all-caps: "THIS MEETING HAS NOTHING TO DO WITH SOLICITATION OF FUNDS!"[59]

No record of the January 11, 1965, meeting survives.[60] But three days afterward, a letter dictated by trustee Rev. William A Thompson was distributed to faculty and staff. It contained a single question, to be answered Yes or No by 1:30 p.m. on Friday, January 15: "Will you remain as a teacher or staff member at Heathwood Hall School if it is integrated?"

The results of this confidential survey are not memorialized, nor does the Heathwood Hall Archive record subsequent staff resignations. But of the 17 faculty members listed in a 1964-65 school handbook, 16 remained at Heathwood in 1967-68—including everyone who predated Elsie Lamar's 1960 appointment as headmistress.[61] It is not apparent that any Heathwood Hall teacher resigned on account of the school's integration.

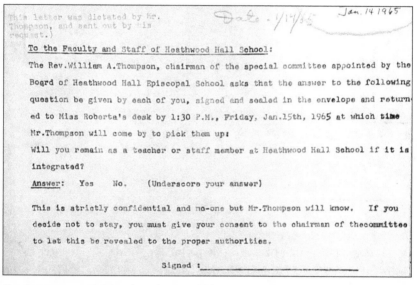

Faculty survey on integration, Jan. 14, 1965.

About a month after Pinckney's all-hands-on-deck meeting and the faculty survey, the *Columbia Record* published its brief report noting Heathwood's new policy. Heathwood Hall would be open to all families on equal terms.[62] Four weeks after that, on March 19, 1965, Elsie Lamar and Hallie Perry met in person. Their meeting was documented in the form of a detailed script of their conversation, presumably by a secretary. They discussed the admission procedure, curriculum, class sizes, and grade placement. "We find, for the most part, that girls mature faster than boys," Lamar observed, "but if we feel that a child is not ready for 1st grade, we notify the parents, and advise that they let him repeat the 5-yr kind[ergarten]." Lamar added: "We try to develop the whole child, and not let him be frustrated by trying to do things that are beyond him." Perry indicated her desire to start Michael, who was on the cusp between the 4- and 5-year-old cohorts, in the older group.

On April 6, Lamar met with Mrs. Lindsay Crumlin, the mother of a Black fourth grader and four-year-old kindergartner. This meeting too was documented in playscript style by secretary Roberta Aldrich.[63] Lamar explained that Heathwood Hall was an Episcopal School "but not limited to Episcopalians." After some discussion of grade placement and tuition fees, Mrs. Crumlin asked: "Do you think that the children at Heathwood will accept my child?" Lamar's response was forthright. "That I cannot answer you, because at present Heathwood Hall is not integrated, and I have never had any experience with an integrated school," she said. "You know your own child better than anyone else does and it will have to be your decision as to whether or not your children will be happy here."

Crumlin confided that she had "no fear for my little girl, but my boy is sensitive." She added, though, that her son had played with an integrated group in Boston. "I believe he will adjust all right here."

"Does he know that there is a possibility of his coming here?" Lamar asked.

"Yes," Crumlin replied, "and he wants to come."

In a letter of April 12, Lamar informed Crumlin that her children had been accepted onto a waiting list (which had been a common practice for white applicants as well). Ten days later she wrote again: Heathwood now had a place in fourth grade for her son, Lindsay.[64]

Detail of Apr. 6, 1965, meeting between Elsie Lamar and Mrs. Lindsay Crumlin.

On May 21, she wrote to Hallie Perry, informing her of a cancellation for 5-year-old kindergarten, freeing a space for Michael. "I wanted to let you know at once," Lamar wrote, "as you have had to wait so long for an answer."[65]

꙰

When Michael Perry arrived at the mansion that fall, he felt a mixture of emotions that would become familiar to many African Americans who would trace the same path: a sense of safety and welcome mingled with feelings of racial isolation, all tumbled together with the ordinary joys, inhibitions, uncertainties, and excitements that mark the school days of children everywhere.

"From five years old until junior high," he would recall, "even if there were other Blacks that might have been out there, I didn't interact with them because they were not in my class. So I was really by myself at Heathwood as far as being Black was concerned. My friends were my white classmates." He felt at times like a stranger decoding the habits and assumptions of a subtly foreign land. "The awkwardness that I might have had in certain situations was because I wasn't part of their community," he recalled. "And other than putting me out there because my parents and other people thought it was a good thing to do—and I do think it was a good thing to do—they didn't think it through past that, as to what to do with me once I was out there."

Yet the friendships were authentic and for the most part untroubled—especially when permitted to flourish in the safe harbor of a close-knit school whose teachers projected an ethos of care.

"There weren't any Black people—there were like three in the school," remembered Steven Larkin, who came as a fourth grader in 1968. "But my experience at Heathwood Hall was fun and great. I didn't run into the same racism that was going on in the streets of Columbia," he added. "You know, they had the Orangeburg Massacre—there were some mean white people down there in Orangeburg. And I'm sure there were just as many mean white people in Columbia. Or more. But I didn't run into that, at that age.

Remember, I was nine or 10 years old. Had I been 16 or 17, you can bet I would have encountered that. When I got to A.C. Flora, I encountered it."[66]

Larkin would describe his three years at Heathwood in almost beatific terms. "It was like family. It gave me confidence, and humility," he said. "It gave me a sense of peace." Mrs. Lamar was "nice and very gracious—and always very supportive." His classmates seemed to like him for who he was, and he made friendships that lasted well beyond his graduation from sixth grade.

Heathwood's integration was also a momentous development for existing students who experienced it as a before-and-after transition. "I was blissfully enjoying white privilege as child," recalled Will Prioleau, who'd started at Heathwood in 1962. "I remember seeing separate water fountains." Then, halfway through his time at the mansion, the social possibilities suddenly expanded. The realm of adults remained starkly divided but new friendships could bloom among children. The significance of his schoolyard bond with Steven Larkin, for instance, was clear to Prioleau: "Our parents couldn't go out to dinner together in public, but we could sit next to each other in the same classroom."

Library at the Heath Mansion, circa 1969.

Heathwood appealed to African American families primarily as a place where academically motivated children could thrive. Fredrina Tolbert, a graduate of Charleston's renowned Avery Normal Institute[67] who held a master's degree in music from Boston University and sang arias in four languages,[68] enrolled her daughter Charla Tolbert McMillian in kindergarten in 1968. Her son Charles, who followed the next year, remembered the "pep talk" with which their mother prepared them for the transition from an all-Black neighborhood to an overwhelmingly white school. "I remember Mom telling me that I'm smart, I'm cute, I'm witty—and that I would look different from my classmates," he recalled. "She talked to us about the n-word—and said that this is something you might encounter. So we were prepared for the worst.

"And I don't remember, in the early years, encountering anything adverse," he continued. Yet the school did single out his older sister from her classmates in another way. "By the time she got to third grade, the headmaster called our house and said, 'The teachers don't know what to do with Charla—because she already knows everything.'" So one of Charles' early memories of Heathwood involved a family meeting where the school decided to skip Charla directly into fourth grade.[69] That would become something of a pattern for Charla, whose prowess as a runner eventually earned her a spot on the boys cross-country team—an apparent school first. Her achievements in scholastics, music, drama, Spanish declamation contests, and high school debate propelled the Class of 1981 graduate to Dartmouth University at a time when Ivy League acceptance was an exceedingly rare event for Heathwood's small graduating classes.

As positive experiences spread through word-of-mouth, a small group of upwardly mobile Black families trickled into the mansion. So the Cooper boys—Noble, Ford, and Martin—followed their neighbor Michael Perry; Claudette Stewart paved the way for Marshall, Michael, and Beth James; and so on.

"It wasn't all rosy," conceded Charles Tolbert. These children were often the only Black students in their elementary grade class sections—though Middle School (which coincided with Heathwood's move to a bigger

Kindergarten dance, circa 1969.

campus) brought a modicum of relief from that sometimes isolating circumstance. The sailing also seemed far smoother for children of "bourgeois" families like his own, he noticed, than for Black peers who projected a more assertive "urban" bearing. Like Michael Perry, Tolbert retained a keen memory of several early African American students who were teased by white peers and "singled out for [their] race while I wasn't." Yearbooks from this period attest to the departure of a number of Black students not very long after their arrival. And friction occasionally came his way, too. He remembered one white classmate jeering, "Work, slave, work"—provoking a physical retaliation. A second would inscribe the initials KKK on notebook covers and "joke" about attending nighttime meetings with his grandfather. Ridicule of Columbia's historically Black Benedict College emerged as another unwelcome, albeit more socially acceptable, form of derogatory humor.

Yet those were exceptions to a far more welcoming rule. Heathwood's Episcopal affiliation, Tolbert felt, "added a level of graciousness and acceptance" during his early years at the mansion. "I just remember going to chapel, and it was more about inclusion and accepting everyone," he said. "And we weren't treated as *other* in those early years." He fondly recalled

Recess at the Heath Mansion.

middle-school slumber parties at the homes of white classmates like David Nidiffer and Marty Belson—and reciprocating with sleepovers at his own house.

A memory from fifth grade suggests that Heathwood's faculty approached the integration of non-white children by explicitly setting expectations for the behavior of existing students. In the fall of 1975, Tolbert recalled, "Our teacher said, 'Two students are coming to school today, and we don't want you to stare at them. We want you to welcome them. Their names are Yoon-Sun Lee and Yoon-Young Lee." These musically virtuosic sisters were not the first students of Asian descent to attend Heathwood, but the manner in which they were received midway through a fall semester bespeaks a proactive attitude towards inculcating a school culture of openness. Will Prioleau, Steven Larkin, and Mary Bentz Gilkerson would identify Elsie Lamar as the original source of that ethos.

B y the time Noble Cooper was in the middle grades, he felt surrounded by "lifelong friends" in a setting whose tone was set by Ms. Page, Ms. Gilpin, and the Kindness Club. "We spent the night at each other's house," he recalled. "Everyone looked at me as a regular person—it wasn't as an African American. I was welcomed in houses. We were really close. A lot of us were very talented in many respects, and we respected each other's talents."

Conceding that the escape from racial animus could never have been total during that era, Cooper credited his peers and faculty members with fostering a more humane culture within the cloistered atmosphere of the school. "The school and the students, they protected me," he said. In middle and high school, sports could be particularly prone to outbursts of reactionary racism,[70] but for Cooper these incidents underlined the sense of belonging he felt at Heathwood. "My teammates were so nice about making sure I was with someone, and making sure I was treated properly. They gathered round me, and made me feel like family. So I didn't really notice the discrimination—but again, I was protected by the students, and the staff, and the culture."

Meanwhile, integration began to change the school in other ways. When James and Maxine Dickey moved to Columbia from Virginia in the late 1960s, intent on sending their son Kevin to private school, they had choices. "They didn't make a big deal of it," Kevin remarked later, "but they did not like idea of a segregationist school like Hammond Academy was. They liked the idea that there was some element of diversity in the school ... they liked that Heathwood had that emphasis—which was a small amount, but a large amount at the time."

This dynamic would take on a self-reinforcing quality, especially when Columbia's public school system finally implemented a comprehensive desegregation plan in 1970. Having spent so much time and energy trying to evade the *Brown* integration mandate rather than plan an orderly transition under it, the state's public schools had set themselves up for an organizational shock to challenge any complex bureaucracy. It led both to sweeping intended changes—93 percent of African American students in South Carolina attended integrated schools in the 1970-71 academic year, up from 29 percent the year before[71]—as well as anxiety that affected virtually everyone with a stake in schools, from parents to principals. In the resulting flight to private education among many Columbians who could afford it, Heathwood emerged as a choice that appealed to certain families whose wariness of an unsettled public school system coexisted with a desire for a multiracial educational atmosphere. In this way the Dickey family was followed in turn by the Walkers, the Haynsworths, the Edgars, the Rices, and in fact far too many families to name, in a process that continued to influence school selection well into the 1980s.

The trustees worked to make Heathwood more attractive to minority students by diversifying their own ranks. "I had expressed a desire to have a school that had a diverse group of students, and a diverse board of trustees," recalled Bob Royall, who credited his selection as chairman of a reorganized Board in 1973 to those priorities.[72] Noble Cooper Sr., a dentist who was active in the NAACP, served on the board. He was soon joined by Henry Ponder, the president of Benedict College. Royall was succeeded by Bob Burg, one of at least two trustees of that era whose religious heritage included Judaism.

Within the mansion and its grounds, the success of integration had perhaps more to do with the women who spent every day there. They created a culture robust enough to outlast them. When Patsy Malanuk (then known as Patsy Moore) interviewed with headmaster Richard Nevius for a teaching job in 1970, she came away with the impression that he had hired her on the basis of her single year on the faculty at Waverly Elementary School. "I'm sure there were a lot of other people interested in the job," she recalled, "but he was very impressed that I had been so bold as to teach in an all Black school in 1969. And I think that's why he hired me. He had a progressive view of the world." Yet she came to attribute the school's open culture to earlier leaders. "There was something about Elsie Lamar," she said. "She was one of the most generous people. She was self-effacing. Her life had not been easy—she raised Billy after his father had died early. Elsie had this arms-wide-open way of being. As of course Page did," Malanuk added, referring to kindergarten teacher Page Steinert. "There was an ethos of those women who had led the way at the school."

The greatest testament to their achievement—which was authored in equal measure by the students themselves, who are prime culture-creators in any school—has less to do with Heathwood's attraction of like-minded parents than with the way the school fostered a certain social and spiritual growth among families for whom racial openness was not, in fact, a preexisting priority. For the truth is that the friendships the children cultivated at school did not always slide without friction into the adult world beyond it. As many people would later recall, classroom closeness did not always translate into birthday party invitations.

"I remember awkwardness about Steven coming to our house," remembers Will Prioleau about Steven Larkin. "I wanted to believe for a long time that my father was a Kennedy Democrat and that part of the reason we went to Heathwood Hall was that it had integrated—but that wasn't true." But ultimately another fact mattered more: "It didn't *stop* him from sending us there."

About one thing, at least, Herbert Ravenel Sass had been right: familiarity can breed affection. And as Michael Perry would recall, with fondness and amazement, narrow-minded attitudes could sometimes open up with unpredictable speed.

"There was a time I was going to go home with one of my buddies," he reflected. "We made arrangements, as you do when you're kids like that—and then, last minute, instead of me getting in the car, he had to come back and tell me his mom said no." Considering how quickly they'd become friends in first grade, this was painful. "Second grade, I thought I was going to his party—then come to find out I wasn't." But then the script flipped. "The very next year, his mom confessed to my mom: that she had been raised in a racist—well, let's say, with a type of a racial resolve. She was very ashamed, and apologized profusely. And over the next few years—it's funny how it happened so quickly—she just turned quite the opposite. Who knows why?"

Pausing to remember his friend's mother decades later, Perry surfaced another memory that seemed to answer his question. "In fact, the last time I saw her was at Jim Gasque's wake," he remarked. "And it was like whenever you see people you grew up with: It was like I had seen her the day before."

chapter three

BIRTH OF THE HIGHLANDERS

Rev. Richard Nevius—a new Board—Burwell Manning and a gift of land—Earl Devanny—the Dewar's Highlander—Ms. Polly and her puppets—"What does honor mean to us?"—Q—from the mansion to the mud fields

[*1969-1974*]

In January 1969, after nine years as headmistress, Elsie Lamar resigned. "We have come through some trying times," she wrote to Board Chairman James Stirling, "but we have weathered the storm, and I feel that we now have no way to go but forward."[1] The next five years would bear that out, and Heathwood Hall would emerge as though from a cocoon, fundamentally transformed.

The school's final years in the mansion were marked by a focus on growth. The addition of Middle School grades on the original campus was the first step toward realizing an expansive K-12 vision, which would be completed on virgin ground. The leaders who guided this transition recognized that its success would depend largely on two things. For the trustees, the primary challenge was generating philosophical agreement and financial support from the parent body. Administrators and teachers

Math class on the grass, circa 1969.

faced a more subtle task: forging a school culture and identity robust enough to withstand a doubling of the student body and the addition of high school, while preserving some of the characteristics that had long distinguished Heathwood as a close-knit elementary school.

Lamar was succeeded by the Rev. Richard Nevius. His short tenure was significant in two ways. The first lay in the wide-ranging and unapologetic intellectualism that marked his approach to learning. "Whenever I find myself getting too complacent about the purposes and results of education," Nevius began a speech as headmaster, "I re-read Philip Magnus' biography of King Edward VII." After that opening salvo, Nevius mused about the miseducation of George III, David Reisman and Christopher Jencks' seminal analysis of mid-20th-century American academia, the liturgical history of the Roman Catholic Church, the limitations of IQ tests, the legacy of Charles Darwin as considered in light of Thomas Aquinas' theological commitment to scientific rationalism, and the salutary influences of interfaith dialogue and cooperation. Into this cerebral panorama he also managed to weave a Sigmund Freud joke and a reference to a *New Yorker* cartoon.[2]

The second noteworthy thing about Nevius was his sex.

"His leadership," in Kevin Dickey's estimation, "turned Heathwood Hall from kind of a sweet matriarchal place into one that broadened out the scope of the school ... He was kind and caring without it being such a matriarchal environment. Under Elsie Lamar it had a really motherly feel to it. With him it felt more like a school. And that was great."

Nevius moved to replace recess detention with a demerit system (children "need recess") and cashiered what he characterized as a "totally confusing" E-G-F-P assessment system in favor of traditional A, B, C grades.[3] He also—like Rev. Stirling—embodied the progressive wing of the Episcopal Church, particularly with regard to racial issues. "Non-Public schools are springing up all over the South," he remarked in that speech. "The reason for this sudden growth of private schools is completely obvious to all of you. One of the strongest reasons for our seeking membership in the National Association of Independent Schools is so that we will not be identified with this new kind of private school."[4]

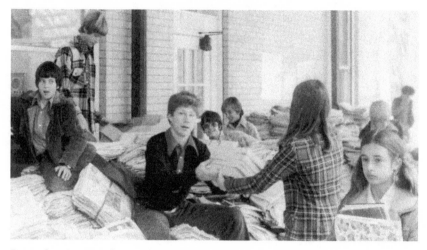

Bruce Stanley, Rick Stanland, Frankie McCrory, Jim Maass, and Claudia Barton run the paper drive, circa 1974.

Despite all this—or because of it, or for different reasons altogether—Nevius inspired insufficient confidence to last long at the helm. He proved to be a transitional leader, paving the way along with interim headmaster Frank S. Morris for the 1972 installation of Earl Devanny, who cemented Heathwood Hall's masculine turn.

Devanny's selection by the trustees was tightly bound up with expansion plans, for which Bob Royall ran point at the behest of Gayle Averyt. Averyt, the CEO of Colonial Life & Accident Insurance Company, served on the board of directors of Citizens and Southern National Bank, which had transferred Royall to Columbia in 1970. Royall enrolled his daughter at Heathwood, where Averyt was an active parent. "He approached me with the concept of taking the school from six grades to 12 grades," Royall recalled, "and indicated that he felt that we could get a gift of 100 acres of land for the school. So the challenge became one of convincing the parents of those involved with Heathwood ... that we needed six more grades."

The further challenge was to "convince them that we could build a campus on this 100 acres of land," he added, "which was along the Congaree River, and farmland at that time."

Parent opinion was split. A four-classroom and chapel annex had augmented the mansion campus in 1970-71,[5] and not everyone was sold on adding high school. Skeptics voiced concerns about the location's distance from town and its low-lying elevation. Proponents envisioned a blank slate that could sustain a K-12 school with a full athletic complex and ample room for growth. The land in question belonged to Burwell Manning, whose family's connections with Heathwood went back to the Heath Mansion.

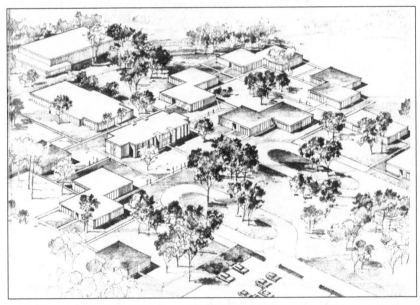

Architectural rendering of the Congaree campus, and a classroom pod.

Burwell Manning, Robert Royall, Arthur Simons, and headmaster Earl Devanny
look on as Bishop Alexander helps Leslie Haynsworth and Chalmers Poston
break ground for the Congaree campus, 1974.

Manning, who died in 2005, was a farmer and real-estate investor who
had multiple motivations for making a gift of land. "He was always proud of
the school," said his daughter Lynn Manning Cooper, a 1996 Heathwood
graduate who returned in the 2000s for a long teaching career. "He was proud
of the early decisions of the school. He was proud of the way they used the
family home to improve the community ... I think when he made that decision, he saw a need. He knew he had the land. He didn't want to see the city
of Columbia lose an asset. He thought that Columbia had great potential."

Cooper reflected that her father, who was not particularly religious,
hoped Heathwood Hall would become a boarding school. "He always
thought it was a shame everybody would go up north. If we had a decent
boarding school, people could stay closer to home," she said. "I think he
saw an opportunity for a beautiful campus, and he believed that being
outside was good for children."

Manning was also savvy enough to envision the ways a successful school might increase the value of his family's surrounding holdings, which were largely planted with corn, wheat, and soybeans.[6] Whatever the case, in 1974 Manning conveyed to the Foundation for Heathwood Hall[7] a five percent interest in a 133-acre parcel on the east bank of the Congaree river, contingent on the construction of a private school that would offer 12 grades by no later than 1985. The remaining interest in the property would be transferred over an unspecified period (later capped at 20 years) as a charitable contribution to the trustees, who would meanwhile have the right to lease the entire parcel for $1 per year.[8]

Earl Devanny appealed to the trustees as a man capable of essentially rebuilding the school from scratch. "He had a military background," Royall said, "which was good ... He was a disciplinarian. An organizer. The military is something we all ought to have." That certainly appealed to Royall, who considered his 10-year stint in the US Marine Corps the best education he ever received. "He was very aggressive. I thought he was perfect for the job and I think the results proved it. There are lots of problems that jump up and bite you when you've got something that's brand new, and it didn't seem to shake him. He handled everything that came his way—including a flood. He just was a go-getter, and he didn't back off when the problems would come."

Devanny came from Presbyterian Day School, a boys elementary school in Memphis, Tennessee. Before that he had been a tactical officer at Indiana's Howe Military Academy, where at least one cadet remembered his zealous enforcement of short hair.[9] During Heathwood Hall's final two years in the mansion, where seventh and eighth grade were now offered, Devanny grew the school's boys and girls athletics programs—though they inevitably ran up against the limitations of the old campus, where teams occasionally opted to walk to the basketball court at Heathwood Park rather than practice on the school's barebones blacktop.

The 1974 Middle School boys basketball team.

It was under Devanny's leadership that Heathwood Hall officially adopted the Highlander as a mascot.[10] Although the reasons for its selection are murky, the school's original choice of visual imagery can be traced with some specificity. Pictorial depictions of Scottish Highlanders have taken varied forms in popular culture. The particular image Heathwood Hall landed on was a product of happenstance, possibly blended with a touch of droll humor on the part of an institution celebrating its 21st birthday.

In the telling of Jimmy Walker, who in addition to teaching and coaching served as Devanny's assistant headmaster, the Heathwood Hall Highlander took shape courtesy of trustee Bob Burg. As the head of one of Columbia's major liquor distribution companies, Burg at some point found himself in possession of a life-sized cardboard replica of the Scottish character used to promote Dewar's "White Label" Scotch Whisky. One thing led to another, and soon the mansion gained a new tenant: a spirited Scottish laird decked out in a plaid kilt and Gaelic hose top socks, with a traditional sporran pouch suspended from a waist belt.

Devanny may have arrived with a reputation as a disciplinarian, but at Heathwood Hall he exhibited a softer touch than he likely had at

Howe Military Academy.[11] In Walker's judgment, Devanny's enthusiasm wasn't so much for discipline as for order. (And the assistant head, it must be said, sported a shaggy hairstyle more in line with *Scooby-Doo* than any drill sergeant's manual.) Leslie Haynsworth, who as a small girl rode in Devanny's car to the site of the new campus for a ceremonial groundbreaking, remembered him as a gentlemanly figure with a facility for putting young people at ease.

For Heathwood students he was a more remote presence than Elsie Lamar had been—which was a natural consequence of an expanded administrative burden at a school that now went through eighth grade and was planning a major expansion. So classroom teachers set the tone.

Marshall James, who started first grade during Heathwood's last year at the mansion, remembers his mother walking him to the outbuilding where Polly Nettles—Ms. Polly—taught. "Even though I was really young, it seemed a little unusual—because there was this big house looming over campus," said the Class of 1985 graduate. "What I remember more than anything about my first-grade year was Ms. Polly."

The original Highlander, and its inspiration.

Along with Ms. Page, Ms. Polly would become a bridge between the Lamar/Mansion and Devanny/Congaree eras. Both women helped to preserve some elements of a school culture that was swiftly changing. "When I was in Ms. Polly's class, the big issue was whether or not, during the course of the year, we had been good enough to make those puppets at the end of the year," James said. "She held that over us. And I think we were able to make the puppets. But that was my major concern in first grade: whether or not we were going to get to make those puppets."

Page Steinert and Polly Nettles were also among the 17 signatories—all women—of a remarkable document produced by the faculty in May 1971. It was an addendum to a proposal to establish an Honor Court composed of six students and eight teachers who would "decide guilt and punishment of extreme cases such as cheating, stealing, lying, severe fighting, severe insolence, or the accumulation of 10 demerits." The proposal stipulated that each class create its own list of rules and punishments for the coming year, bearing in mind that "rules are not to restrict, but to protect," and that "children often do misdeeds for a reason, and we should try to get at the root of the problem as well as the correction."

In this way the faculty affirmed democratic deliberation as one pillar of Heathwood's governing ethos. Additionally, the group submitted a "Statement of Principle" that was equally striking. "We have spoken of an Honor Court for our students," the letter began, expressing a hope that it would give rise to a "renewed sense of responsibility ... springing from student organization and participation." Then it asked: "But what of ourselves—faculty, staff, headmaster? What does honor mean to us?"

Over the course of four pages they laid out an expansive answer. It meant finding a "suitable curriculum for as many of our children as possible, not just the brightest and best."[12] It entailed the "sacrifice" of time "to a child who needs an extra quota of love or understanding." It meant being "mindful of the needs of others" and honest in dealings with pupils, parents and colleagues—including a mandate to "examine ourselves to see whether we are contributing to a personality conflict with a student, and how we might correct the situation." They forswore the use of "sarcasm, especially around children." Their ideals extended even to "informing the public that it is welcome to use the grounds after school," as long as that privilege was not abused.

"Heathwood could become an academic preparatory school," they declared in a section subtitled *Love*. "It could become a school associated with social prestige. Let us not forget, however, that a good education can be obtained anywhere with enough initiative and background on the part of the individual. Let us not forget that Heathwood basically was established that children might come and learn in an atmosphere of peace and love, in an atmosphere where each might be accepted as an individual with his own special talents, in an atmosphere where he might develop those talents to the best of his ability."[13]

Although Board Meeting minutes and yearbooks offer no clear verdict about the fate of the Honor Court proposal, the faculty's accompanying "Statement of Principal" offered a confident, full-throated mission statement from the adults who ultimately mattered most: the classroom teachers who charged themselves with carrying it out. Sensing that the school was on the cusp of a momentous shift, these educators issued a clarion call asserting that "the change which comes from growth need not eradicate the traditions and ideals upon which Heathwood Hall was established."

Several new faculty members who came at the tail end of the mansion era would also help to smooth the coming transition. Claudia Barton would recall science class with Sarah Magoffin—a "trooper" who spent that final year on Heathwood Circle teaching in the basement. Nancy Reeder, who would serve as Heathwood Hall's librarian for 44 years—a tenure exemplified by the "Please Disturb" sign she hung on her door—also began around this time, in 1972. Her interactions with children across the grade spectrum gave her a fine sense of student life beyond the classroom. "It was strictly forbidden that any student go up to the ballroom," she would later recall about the mansion's top floor. "Of course, if you wanted to cut class, that's where you went. So if anyone was missing they looked first in the ballroom."

Librarian Nancy Reeder.

Insofar as the school's culture was transmitted from one cohort of students to the next, Heathwood's final years in the mansion retained the same familial warmth that had imbued the school from the beginning, augmented by a certain free-wheeling spirit that marked the upper grades. The 1972 yearbook featured a series of mock bequests from the eighth-grade "seniors" to the seventh graders coming along after them.

"I, Robin Nettles, will to Sandra Reed, my most prized possession, a 99 which I made on a French test," read one. "I, Buddy Cole, hereby leave my lunch to August Krickel. It's been sitting in the corner for five months and not a bite of it is gone," went another. Allen Green bequeathed to Chris Sox his ability to do Gamecock cheers in class. Desks near the radiator featured in more than one will. "I, Nancy Welch, not being of sound mind, will to Alice Garrett and Suzanne Powell my hangup about naming things after boys."

Devanny's tenure would ultimately prove more remarkable for the development of a new campus than for the implementation of a distinctive pedagogical vision. But he cemented his most lasting legacy with a single faculty hire in 1973. Poached from Dreher High School's English department, the man in question would teach for one year in the mansion before carrying its familial spirit to the banks of the Congaree River, where over the next four decades he would become perhaps the most iconic personality in the school's history. In the scores of interviews conducted for this book, no teacher evoked more declarations of devotion than Jimmy Gasque, known to two generations of students as Q.

"The greatest teacher that I ever had in my life was James Gasque," declared Michael Perry, who first encountered him as an eighth grader in the mansion. "The first day that we saw him at Heathwood, he told us he was going to teach us from the guidelines of his twelfth-grade advanced class at Dreher. And everybody moaned and protested. And he laughed! That was Jim Gasque. He was brilliant … He was irreverent—he didn't coddle you. He was so honest. And that was the best thing for me."

To call him a consummate Southerner, or to echo his 2014 obituary's proud claim that he came from Carolina Soil, is to flail in understatement. Jim's world, as his Heathwood colleagues would come to jest, was bounded in the south by Pawley's Island and in the north by Kanuga, the Episcopal Church retreat 10 miles over the mountains dividing South Carolina from North.[14] The lone geographic loyalty rivaling Gasque's home state allegiance was the affection he held for the British Isles, and specifically the Anglican trappings of the Episcopal Church, which were inextricably bound up in his devotion to the English language. He relished Shakespeare above any other writer, but had a soft spot for C.S. Lewis and the Scotsman Kenneth Grahame's 1908 children's classic *The Wind in the Willows*. Forever dressed in jacket and bow tie—one day tartan plaid knotted atop a white Oxford shirt, the next day canary yellow bursting above a plaid button-down—he vibrated with joy in the presence of high ritual and regalia. In his living room hung a framed photograph of Queen Elizabeth on ceremonial horseback, Trooping the Colour down the Mall from Buckingham Palace on her birthday. His affection for the Baroque cadences of George Friderich Handel could only have been amplified by

Jim Gasque in his classroom.

the German-born master's final resting place, in Westminster Abbey of London, where the composer spent his last three decades creating anthems and oratorios as a naturalized British subject.

As a writing instructor Gasque cast spells over many and provoked curses from a few, pressing his students to fling themselves toward ever more emphatic verbs. Some English teachers idealize thrift and austerity in the written word. Others favor purple prose. Purple, in mere monochrome, would not do for Q. Gasque prized sentences woven from lilac pompoms and lavender stems, rolled in crushed violets, plastered with mulberry-slathered fuchsia petals and dunked in grape must so that the squeezed liqueur might drip down every comma tail like spilt sangria, slip-sliding toward a final clause stopped not by a period but a port-soaked plum.[15] Years later his former Upper School principal Bob Haarlow, a Princeton alumnus, would cop to having kept letters from Gasque whose language strained his own vocabulary: "It couldn't have been more flowery if they had been written by a very sophisticated Southern woman."

The man was inimitable: neither by acolytes like Class of 1994 graduate Mel Pennington, who dropped $150 on a Mont Blanc fountain pen to sport in his own lapel in homage; nor by the irreverent impressions of Ryan Waldron and Todd Robertson in the Class of 1993, who play-acted their instructor's perpetual swoon behind his back and sometimes in front of his nose—for Q loved his students enough to laugh, if through stiffened lips, at himself. Imbuing his staunch fealty to the Anglo-Saxon canon with a florid theatricality that belonged to him alone, Gasque telegraphed a species of aesthetic conservatism whose flamboyance marched so close to the edge of subversive parody that one occasionally wondered if he meant to cross the line. Students nearing the turn of the 21st century would search his extravagant Southern mannerisms for hints of concealed irony. But they searched in vain, for Gasque disguised nothing: he wore it all on his sleeve, right next to his heart, which beat for his students and was upholstered in Heathwood plaid.

In many ways, the task that faced Earl Devanny during this period mirrored the one expressed by graduating eighth graders in the 1972 yearbook just before he arrived. "We are now maturing and preparing to face the adult world," they wrote. "We will be questioning old traditions to make way for newer, creative thinking. We must be careful, however, to carry over the best from the past. Our goal is to combine the old with the new, the traditional with the creative, and contribute something worthwhile to our world."[16]

Strong personalities and a fortified school culture would prove important as Heathwood Hall prepared to leave the mansion and resettle five miles to the south-southwest. For when students, teachers, and families rolled into the new campus at 3000 South Beltline Boulevard in the fall of 1974, they entered a realm of stunning rawness.

When Jimmy Gasque looked out the window of his new classroom, "there was not one green thing in sight. There were no trees, no bushes," he recalled, "nothing but endless fields of mud."[17] The absence of vegetation struck nearly every person who joined him there. "There was not a blade of grass on this whole campus," remembered Nancy Boyle, who came in 1976 as a teacher and chaplain. "It was red mud—the ugliest place I had ever seen in my whole life."[18]

Transforming this site into a flourishing campus where children could thrive became a project that combined the commitment of trustees and administrators with community volunteerism on a scale without precedent in the life of the school.

chapter four

OUTWARD BOUND

*a barren plain—a grass campaign—56,000 pines—the tractor
rustler—Highlander Games—the sporting life—culture creation—the
"enrollment certificate exodus"—Nancy Boyle v. Detention—
the flood—an untimely passing*

[1974-1977]

American education in the late 20th century was partly a matter of the accessories: backpacks, lunch boxes, Trapper Keepers, No. 2 pencils. From the opening of the Congaree River campus, an additional item became paramount for the students of Heathwood Hall: rain boots.

Jay Hennig, a Class of 1982 graduate who later chaired the Board of Trustees, recalled moving from the mansion to the new campus in fifth grade. "It was new construction, and there was no grass," he said. "The wind would howl through there," he continued, for there were no mature trees. "When it rained they would put down these raised wooden platforms for us to walk on, because there was mud everywhere. It would get all over everything, and in the classrooms, and all over you. I think some of the cement sidewalks weren't even installed."[1]

In dry weather it was "dusty and barren," said Class of 1978 alumna Claudia Barton. "I don't even recall if there were any shrubs planted."

Welcome to the new campus, circa 1974.

Mixing cement for sidewalks.

Neither did Class of 1985 graduate Marshall James, who was in second grade for the transition. "It just seemed like four pods and a breezeway. There wasn't much vegetation. There wasn't much landscaping." The ground beneath the pods—single-story buildings that held eight classrooms apiece—had been modestly raised with earth excavated from what became a pond on the northern part of campus. The old chapel and classroom annex was moved from the mansion and reassembled on somewhat elevated terrain, becoming the Commons. But pathways linking these structures to other campus buildings, especially the gym, flooded readily with rain.

Students had to stick to prescribed paths no matter the weather.

"They were trying to plant grass and get it to grow," James recalled. "And it was a huge deal for students not to walk on the grass. It was a mantra: *Do not walk on the grass*. Teachers had eagle eyes." Faculty vigilance was hardly limited to that first year. "I do remember walking on the grass once. Mr. Newell chewed me out," James laughed, referring to Al Newell, who joined the Middle School faculty in 1976. "I was the last of 10 who had walked on this patch of grass in front of the pods. And of course I was the one who got caught."

Campus beautification quickly involved the entire community. "One of the first events we had was an Arbor Day," Hennig said. "All the families were supposed to come … and I remember everyone going out there and digging a hole to plant a bush or a tree." Although professional crews planted most of the 56,000 pine saplings that would become wind breaks and shady groves,[2] the near-universal participation of Heathwood families in volunteer efforts instilled a deep sense of community responsibility and pride.

Saplings grew so quickly in the fertile soil that successive waves of students would struggle to imagine the campus's initial starkness. "Those live oaks in the quadrangle," Jim Gasque would regale them, "used to be so small that we'd have to stand them up in the morning after a heavy rain."[3] Where later generations would gather in the shade of towering pine trees to board school buses, mid-1970s students would remember massive collective labor.

"We planted those pine trees," said Class of 1982 graduate Anna Ponder. "Kids planted those. We did all kinds of stuff like that. And the parents—the volunteerism and philanthropic contributions of the parents really kept the school afloat. Including the donation of the land itself!"

In fact, Burwell Manning had made a further contribution by grading a section of land for conversion to athletic fields. This was "a gift that Heathwood didn't ask for," said trustee Julian Walker, "but it was a gift." The school had neither the money nor the staff to plant and maintain these areas, which would be ruined by erosion if not covered with grass soon. So Walker, who served on the buildings and grounds committee before becoming chairman of the Board, took the task upon himself.

He started by approaching a psychiatrist named Jack Dunlap.

"I remember saying, 'If I'm crazy, you're the person to tell me.' He said, 'No, you're not crazy.' So I said, 'Great, I need $500.' … And he was the first of many interested parents, mainly, who contributed."

"We had not yet had a graduating class," Walker explained. "We were struggling with enrollment. My vision was that to really help with the growth of the Upper School, we needed to do what we could to get those athletic fields up and operational."

A donation from Bob Burg enabled the installation of a rudimenta-
ry irrigation system. Walker arranged for deliveries of hybrid Bermuda
grass from Tifton, Georgia, on a series of Saturdays. As the trucks drove
around the fields, Heathwood students and staff members would stand
in the cargo holds, casting sprigs. "We would spread it by hand on the
football and baseball field," Hennig remembers. "There was a lot of community service then."

Volunteer landscapers Caroline Averyt, Lee Ann Culbreath, and Mrs. J. Thomas
Culbreath plant perennials around the pods.

Having solved the problems of planting and watering, Walker soon confronted the next one. "The grass was not only growing, it was growing with a vengeance"—and the school had no way to mow it. Which is how Walker, an attorney who headed the trust department of First National Bank of South Carolina, found himself calling upon a facilities manager next-door at the Columbia Metropolitan Wastewater Treatment Plant.

"They had a tractor that was designed to pull a lawnmower device. And I told the guy that I'd really appreciate it if I could use that tractor on the weekends. He said, 'Well, nobody's using it on the weekends. I'll tell you what I'll do: I'll fill it up with gas and I'll just leave the key in it and you come get it whenever you want.' I remember he said, 'Now you know how to run a tractor, don't you?' And I said, "Oh yeah, man, I grew up on a farm.' Well, I didn't grow up on any farm. I grew up in downtown Charleston."

Overcoming the handicap of his urban upbringing, Walker would spend countless weekends driving that tractor-mower over Heathwood's football, soccer, and baseball fields. Occasionally he would dismount only to proceed directly to chair a meeting of the trustees.

For students, the new campus was suffused with a spirit of collective effort and possibility. "We just had this feeling that we had this new exciting school and campus, and everyone was going to work together to overcome the challenges," recalled Class of 1986 alumnus Wade Mullins, who later served as Board chair. "I'm sure there were complaints about the running water, and the mice in the air conditioners, but I don't recall moaning and groaning. I recall everyone just being excited about being out there on that new campus."

The school's spacious new setting—and the influx of new students it enabled—also cemented a profound attitudinal shift that had begun during Earl Devanny's final year at the mansion. "It was a huge change," said Michael Perry, who was in ninth grade for the move. "The way it was when we were in the mansion, it was a little neighborhood school. We had

The Congaree campus takes shape, circa 1974.

something called the Kindness Club. And we were very tight-knit ... It went from being a very closed, coddled environment, to where we started to open up to the world, and become a more worldly place.

"I didn't realize until later that some of my classmates might have been getting scholarship money—or that people were going to summer school," he continued. The mansion had struck him as a place where affluence was the common coin of Black and white families alike. The new campus seemed to open Heathwood to a greater diversity of social backgrounds and intellectual orientations—from Cheryl and Anna Ponder, whose father Henry Ponder was president of Benedict College, to teenagers who had failed to thrive in public schools and sought the fresh start of a disciplinary record wiped clean. "We opened up to a wider variety of families and students," Perry concluded, "and that was a good thing."

The addition of high school was one driver of this social (and to some extent economic) diversification. Another was the implementation of an unfunded financial aid program at the recommendation of

Robert Meriwether and Michael Perry play to a crowd, circa 1975.

Julian Walker, creating a budgetary mechanism to attract families unable to afford full tuition. "It basically recognized that we had empty seats," Walker explained, "and what we needed to do was help as many students as we could identify that we wanted to have at Heathwood, and give them as much aid, in terms of tuition, so that we could fill up some of those empty seats."

Annual tuition in 1976-77 was $910. This represented a slightly higher burden (6.2 percent of median family income in the South) than it had in 1966-67 (5.1 percent).[4] Heathwood's tuition would roughly double every six years for the next two decades, during which financial aid would become an increasingly significant enrollment tool.

"Heathwood was very important as far as showing me a great deal of society that I wouldn't otherwise have had access to," said Class of 1978 alumna Sarah Sturtevant, a clergyman's daughter. "I made friends in all walks of life there, and it gave me the opportunity—because it was a close community and we had such small classes—to learn and grow, and bloom. I really believe that."

Noble Cooper was another who viewed the move to the new campus largely in terms of the breadth of newcomers joining Heathwood's student community. "It brought new talented people," said the Class of 1980 graduate. "It brought in even more ideas and thought. I think Heathwood Hall started becoming more of a think tank then; it got a little more college-prep."

This sense of expanded horizons was evident to a remarkable degree in the first yearbook produced on the new campus. In striking contrast to prior editions, the 1975 *Highlander* opened with a four-page spread of captioned photographs depicting wartime Vietnam and Cambodia, Palestinian Liberation Organization leader Yasser Arafat, the West African food shortage, illegal CIA activity in Chile, the Watergate scandal, and Mercury's South Pole as seen by the Mariner 10 space probe. Under the leadership of sophomore editor-in-chief Becky Meriwether, this yearbook edition would set a standard rarely to be surpassed. "What world-wide event has influenced you the most this year?" the editors asked 24 ninth graders, 13 of whom answered "Inflation."[5] (Younger students addressed somewhat more classic concerns. The most influential event for fifth graders was the State Fair. Gym and P.E. emerged as the "most fun" activities for first graders, and the majority of the seventh grade ranked the new gym as Heathwood's "most far-reaching" change. Parachute games would stand out in the memories of many early Highlanders as a big reason for that enthusiasm.)

Among the faculty, French teacher Benjamin Slavich stood out as something of a countercultural forerunner of the questing progressivism beginning to find a foothold amid more traditionally minded teachers on the banks of the Congaree. "He was sort of contrary to the Heathwood mold—not a part of what I called the 29205 Set," said Class of 1983 alumnus Charles Tolbert, referring to one of Columbia's tonier ZIP codes. A freewheeling teacher whose interests ran toward practices like transcendental meditation, Slavich was "the most exotic person I'd ever come across," said Tolbert, who credited him with his own fruitful decision to study abroad at the Sorbonne as an undergraduate. "He taught us to question authority—question him, question all authority," he went on. "He was just an inspiring intellectual who encouraged independent thinking … and he encouraged me academically at a time when I was just sort of a partygoing, social, comic guy."

Earl Devanny's Highlander Games, still going strong in the mid-1980s.

As headmaster, Devanny recognized a need to knit together this increasingly broad range of children and teenagers and faculty. His signal achievements were in the realm of culture creation. A hallmark initiative was the creation of the Highlander Games—a field day that brought the entire student body together in massive mixed-age teams that squared off in relay competitions, three-legged races, and other fair-style games. Devanny modeled it after a similar event he had supervised at Presbyterian Day School in Tennessee. At Heathwood, some of the high schoolers would wear kilts, and legions of kindergartners would carry fond memories of riding piggyback on their shoulders, holding up buckets of water that rained down through holes as the burly and pint-sized partners dashed back and forth in wild relays.[6]

"It was to create that school unity," recalled Jimmy Walker, Devanny's assistant headmaster. "You know, not everybody had younger or older brothers. It was a way to create that for a lot of kids. And it did. You were proud if your team won!"

Michael Perry is trailed by Noble Cooper, Gil Martin, Steve Lunceford, and Cal Harrelson during the 1974 football season.

Mena Hope drives for a layup, circa 1976.

Varsity, junior varsity, and Middle School athletics—with three-season offerings for girls and boys alike—were another facet of Heathwood Hall's transformation. The school fielded its first football team in 1974-75, when tenth grade was the oldest cohort. Playing on what the yearbook editors archly dubbed a "semi-football field, presently containing more soy beans than grass," the 29-man junior varsity squad won a single game while losing four, but it combined with other teams to make a big impact on the school's culture.

Beyond the inherent rewards of team competition for student-athletes, the most appreciable impact was the propensity of sports to engage fathers in the life of the school.[7] "That was important too, in our psyche," Jimmy Walker reflected. "We were trying to make sure it wasn't just a little neighborhood day school. It was really a vision that this was going to be a strong independent school in Columbia. And we had to find ways to get beyond moms driving carpools, and the Parents' Guild. We wanted to get fathers involved."

Attempts to foster school spirit—which in 1976 grew to include a drama production, a faculty-student softball game, and a Booster Club exhibition scrimmage pitting the boys varsity basketball team against a group of University of South Carolina Gamecock seniors including future NBA star Alex English—carried more weight than the typical rah-rah pep rally. It was around this time that the trustees, facing financial pressures, imposed a requirement for families to purchase "enrollment certificates."[8] These lump-sum deposits came on top of tuition and were to be redeemed upon a child's departure from Heathwood—though the trustees hoped that many families would opt instead to convert them into charitable donations.

The school's need for money originated in challenges stemming from the initial development of the new campus. In July 1973, the Board had estimated a need to raise approximately $1 million to finance construction. The following winter, in response to a series of geopolitical events and domestic oil production policies, the price of oil quadrupled and never fell back.[9] Steel prices rose roughly 50 percent between 1972 and 1974.[10] And the rising building costs coincided with the 1973-75

Alex English looks on as Gamecock teammates take Ms. Polly up for the easy
deuce, circa 1975.

recession, during which the Dow Jones Industrial Average lost 45 percent of its value. The attrition of some $335,000 in pledges for the new
campus had left the school in a "very bad debt position" as of January
1976, with payments looming on a $970,000 loan.[11]

The enrollment certificate plan answered a clear need, but at a regret-
table cost. It precipitated what Scott Devanny, a Class of 1977 alumnus
who would go on to serve as an ex-officio member of the Board, later
dubbed the "enrollment certificate exodus"[12]: the student body shrank
from 674 to 502 between 1976 and 1978, as many families left and the
certificate requirement discouraged new ones from entering.

O ne way to view Earl Devanny's tenure is through the lens of a certain brand of masculinity that was gaining currency in the United
States in the 1970s. Its manifestation at Heathwood ranged from major
programmatic priorities, like the newfound emphasis on athletic competition, to subtler shifts. For instance the school's Maypole ceremony,
in which boys and girls had once played equal parts, became a largely
female affair.[13]

The trustees were not necessarily of a single mind about these developments. In 1974, for instance, they engaged in "considerable discussion"
about whether Heathwood should have a football program at all, with
trustee Rab Finlay suggesting that it was "not necessary." The balance of
opinion favored the sport's inclusion—on the same terms as "golf, tennis, etc."—as part of a "well-rounded curriculum."[14] At any rate, there
was some diversity of views about the school's intended direction. "The
fact that we didn't have a high school sports program never bothered us
one minute," recalled trustee Dick Stanland many years later, but sports
"seemed to be what was driving Hammond at that time."

Insofar as Heathwood was "muscling up" in an attempt to gain
ground with its crosstown rival—as one observer later put it—the school
found a counterbalance in Nancy Boyle. Heathwood's early-childhood
faculty remained a bastion of charismatic matriarchs like Ms. Page and
Ms. Polly. But Boyle, who arrived as a religion teacher for middle and
high school in 1976, would exert a stealthy and lasting influence on the
nascent culture of the upper grades. An emblematic example came in her
first experience of detention hall.

Devanny "was exactly the person" to oversee the transition to the
new campus, Boyle later reflected.[15] "He was a military man, and what
he knew about education was really getting it organized." But by her
lights, he had implemented a disciplinary regime whose results suggested a deficit of purposeful engagement in the classroom. This hit home
during her first shift overseeing Thursday afternoon detention.

"The school bell rang and everyone ran for the bus except those
people who had these detention slips," she remembered. "And they
started coming in … and they came and came, and we had to borrow

chairs from this room and chairs from that room, and pretty soon I had about 75 people."

Dismayed by the sheer volume of alleged miscreants, Boyle produced a pile of comic books for them to read. Presently Jimmy Walker, the assistant headmaster, came by to survey the scene.

"There we were," Boyle recalled, "all propped up with feet on the desks reading funny books."

"Mrs. Boyle," Walker said sternly, "This is detention."[16]

She allowed that it was, but could not abide it. After the period ended, she found her way to Walker's office. "I have one thing to tell you about detention hall," she declared. "If detention hall was an effective means of punishment, it would be empty. But the fact of the matter is that some of these kids are booked up the entire year. And when you keep calling somebody bad and making that kind of behavior get them attention, it doesn't work." She pledged that if she was ever charged with keeping detention hall again, passing out comic books would be her first order of business.

Boyle had a pretty good idea of what Earl Devanny thought about this: *Who is this crazy woman we've brought to this school?* she imagined him wondering. "But we kept talking about it, and they all realized that it wasn't very effective," she said.

"My notion," she went on, "was that if kids had enough to do, and if they enjoyed what they did, then they tended to behave. And if you treated them with respect, they tended to respond. And I decided that if I was going to be teaching religion, that what I would do is to have that happen in my classroom—and that if we treated each other like that in my classroom, that we would go out from that room and treat others with the same respect."

The power of Boyle's example—both at Heathwood Hall and at Trinity Cathedral, where she was an active advocate for progressive causes—seeped into the school's culture in subtle ways. "She wasn't afraid or ashamed or quieted," reflected Patsy Malanuk, who confessed to having been intimidated by Boyle at the outset of her own involvement at Trinity. "She knew what she believed in, and she was going to stand right there and say it, without any hesitation," Malanuk said. In time Malanuk came to regard Boyle as a "prophetic voice in the community" whose moral compass was trained on the Episcopalian insistence on the inherent worth and dignity of every human being. "At one point, I remember she said, 'Well, I guess we're just part of what's left of the Left.'"

As a new series of productive tensions shaped the school's evolution—a slightly more diverse mix of students pressing gently against an abiding inclination toward insularity, traditional discipline rubbing against a child-centered view of ethical development, competitive pride counterbalanced by Episcopalian humility—Heathwood continued to hone its identity in deliberate ways. The search for traditions often led to Sewanee, The University of the South, and an iconography steeped heavily in plaid. Jim Gasque modeled Heathwood Hall's Commencement after Sewanee's ceremony. Devanny's tenure saw the establishment of the Order of the Tartan. Described as Heathwood's "only nonworking club," this was a select honorary society of people who had "already done

Nancy Boyle.

the work," in the headmaster's phrasing.[17] With its unstated admission requirements and the surprise conferral of membership, this too bore some resemblance to Sewanee's by-invitation-only Ribbon Societies.

Yet arguably the most consequential thing to happen during Heathwood's new beginning was an event for which no one had planned, though some had feared.[18] In early October 1976 a cold front stalled over the western Carolinas, spilling an unusual amount of rain. As the water moved down the Broad River Basin toward Columbia, it set off some of the worst flooding in living memory. Lake Murray rose four feet in four days. In Columbia the Broad River crested at 29 feet, the highest level in 40 years, and all that water was bound for the Congaree.[19]

Jimmy Walker's telephone rang at four o'clock in the morning of October 11. It was Earl Devanny. "Get out to Heathwood," the headmaster said. Water had breached a dike and a pressure differential had also reversed the flow of the school's drainage system, flooding it from within. Walker picked up Al Newell and the pair drove most of the way down the road to the school.

"We started to see so much water, and it was dark," Walker recalled. "So we parked and started walking in, not knowing how deep the water was going to be." A little ways in, they spotted one of Burwell Manning's farm workers. They asked him if it was safe to proceed.

"Yes," the man replied, casting an eye over the fields. "It's not as high yet as it's going to get."

They found Devanny standing near the office alongside several trustees: Bob Royall, Bob Burg, Richard Stanland. After calling in a bulldozer in an unsuccessful attempt to close the breach, the men took stock of the school library and administrative records, then summoned several tractor trailers and started a phone tree to scare up volunteers.

The sun came up and the sun went down. "We loaded up three trailers, I think, with books and records and things we were trying to save," Walker said. (The Board later recognized Bill Edens for risking "a large amount of very expensive equipment" to facilitate that effort.)[20] "By eight or nine o'clock everybody realized we weren't going to stop the water. Nobody knew how high it might get." Exhausted, Walker went home around 10 p.m. "Earl Devanny stayed until everybody left, close to midnight," he remembered.

The next day brought a measure of relief. The water was only about three inches high in the classrooms—and crested below the in-wall heating and air-conditioning units. The gym suffered some floor damage, but overall, the campus had been spared total catastrophe. After a faculty meeting in the Devannys' home, the administration arranged to spread classes around several Episcopal parishes in town, having no firm idea how long that might last.

"We were fearful it would be two or three months," Walker said. In the end it lasted about four weeks—and affected the school in some unexpected ways.

In physical terms, the flood's biggest impact was not on the existing buildings but on future campus development. When the Army Corps of Engineers subsequently declared the area a flood plain, the school lost the ability to erect permanent structures at ground level. From that point on, Heathwood Hall would have to build everything up in the air, on concrete pillars—which raised construction costs dramatically. The damage to the gymnasium's rubber floor would plant a decades-long fear of upgrading it to hardwood—consigning a generation of winter athletes to play on thin carpet laid over hard concrete.

Yet the flood's more important legacy may have been less tangible. In a phrase that would become a Heathwood Hall mantra in the late 1980s, teachers had to learn how to implement the pedagogy of *less is more*.

"I ended up being thrust into a classroom with a lot of seventh graders, and it was the size of a small kitchen," recalled Lark Merrill Palma, who had joined the English faculty that year. "I learned quickly about class management."

Part of that involved a return, in some ways, to the spirit of improvisation and experiential learning that had animated Susan Robinson many years before.

"They had to find stuff for us to do," exclaimed Anna Ponder. "There were 150 kids running around Trinity!" She vividly remembered taking tracing paper to the cathedral's cemetery to create charcoal rubbings of tombstones—an art and history project that many subsequent class cohorts would reprise. Stranded in many cases without textbooks, teachers in all disciplines had to get creative with their lesson plans—again foreshadowing some of the practices that would come to be emphasized in the 1980s and 1990s under headmaster Bob Shirley.

In Nancy Boyle's estimation, the flood was a spiritual turning point. "There was another thing about early Heathwood," she remarked in 1991. "Not only were the buildings ugly, and the yard was ugly, and all was raw and new, but we hadn't learned how to live together in community ... We were all struggling with that." Faculty members, she said, often ate their lunches alone and rarely spoke to one another—at least not as much as Boyle felt was necessary to foster a thriving place of learning.

But when the dike broke and classes were scattered between several churches, a new spirit of collaboration arose out of necessity. "The faculty met every day to plan how to cope with the next day," she said. "As we met after school and talked about what we needed and how we could help each other, we got to be friends ... the whole faculty got to be a community and a family, and so did the students."

By the time everyone reassembled on the campus, shared hardship had cemented the bonds between them. "Somehow, because of that emergency, people began to cooperate and care about each other," Boyle reflected. "I believe if we hadn't had that event, and hadn't had that experience of coming back out here and moving into this place together, that we wouldn't have become quite the same family."

If that was so—if the flood was indeed a fortuitous adversity—the Heathwood family would not have long to bask in their triumphant return to campus. For no silver lining would be apparent in the tragedy that struck the following fall.

News of it reached Julian Walker on his borrowed tractor. It was Sunday afternoon, September 11, 1977, and he was mowing left field. "My wife Ellen walked up," he remembered, "and told me Earl had had a heart attack." Devanny had collapsed on the tennis court during an afternoon game with his eldest son and had been taken to intensive care at Richland Hospital. Visitors were not allowed. Walker continued mowing until he saw a second figure approach. "About an hour later Jimmy Walker came across the field. I could see tears coming down his face, his cheeks, so I knew Earl had died."

chapter five

PROGRESSIVE PIVOT

*Bob Shirley—moments in race relations—birth of a sports rivalry—
faculty metamorphosis and "happy noise"—"trash detail" and ice
cream—The Chronicles of Narnia—the Legend of Congamomma—
the inimitable Coach Cy—philosophy for children—from the Learning
Center to Advanced Placement—Campus Center—Bill Cherry and
"the microcomputer"—Shirley's Sizerian vision*

[1977–1987]

In October 1977, a trustee committee asked five students representing the fifth through eighth grades what they liked about Heathwood Hall, how they would make it better, and what qualities they sought in a new headmaster.[1] The pupils agreed about many things. They liked small class sizes and the fact that "you get to know almost everyone." They were emphatic in their desire for a bigger and better library—which was still shoehorned into the trailer modules containing the administrative offices. They wanted more activities, more sports, and more opportunities to engage in the arts. For a headmaster they wanted someone who liked the school, liked the teachers, and expressed interests that went beyond discipline and punishment. Asked to describe the typical duties of a headmaster, the Middle Schoolers expressed a somewhat fanciful view. *Talk with bad students*, several said. *Fill out papers*, another volunteered. *Have board meetings. Is sometimes nice.* By one student's reckoning, *I don't think they do much but sign papers and give orders.*

Among the questions they proposed to ask candidates for the job was this one: *Will you ask students what they think and what their ideas are?*

After Earl Devanny's untimely death, the trustees named Jimmy Walker as acting headmaster. The 29-year-old made no bid for permanence, but provided critical continuity at a challenging juncture. He proceeded with a blueprint that had begun to take shape the year before with the assistance of Russell Frank, an educational consultant and executive director of the Mid-South Association of Independent Schools.[2] Walker implemented his recommendation to establish administrative clarity and divisional autonomy by formally naming heads of the Lower, Middle, and Upper Schools. This provided parents and faculty alike with clearer and more direct lines of engagement. In 1976, Heathwood gained accreditation from the Southern Association of Colleges and Schools—an important step in establishing credibility as a college-preparatory school.[3]

Meanwhile Walker stepped up a program of community outreach meant to quell the furor over enrollment certificates, reassure existing parents about the state of the school, and recruit new families. This volunteer-heavy initiative took the form of in-home, multi-family meetings hosted by Heathwood parents to bolster confidence about the school's direction.

"I think it was important, when I was appointed acting head, that so many members of the school community had seen me in an administrative and a communications role," Walker reflected. "I could talk a lot about the kids—but I could also talk about curriculum, finance … That helped the Board have a good deliberative search, interview a number of candidates, and not have to feel like they had to get somebody in by Christmas."

In the spring of 1978, the trustees selected James Robert Shirley as the next headmaster.

On paper, Bob Shirley was an almost uncanny fit for a school seeking to cultivate a patrician Southern brand even as it grappled with the financial and organizational challenges of expansion. The Greenville native had attended Sewanee for two years before moving back to South Carolina and graduating from Furman in 1958. After a four-year stint in the US Marine Corps, he spent three years working as a banker for Wachovia in Winston-Salem, North Carolina. It was there that he became, at 30, an English teacher at the Summit School, an independent preschool-through-ninth-grade institution that traced its origin to 1933. In 13 years there he rose to become assistant headmaster, running Summit for six months toward the end during a headmaster's sabbatical. Meanwhile he earned a master's degree in English from Wake Forest University, writing a thesis on the poetry of William

Carlos Williams. In short, Shirley combined the military bona fides that had attracted some trustees to Earl Devanny, the clubby conviviality of a Sewanee SAE brother, administrative experience at a non-segregationist Southern independent school, and a financial background whose value was self-evident.

He was also a Trojan horse. Shirley was the son of a train dispatcher who had joined the Brotherhood of Railroad Trainmen shortly before it carried out a nationwide work-stoppage amid the largest wave of strikes in American history; the Shirley family's prosperity owed much to the power of labor unions. He experienced the Marines—"one of the strongest cults of manhood in the United States"—simultaneously as a master class in discipline and leadership and "a dangerous way to view one's purpose here on earth." Heathwood attracted him partly by dint of its tension between Deweyan progressivism and the school's traditional Episcopal ethos—yet in Shirley's view, that tension was "blessed by the weakness of the Church." And although the former banker rubbed elbows easily in Carolinian parlors, where he became a prodigious fundraiser, he appraised Heathwood with the steely eye of someone with a clear idea of what he wanted to change. "There was an ambient culture that wanted to be progressive but didn't want to give up the Confederacy," he would later say.[4] The defining mission of his tenure, as he would come to see it, was to "slip a progressive education under the cover of a country club environment."

The "ambient culture" Shirley aimed to change had multiple dimensions. One of them manifested in terms of race. In the decade since Heathwood had welcomed its first Black students, the school had progressed beyond tokenism (which was typical of integration's first phrase everywhere) to incorporate African Americans more meaningfully as participants in the life of the institution. Yet it still had some distance to go to achieve a culture that afforded Black families a sense of proprietorship commensurate to the intellectual and curricular insights they might bring to bear.

Bob Shirley and his 1985 Homecoming escorts.

A particularly visible example of this came in the 1976 *Highlander* yearbook. An opening section keyed to the theme of America's bicentennial featured a composite photograph depicting South Carolina's postbellum Reconstruction legislature. This assembly, which among other things created the state's first constitution to provide for a system of free public education, was composed substantially of African Americans. Its portrayal in the yearbook reproduced a racially slanted historical interpretation that persisted in regional textbooks despite having been widely rejected by historians.[5] The yearbook caption read, "The S.C. Legislature during the Reconstruction era was composed of radicals who were responsible for hard times in the state." Two additional images appeared on the same page: one celebrating the "elegant ante-bellum mansion" of the Hampton Plantation (where rice had been cultivated by intensive slave labor);

and another glorifying Confederate calvary officer Wade Hampton as a "beloved governor of the state and a leader of the Redeemers," a group whose central project had been the violent disenfranchisement of Black South Carolinians and the restoration of white supremacy.

To Henry Ponder, the president of Benedict College and a Heathwood trustee, the most disappointing thing about the copy editor's "racial slur" was the lost educational opportunity it represented. "I think that if we had a Black faculty member back then and if he or she had known about the galley proofs, the teacher could have helped the student. It would have been a good educational lesson," he reflected several years later. "Of course the teacher wouldn't have to be Black to catch it, but when a faculty has minority representation, these issues tend to be discussed more often. It gets into the air."[6] Observing that Heathwood had enjoyed more success recruiting African American trustees—he counted himself as one of three in the early 1980s—than faculty members, Ponder nevertheless drew attention to the fact that real integration involved more than inviting a handful of Black students into a given grade cohort.

Yet even the retention of Black students became a matter of concern immediately following this yearbook incident. In a June 1977 Board meeting, Earl Devanny lamented that between the 1975-76 and 1976-77 school years, the number of African Americans in Heathwood's student body fell from 38 to 19—and only 11 were enrolled for 1977-78.[7] This drop came amidst a broader decline in enrollment spurred partly by displeasure over the financial burden of enrollment certificates, but attrition among Black families was unusually severe. Rectifying that situation would take work. By 1979-80 the school had swung the momentum back in the positive direction, with approximately 25 African American students.[8] But Heathwood's leadership aimed higher.

Ponder counted Devanny as an attentive ally in that regard, and Bob Shirley as a wholehearted one. The experience of Ponder's youngest daughter, Anna, who straddled the Devanny and Shirley eras as a 1982 graduate, attested to both a gradually improving social atmosphere within the Heathwood student body and a desire for that forward momentum to be carried further.

Contrasting the deep sense of belonging she felt at Heathwood with the somewhat more isolating experience of her older sister Cheryl, who was the school's lone first Black graduate in 1977, Anna emphasized the extent to which she and her two fellow African American classmates fully participated in the life of the school.

"All three of us had really, really positive Heathwood experiences. We were all popular. We were in the Order of the Tartan, we were in student government, drama, athletics. Ford Cooper was hugely popular. We had a great time. We got invited to parties.

"At the time," she emphasized, "there was so much segregation in Columbia. Even after I got out of college, I was supposed to go to a wedding at Forest Lake Country Club—it was a Heathwood person getting married, and I was invited. And the general manager of Forest Lake Country Club called the mother of the bride and said, 'Now you know there are no Jews and no Blacks allowed in this club, and I see these names on this list and I know who they are.' ... We were never invited to formals, either—and a lot of that has to do with the fact that our parents didn't socialize. Black and white people in Columbia at that time just didn't socialize together. It was extraordinarily sad." By comparison, Heathwood was an oasis. She could feel the school pushing its home city in a better direction. Yet something was nevertheless missing, and by senior year it became impossible to ignore.

"When we graduated from Heathwood, all three of us went to historically Black colleges and universities," Ponder reflected. "And I don't think that was an accident."

"I *loved* Heathwood Hall Episcopal School. I loved my years there, I loved my classmates, I adore my teachers, I adore Bob Shirley," she stressed. "And I studied Fitzgerald, and Faulkner, and Shakespeare, and Hemingway—but I never read a single book by Toni Morrison. I never read a single book by Alice Walker. I never read a poem by Langston Hughes for a class until I left Heathwood ... And it's more than just that I wanted it, we *all* should have had it," she said, indicating the entire student body. "We *all* should have read Alice Walker. We *all* should have read Toni Morrison. We *all* should have read Langston Hughes."

Such curricular gaps were hardly unique to Heathwood Hall.[9] Inattention to African American historical and literary figures remained endemic in US secondary education during the 1970s, especially in textbook editions marketed in Southern states.[10] The question was whether Heathwood wanted to be a leader or a latecomer in mounting a more comprehensive education. The way Anna Ponder's college decision played out on the Congaree campus suggested that certain intellectual attitudes were ripe for change—for when she decided on Spellman after an eleventh-hour college visit, she found herself very suddenly cast into a role that had been unfamiliar to her at Heathwood: the object of paternalistic dismissal of Black accomplishment.

After leaving Spellman with application paperwork she had worked to complete all Sunday night, Ponder turned up in Jim Gasque's room to get his official sign-off as the college placement advisor.

"I was so excited," she recalled. "I rushed in to see Mr. Gasque, because I had to get it done really quickly or else I wouldn't be eligible for the honors college or a scholarship that they wanted me to get. And Mr. Gasque looked at me. He was at his desk. I will never forget this: he shook his head and said, 'No, I won't do it.'"

The declaration stopped Ponder cold. "I loved Mr. Q," she emphasized years later, long after earning a master's in international economics from Johns Hopkins and a doctorate in political science from Yale. "*Loved* him. And my facility with English usage, I absolutely credit him with that. I learned an awful lot from him. And I appreciate it. Daily." But in this moment, she felt like the air had been knocked out of her lungs.

"It was like I stopped breathing for a minute. And he said, 'There are better places for Anna. I will not do it.' Because he wasn't going to send me to a Black college. He wanted me to go to, at minimum, I guess a Georgetown-level place, but really probably an Ivy. And I was stunned. I was in shock. I got red-faced, and I was hurt and embarrassed, and I didn't know what to do. I was 17. So I ran all the way through campus, all the way down the center corridor and up to the breezeway, which was where you had to go if you wanted to use the telephone. And I called my mother."

As Eunice Ponder piloted her Cadillac Fleetwood down Heathwood Road to set her daughter's situation right, Anna replayed the final moment of her dizzying confrontation in Room 17.

"I was so hurt, and I was a favorite of his—I mean truly a *favorite* of his," she remembered. So the dismissal of an historically Black college by Heathwood's most iconic teacher hit her more painfully than simple indifference toward African American contributions to the country's intellectual life; it felt like a dismissal of her entire family. "I remember looking him. I just looked at him. He said, 'There are better schools for Anna.' And I said, 'A Black college has put food in my mouth and clothes on my back my entire life.' And I just ran."

Yet for all the work that remained unfinished in this regard, Heathwood's commitment to traveling further down that path continued to distinguish the school from other private competitors. And in the early 1980s, the school's varsity athletics program would play a modest part in catalyzing a broader shift within Columbia society. The ramifications would ripple beyond Heathwood, and for neither the first nor last time, it would largely be a story of young people leading their elders.

When the 1979-1980 school year began, Heathwood Hall had never faced Hammond Academy in athletic competition. Though the schools largely drew from the same social strata, which gave rise to a natural rivalry in the competition to attract families, Hammond's commitment to segregation extended to a refusal to face Black opponents on the field of play. (Well into the mid-1980s, Heathwood yearbooks would name Cardinal Newman, not Hammond, as the school's athletic archrival.) But as the Highlander varsity basketball team blazed through opponents of all stripes that season—including several public schools in addition to the usual private-school slate—a buzz began to build.

The team's record of 25 wins and a single loss—on a long-distance heave at the buzzer—was probably an insufficient measure of their prowess. So was their 25-point average margin of victory. A better gauge could be found in the juxtaposition of two remarkable facts: senior Noble Cooper, a six-foot-four wing guard, would proceed to play for the scout team and junior varsity at University of North Carolina, going up against

Michael Jordan, Sam Perkins, and James Worthy[11]; yet on the offensive end of the court Cooper didn't hold a candle to his teammate Richey Taylor, who poured in 30 points per game.

The upshot, as Cooper recalled, was that the boys on Hammond's squad ached to challenge their crosstown peers. But they were obstructed by their own school's administration, which would not sanction an official game. A solution emerged: "We played a scrimmage at Heathwood." In that way, the Heathwood-Hammond sports rivalry began with an off-the-books contest on the Congaree River campus. "Of course we beat them pretty good," Cooper laughed. "By about 20 points. They shouldn't have given me an opportunity. That wasn't wise."

The first official basketball game between the schools came in the 1981-82 season—which was the first to feature Cy Szakacsi, a coaching legend in South Carolina high school athletics, at the Highlanders' helm.[12]

"It was a big deal," remembered Jay Hennig, a senior on that team. "It was very controversial, because we had two players who were African American and they had never let an African American play in their gym before. So we actually had to go through protest signs by parents—there were people protesting having that game there.

"But it was a great thing," Hennig continued, "because the players were friends—we played pickup at parks. That was a big deal to have that first game between the two schools. It was a big event for both schools—for the whole community."

Anna Ponder echoed Hennig's sentiment. Although Hammond won the contest on a buzzer-beater, she located the game's deeper significance in a gesture that occurred off the court.

Ponder's desire to attend that game went beyond her role in the pep club. "I was not going to miss an opportunity to go to Hammond, for anything, since they didn't want us there," she recalled. But halfway through, the president of Hammond's student body made a momentous decision. "At halftime, Laurel Seibels walked from the middle of her bleachers, all the way around the basketball court," Ponder said, "and sat by me—not only during halftime but during the entire second half of the game. And that was a huge moment in race relations. Huge.

"I knew her," Ponder added. "We were friends. We just sat and talked about whatever, but it was a big deal."

꽃

Bob Shirley's chief ambition was, in some ways, a heavy lift within a school that had come to think fairly well of itself. It boiled down to elevating expectations about what constituted a truly excellent education—and persuading Columbia parents to pay what it cost to deliver. This became a central challenge for Tate Horton, who served the Board as treasurer in the early 1980s before chairing it between 1987 and 1990.

"The core of the Columbia parent market who could afford Heathwood," Horton reflected, "was in large measure made of people who'd grown up in Columbia, and whose parents had grown up in Columbia, and were used to doing things a certain way, and didn't have high expectations for what schools could provide. Because they'd figured that they'd managed okay with the education they'd gotten, and why spend more—or why try to get more than what they'd had, growing up in the '50s and '60s?" Even if Heathwood's parent body broadly embraced the higher expectations that Susan Robinson had articulated from the very beginning, growing the school's enrollment was a challenge in a marketplace that regarded the past as a valuable source of insight and perspective.

Shirley was emphatically uninterested in reproducing mid-century American educational norms. But by his own admission, he began his tenure with an underdeveloped sense of how to pursue his goals effectively. "I wanted to lead but did not really understand what that meant."[13] One of his first acts yielded a lesson in how to alienate potential allies. "On my first day in the office I told the bookkeeper I wanted to use NAIS standard accounting," he recalled, referring to the National Association of Independent Schools. "She closed the book and quit. That should have been a hint." If tweaking accounting standards could ruffle feathers that dramatically, what minefields awaited him in realms of actual philosophical disagreement? "From then on, I did a lot of listening and patient operation."

Having quickly discovered the drawbacks of administrative fiat, he began slowly but methodically remaking the faculty.

Noble Cooper's view about what distinguished Heathwood Hall— that ultimately "it's the students you interact with each day that really transform you"—may be true of every school. But no educational institution can thrive for long without a teaching corps capable of directing youthful dynamism with purpose. Highlanders from the late 1970s typically felt prepared for college, especially in the area of writing. But when compared to well-regarded independent schools outside of the South, Heathwood reflected the inexperience of its own institutional youth. One of the few students afforded the opportunity to grasp that difference was Michael Perry, who enrolled in St. Albans School in eleventh grade when his family moved to Washington. "Once I got to D.C., and saw what the real competitive world looked like," he recalled, "I thought, *I should have gone to summer school.*" He also came to the conclusion that many of his scholastically motivated friends in Columbia public schools emerged "more academically proficient" than he had, particularly in math and science.[14]

Shirley felt that the Upper School, in particular, needed a more galvanizing vision. He set about building one, moving outward from the twin pillars of Jim Gasque and science department chair Sarah Magoffin[15]—a pair remembered as "fabulous mentors and curmudgeons at the same time" by Anne Weston, who came as a Middle School science and math teacher in Shirley's first year before moving into Upper School biology. Lark Palma, who had left for Charleston the year before, returned to teach English and oversee drama productions. Carlo Haigler joined the math department. In their own distinct ways, each of these women would conjure classroom atmospheres in which the traditional teacher-pupil hierarchy took a backseat to a feeling of common endeavor—a dynamic that would deepen with the arrival of Bob Haarlow as Upper School principal several years later.

In 1979 Shirley cold-called Bill Cherry, a Vanderbilt graduate and soccer player who'd been teaching at the Ensworth School in Nashville, Tennessee, and coaxed him to visit Columbia in August.

Cherry's first drive down the Heathwood Road was unforgettable. "It looked like something that could have been out of the Vietnam War," he recalled. "There were potholes … and the heat was smoking up off the road, coming up in vapors. And my wife turned to me and said, 'You're not seriously considering taking a job here, are you?' And then we had the interviews in trailers." But Shirley sold him. "I found him to be a very interesting person," said Cherry, who signed on to teach math and coach athletics while helping to develop the Lower School curriculum.

That would become a recurring pattern as Shirley increasingly cast his net beyond South Carolina. John Pulford, who'd grown up in Brazil, had taught along with his wife Marsie in Iran and St. Croix before being lured to Columbia, where neither of them had roots. "Here you've got this head-master of this small private school in the middle of the farmland in South Carolina," John Pulford remembered, "and little did you know he was an intellectual dynamo—bursting with ideas, and very personable."

"Heathwood was very, very different from what it became later on," the longtime history teacher continued. "In 1983, it was a lot of good-old-boy stuff: pickup trucks with shotguns in the back[16] … But the kids were really nice. That was what got me going."

The Heathwood Hall Hunting Club, circa 1983.

In scholastic terms, Pulford found islands of excellence amid ample opportunity for improvement. "When I got there, the Middle School was where it was at." Don Mayer had just joined principal Al Newell's faculty as a history teacher from Boston, bringing another jolt of energy from further afield. The Upper School struck Pulford as a work in progress. "It changed for me, dramatically, when Bob Haarlow was hired."

Haarlow had founded an independent day school in Southern Pines, North Carolina, and grown it in a dozen years from 35 fourth- through sixth-grade students into a K-12 institution. Yet the new Upper School head, a Midwesterner who'd played basketball with Bill Bradley at Princeton, was still another regional transplant.

And they kept coming. Luisa Gonzalez, a Cuban immigrant who majored in French at Wichita State University, where she also earned a master's in Spanish, came in 1984. Beyond literature-inspired, Spanish-only debates on questions like "Is it better to be admired or loved?," her long career at Heathwood was marked by a dedication to cross-cultural awareness and the instrumental role she played in the development of Winterim, a week-long break in classes during which students could pursue internships, travel, and community service that was originally introduced by Bill Cherry.[17] Francis Broadway lumbered in from Michigan, imbuing chemistry and integrated science classes with sardonic humor and a heterodox brand of Black masculinity.[18]

To reinvigorate the mathematics faculty—traditionally the hardest recruitment challenge faced by US school administrators—Shirley went after a Connecticut teacher named Daniel Venables. "In the area of advanced learning in math and science, there are just not many people around who understand where we are headed," the headmaster would later reflect. "Dan Venables is one." Venables was also unsparing in his assessment of the challenge he would be facing, compared to the high-performing, well-funded public school where he had begun to make his reputation.

"I was shocked by Heathwood," he recalled, reprising a directness whose sharp edges he would have to sand down, at least partially, to become an effective leader. "I thought the educational quality was very low—I thought rigor was nonexistent in the math classrooms." But he also saw an opportunity. "Bob Shirley wanted to really do some progressive things ... he at that time hired six or eight teachers from all over the country who were known to be top-notch teachers, who would head various departments and try to move the school forward."

Something else in the school's atmosphere convinced him that this project was possible.

"When I first got to Heathwood, I was impressed by what I continue to call, to this day, *happy noise*," he recalled. "You can tell, walking the hallways between classes, whether a school is a happy place or not. And Heathwood was a happy place. The flipside was they needed to raise the bar academically—but kids were happy there. And there was a real community—and a community I wanted to be a part of."

As the Upper School's faculty metamorphosis laid the foundation for a progressive pedagogical renaissance that would spring into clearer focus in the late 1980s, Shirley installed a Lower School principal whose authoritative mien harked back to a more traditional style of schooling. Margaret Adams, a former nun with a no-nonsense knack for inducing compliance, came to Heathwood in 1980. She quickly became one pole in yet another productive tension that would shape the school.

Born during World War II in Charleston, Adams had gleaned a desire to teach from the Catholic schools she attended. "At that time it was either you were going to be a secretary, nurse, or teacher," she later reflected about the roles open to women of her generation. "I was always taught by nuns." In 1962 she joined the Order of Cyril and Methodius in Pennsylvania. The strict regimen she found there challenged a young woman whose teenage pastimes had included Friday night drag-racing in Charleston's St. Lawrence Cemetery.[19] But she stayed for 14 years, returning to Charleston when her father developed cancer. To her undergraduate degree in early childhood learning and development she added a master's in early childhood reading instruction and a doctoral degree in school administration.

"She knew a lot about how people learned," recalled Shirley, who took a graduate course she taught at University of South Carolina on childhood language acquisition.

Adams implemented what she called a "very difficult" phonics-based reading program, but the children rose to the challenge. "The academics, to me, had to be strict, strenuous," she said. "They had to know that this was what they were there for: the education. You couldn't just let them sit back and do nothing. Some schools were easy at that time. But putting in a curriculum that was strenuous made us strong, and I think that's why the enrollment increased … Parents began to see that the teachers were doing what they should be doing, and holding the children accountable."

A new building bolstered the Lower School's footprint as well. The Averyt Early Childhood Learning Center (ECLC) opened during the 1981-82 year. Bringing it to fruition was, figuratively and literally, a heavy lift. After the trustees conducted a fundraising drive to build a structure at ground level, a zoning determination mandated that it be raised above the level of a 100-year flood. The cost differential made Board chair Jim Smith reel. "It was like a 50 percent increase, or more, to put it up in the air," he recalled. The "last-minute curveball" appeared to put the entire project in jeopardy. "I was just sick about it," Smith said, remembering an architect's meeting attended by Bob Shirley and Gayle Averyt, the campaign's main benefactor. "I was anguishing over it, and Gayle said, 'Just build it,' … and that was the greatest."[20]

Hoisted above the flood plain by 16-foot columns in the manner of Le Corbusier's Villa Savoye, architect Richard Molten's building featured new classrooms; a scaled-down kitchen where children could practice measuring, mixing, and taking turns; and a dedicated Lower School library. The open area underneath (later enclosed) served as a sheltered space for assemblies and physical education classes.

Adams also ensured that children who demonstrated motivation and aptitude in a particular subject area got the opportunity to advance, either by joining an accelerated group of peers or hopping up a grade level for part of the day.[21] In Shirley's estimation, Adams "put a lot of teeth in the Lower School program" across the academic spectrum.

Lower School Principal Margaret Adams, circa 1985.

She put fangs into its disciplinary regime.

Of all the accoutrements of 1980s school life—Jams shorts, Guess jeans, Jansport backpacks, parachute pants—perhaps no accessory was more commonly sighted at Heathwood than a black garbage bag in the hands of a reprobate Lower Schooler scouring the campus for loose trash. "Trash detail" was only the default punishment in a wide-ranging repertoire. A boy caught chewing gum in class might find himself sitting outside Dr. A's office chewing 50 sticks in a row. An errant spitball could result in the principal's order to produce 100 more, stripping every last drop of saliva from a penitent tongue. There was a fair bit of weed-pulling. "I want to see your eyes," Adams would command at assemblies as she clicked a ballpoint pen, and her preternatural power to spot averted gazes out of the corner of her own inspired an awestruck sensation of inescapable surveillance.

No child shorter than five feet in height had the slightest doubt about who truly exercised power at Heathwood Hall. Once, Bob Shirley was teaching in a pod classroom when two kindergartners rapped upon the door. "I opened it," Shirley recalled, "and one of them looked at the other, and then at me, and said, 'Dr. Adams is going to *get* you!'" The boy then pointed at a classroom wall. "'You know that thing on the wall? It's got an eye in it, and she can see *everything you're doing*.'" Plainly, not even the school's headmaster could consider himself immune.

"She scared me as a Middle Schooler," confessed Class of 1985 graduate Marshall James, who had never even fallen directly under her jurisdiction. "Because you did know about her reputation, even in the Middle School." Many years later—well after Adams had left Heathwood to head Columbia's St. John Neumann Catholic School—a pair of high school boys[22] encountered Adams across the divide of a filling station gas pump. Their memories were long and vivid; they dove onto the bench seat of their sedan, cowering out of sight until their former principal filled her tank and drove away.

"I did have high expectations," she said years later. "And I kept saying, 'There's nothing in life that's free; you have to work for everything you get.' These children, most of them came from money," she reflected. "I wanted to make sure they realized that that was their parents' money—it didn't mean they were going to have all that money. So there was no excuse for not working hard. And they had to take consequences themselves for what they'd done, and not blame other people.

"You have a choice," she would stress to children: "You can do what's right or what's wrong. And there are rewards and consequences."

So Adams—who abhorred the desk-bound, penmanship-ruining rote punishments of her own youth—had developed a straightforward philosophy: "If you take something out of a system, you have to put something back in. When you misbehave, you are taking something away from others. So physically you have to do something, like picking up trash or pulling weeds, because that way you are giving something back to the school."

One measure of the results lay in the experience of students. Duncan Belser, a Class of 1994 graduate who was no teacher's idea of a problem child, recalled the impression a single visit to Dr. A's office could make. "I remember sitting, waiting to be seen, with a lot of anxiety. My infraction was relatively minor, as infractions go; I think I was talking when I shouldn't have been talking. Which, shocker, does happen at age six." They discussed the costs of classroom disruption to the rest of Ms. Polly's pupils. "I may have had the opportunity to pick up trash," Belser said wryly years later. "That's a helpful consequence. The task you've been given to do promotes the betterment of the community you're in. And it's clearly not corporal punishment in any fashion. But the dispensing of that was relatively simple: we acknowledged the facts, we recognized that wasn't okay, and to help you remember, go carry this bag of trash and pick up some stuff for at least an hour, and that'll give you some time to think about it. And that's a valuable thing!"

Another student from this era recalled receiving a vivid lesson of particularly lasting value. "I had said some horribly insensitive, in fact racist thing to somebody," this person recalled, about a species of joke that was more common at that time than it ought to have been. In the principal's office, Adams meted out a devastatingly simple punishment: "I want you to tell me," she said, "*word for word*, the joke that got you sent here." Repeated through tears of shame, the punch line cauterized the stale air with a grotesqueness from which the fourth grader could not hide. "It was like pulling something that you would say in the shadows with your friends out into the open," the offender attested many years later. "It was excruciating. But it was a lesson. Someone needed to impress upon me why that was unacceptable—and nobody else was stepping up to the plate. So I am so grateful that she made me realize it, and account for it. Because that was not the person I wanted to be."

Class of 1994 alumna Jennifer Coggiola Morgan, whose punishment for snapping a tree branch was to hold it aloft in its former airspace for the duration of recess, retained an equally deep gratitude for the compassion with which Adams helped her conquer anxiety in the wake of her parents' divorce. "I pretty much refused to go to school," Morgan said about her third-grade year. "But as long as I made it to the ramp that led to the offices," she recalled, "I could put a penny in a jar. And if I collected five pennies, she would take me out for ice cream on Friday." Almost four decades later,

Morgan would remember the flavors she alternated between during their forays to Baskin Robbins: Bubblegum and Pralines & Cream.

Faculty appreciated Adams for other reasons. "I went to Catholic school for 16 years, so she wasn't anything different than what I went through," said Marsie Pulford, a fourth-grade teacher who rivaled her husband in the affection she inspired among students. "She ran the school with kind of an iron hand. But she would listen to you. Whenever I had a problem I would go there and she was great ... And curriculum-wise, she would listen to what we had to say," Pulford added. "I always felt she was open to things."

There was also the matter of comparison. In a child's eye, a stern principal can make a sweet-hearted teacher seem sweeter still. And student memories of the Lower School during this era ran long on warm fuzzies. Ms. Pennington filled her first-grade classroom with "a motherly energy and an enthusiasm that didn't feel forced."[23] The only bad thing about being assigned to the second-grade homeroom of Patty Lamar—Elsie Lamar's daughter-in-law—was that some of the older kids swore Sandra Johnson was nicer (and vice versa). Pesky bouts of hiccups would send kids seeking the scalp-tickling remedy of Mary Scoville—whose treasured read-alouds of C.S. Lewis' Narnia chronicles set the stage for deeper engagement in Robin McLeod's English classroom.[24] Heathwood at this time was the kind of place where when Caroline Morris received her 1983 yearbook at the end of second grade, and wanted to participate in the tradition of signed inscriptions, she sought just one: from art teacher Sally Ashley.[25]

As the Upper, Middle, and Lower School divisions functioned with increasing degrees of academic independence, Heathwood continued to cultivate cross-class camaraderie in various ways. The Highlander Games remained an all-ages springtime bonanza of sack races, water balloon tosses, and flour-pasted faces freckled with M&Ms. Spirit Week offered the spectacle of fifth graders trying to outdo jaded sophomores on Punk Day—though neither group could possibly have provoked greater school-

Marsie Pulford mobbed by students.

wide mirth than the Upper School faculty's donning of Shakespearean costumes to celebrate the Bard's birthday in 1986. As late as 1984, the school's bus routes were still largely driven by eleventh- and twelfth-graders. But during this era Heathwood derived much of its vitality as a unified K-12 institution from its physical education and coaching corps.

Sarah Roth, Stan Wood, and Lynn Humphrey arrived early in Bob Shirley's tenure. Each one would outlast six headmasters and the COVID-19 pandemic to teach and coach for roughly 40 years. Few adults in the school's history interacted with more students across more stages of childhood and adolescent development.[26] Boys and girls who played parachute games in first grade would wage "brisketball" battles in Middle School, and then reconnect with their old P.E. teachers on any number of varsity and JV teams. Over the years Roth coached volleyball, basketball, and—with the 1984 addition of the Wells-Roberts tennis courts[27]—tennis. Humphrey coached volleyball, softball, basketball, and golf. Wood coached football, softball, basketball, and—with the 1988

Cary Sheely, Alison Sellers, Ainsley Howard, Scott Rhodes, Cindy Wolfe, Josie Bruccoli, Blair Newton, and Kim Butts: Heathwood's 1983-84 bus drivers.

advent of the NCAA-grade Henry Woodward Track[28]—track and field. In this way, athletics became integral to how students felt known and valued by adults over the course of their time at Heathwood. And after concluding a stint as athletic director in the mid-1990s, Wood would draw on his early experience of the Project Adventure ropes course[29] and the annual seventh-grade camping trip to develop the PEAK program, a far more extensive outdoor education and leadership initiative that would come into its own in the 2000s.

The 1983 installation of floodlights on the football field drove school spirit in more and less predictable ways. Friday night games became oc-casions for community tailgates and autumn bonfires, as was the case for American schools beyond counting. But at Heathwood they featured an additional twist: the indoctrination of Highlanders of all ages to one of the most peculiar cheers in South Carolina interscholastic sports. *Come from Bermuda*—it began—*Come from Bahama, Nobody Beats the Congamomma!*

The origin of this strange chant was unknown to the majority of children who parroted it—and considerably more bizarre than most would have imagined. It derived from the fertile mind of Billy Shand, who taught history at Heathwood in the late 1970s. Congamomma, in his telling, was the name of a man sent from Hibernia to bring Christianity to the Charlestonians. Upon arriving in South Carolina's port city to find that it already contained several churches, this unfortunate fellow was cast into the Cooper River by the city's inhabitants, whereupon Congamomma was swiftly swallowed by a pregnant alligator. This reptile—perhaps confused by the presence of live offspring in her belly in place of biologically ordained eggs—swam all the way upstream, traversed Lake Moultrie and Lake Marion, and then proceeded halfway up the Congaree River before spitting out her babies along with Congamomma, who promptly scrambled up the riverbank and established Heathwood Hall.[30]

Football also figured into the female Heathwood experience—at least in the lighthearted spirit of the Powderpuff games, which launched as an annual tradition in 1984. There was no shortage of competitive energy in these flag-football contests, though. Whether it derived from the field players or their male classmates who coached them, the junior class team of 1986 was accused by yearbook editors of resorting to "dirty tricks" in an unsuccessful attempt to overcome their senior class rivals.[31]

Among male student-athletes in the 1980s, no rite of passage rivaled the experience of being coached by Cy Szakacsi. "What we knew about Coach Cy was that he was a legend because of his coaching years at University High and A.C. Flora," recalled Marshall James, who suspected that moving to a small, scholastically oriented private school took some adjusting to for this old-school competitor, whose unfiltered intensity sometimes drew comparisons to Indiana University's Bob Knight. "Coach Cy was very intimidating, he had a raspy voice, he yelled a lot—but you knew the guy had a heart," James continued. "I have to admit, there were times I would do things just to make him mad, just to send him over the rail. But I really enjoyed playing for him ... I loved Coach Cy."

With a mastery of profanity that picked up where George Carlin's Seven Words You Can Never Say on TV left off, Szakacsi could rile

Role reversal: Boys cheer on their Powderpuff peers.

John Pulford (left) gets into the spirit on Fifties Day, circa 1985.

up his own administration as readily as opposing fans. "A wide ass," he might muse in a calm moment of philosophical basketball reflection, "is worth three inches in height—if you know how to use it." The heat of a close contest brought out the real goods. Among the strangest tasks Bob Haarlow ever carried out at Heathwood came at the behest of Margaret Adams after she succeeded Jimmy Walker as assistant headmaster in the late 1980s. "She ordered me, as my superior, to sit behind the bench during one basketball game, jot down all the nasty words that Cy said in the huddles, and then at halftime go into the locker room, unbeknownst to Coach Cy, and write down what his halftime message was," the Upper School principal recalled. "I did as I was told," he added. "But I told her half—a fourth—one-tenth!—of what Cy said. Because Cy was on a roll."

Yet to his players, the grizzled veteran embodied one of the deepest truths about teaching. As John Pulford put it about his own classroom career, which prized authentic relationships as the basis for everything else: "If kids know you love them, they'll let you get away with murder."

Meanwhile Bob Shirley worked, with varying levels of visibility, behind the scenes. To older students—especially contemporaries of his daughters Caroline and Thrace—he came off like a "class dad," or the uncle you actually hope to sit next to at Thanksgiving dinner. Younger ones hoped, perhaps, to be sent to his office rather than Dr. A's. For the faculty, he was at once a headmaster in the old mold—a charismatic scholar who counted Aristotle as a mentor and thrilled to long discussions about Faulkner and Dostoevsky—and a partner in pedagogical experimentation.

"A sage," Daniel Venables called him. "He was nothing short of that. He had a vision that was so far-reaching. He didn't look at tomorrow, he looked 10 years down the road. What do we want the school to be?"

Shirley excelled at fostering an authentically inclusive sense of "we."

"He was so open," said Anne Weston. "He was the kind of leader who inspired you to want to work, but he was as questioning as the next person. He had a way of helping us think about things. He didn't necessarily know what the answers were either," she added. "He helped instill or create this climate where he wanted us to take a risk and potentially fail, but get up and try to figure it out and do something again."

By the midpoint of the 1980s, some of Shirley's own priorities were becoming increasingly clear. One of the few scholastic initiatives he had directed from the top down was a "Philosophy for Children" program implemented with assistance from faculty at the University of South Carolina.[32] It appeared that Heathwood Hall was the only school in the nation to adopt this curriculum across grades 1-10. The component most memorable to students probably came in Middle School via Matthew Lipman's *Harry Stottlemeier's Discovery*, a novel in which a group of fifth graders galvanized by the basic concepts of Aristotelian logic wrestle with questions about the nature of reality, causality, belief, fallibility, rights, and justice. "In school," the titular character observes in this book, "we think about math, and we think about spelling, and we think about grammar. But who ever heard of thinking about thinking?"[33]

With this program as well as his own Upper School ethics course, Shirley wanted Heathwood students to have that chance.

"In a Christian school there is a Christian ethic," he reflected, "but there is an ethic that existed before the advent of Christ—and which is important in Classical Greek literature, in the work of the Stoics and Plato and Aristotle. The fathers of ethical thought are there. And I think that has to be ingrained in people. It makes a huge difference.

"Aristotle is not the be all or end all," he added. "But Aristotle brought us the most important questions. The dialogue that goes on in Plato and Aristotle is the beginning of understanding the depth of what human existence is really all about."

Class of 1993 graduate Nate Terracio experienced Shirley's class as a turning point in the passage to adulthood. "We were really confronted with real-world paradoxes. And you had to come to terms with the fact that maybe up until that point you've always been told there's a right and wrong choice—you know, *do this* and *don't do that*—and then suddenly you realize that the really tough decisions in life are where there are either two 'right' choices or two 'wrong' choices. But you have to make one," he said. "An introduction to that was useful, at a time where our brains were still really maturing."

A second mark of Shirley's early tenure was his expansion of the Learning Center. This resource for children with learning differences (and faculty seeking help to teach them more effectively) had become Nancy Boyle's domain after Boyle's tenure as Middle School principal. Shirley grew its footprint by bringing in Debbie Lamm, Jane Ness, and Dan Palma.

"If you have a learning disability you could be extremely smart in other areas," said Palma, who'd been in the field for five years before coming to Heathwood. "Just because you're a slow reader doesn't mean you're not a tremendous thinker, or a good artist, or really good in math. The Learning Center was there so that we could accept kids who had some of those deficits but could still really benefit from a Heathwood Hall education. It made it more egalitarian." Coupled with the advent of Advanced Placement classes—spearheaded by Lark Palma—it also bolstered the school's commitment to a degree of intellectual diversity. If practices like flexible grade placement had been the mark of child-centered progressive education during the mansion era, the Learning Center and an expanding AP curriculum were central components of what that looked like in the 1980s.

Lifelong Heathwood students tended to perceive this evolution largely in terms of unremarkable philosophical continuity. Newcomers frequently had a keener appreciation for how it distinguished the school from local competitors. Susannah Dunlap transferred from another private school to Heathwood for several years of middle and high school. "I was only there for three or three-and-a-half years before we moved to Thailand," she recalled. "But it saved me. It was like moving out of an industrial box into a green field of possibilities: literature, music, community, diversity, compassion, creativity, and rigorous academics. I had teachers that started the day with yoga, then moved into poetry, then into social justice civics. This was in the 1980s!

"And of course: James Gasque, James Gasque, James Gasque," she added. "I cannot say enough about what that man did for me and so many others."

As a fundraiser, Shirley's signature achievement came with the 1985 dedication of the Smith-Shirley Campus Center, a second building designed by Richard Molten that fulfilled many of the wishes articulated by those Middle School search-committee adjuncts eight years before. The new building's Dorothy and Chalmers Poston Library more than doubled Heathwood's bibliographic capacity, affording space for more than 18,000 titles geared for Middle and Upper School pupils.(The Lower School collection remained in the ECLC.) The 250-seat Mary Rainey Belser Auditorium furnished thespians with a proper stage—and paved the way for a whole new corps of student technical producers. And at long last, Bill Cherry's computer program got a home befitting its forward-thinking creator.

Although he had come as a math teacher and coach, and briefly served as Upper School principal, Cherry's most lasting contribution to Heathwood originated with an eight-page proposal he produced with Jimmy Walker on an IBM electric typewriter in 1982. "It is too simplistic to claim that the goal of the American educational system is to educate or to train in certain skills. The educational process involves preparation of learners for an exceedingly complex existence, one that will certainly change even before the process is completed," it began. "The traditional tools of the classrooms of the past are no longer adequate to meet these challenges,"it continued, before naming a new one: "the microcomputer."[34]

Cherry proposed to buy five 16-kilobyte Tandy TRS-80 computers and cassette tape drives, plus some associated hardware, software, and training time, for a total cost of $17,826. Shirley had the will—but not the money—to experiment. "I told him to go ahead and order the computers," the headmaster recalled, "but not to tell anyone about the program until I had a chance to raise some money to pay for the hardware."[35]

One goal was simply to get students comfortable using machines that were gaining ground in the world of work. But just how to do that in a school context was an open-ended question. In contrast to later decades, the early 1980s had not yet produced a multi-billion-dollar educational-technology industry premised on silver-bullet solutions to age-old classroom challenges. The Minnesota Educational Computing Consortium was one of the closest things to it, but even its blockbuster *Oregon Trail*—which became a touchstone, in successive editions, for an entire generation of American students—was marked by the modesty of its scholastic claims.

Cherry launched Heathwood's program largely on the basis of "pure programming," as he put it. "We had some word processing, but we were teaching kids how to program in BASIC: how to pull data in, how to keep data, how to take that data and use it."

For Heathwood students whose chief desire was for an adult who listened to their ideas, Cherry's computer lab became a constantly evolving digital playground. An early adopter was Class of 1983 graduate Mac Martin. After suffering an injury that sidelined him from athletics, Martin wrote programs to compile statistics for Highlander sports teams. "He would come in after school and program for hours," Cherry recalled. "He just got fascinated. And there were a number of students who did that."

As Tandys led to Apple IIs and then iMacs, ambitions grew. Finding his way from LOGO to software suites like HyperCard, Cherry introduced students to the principal features of what would later become the

World Wide Web. Often enough, the impetus would come from student requests. "Like students were talking about PhotoShop, and wanted to have a class," Cherry recalled, by way of example. "I learned it, I set up a class, and that became the beginning of graphic arts." A similar process led to digital video editing and other innovations.

Cherry was "tremendously influential" for Class of 1998 graduate Jonathan Danforth, who fondly recalled encountering Photoshop 1.0 in his lab. "He was always on the cutting edge," he said. "And he was always happy to let us come in and hack on stuff—by which I mean, attempt to see the very limit of what was possible." Looking back, Danforth would draw a direct line between that exploratory learning and the career he pursued in software engineering.

Class of 2002 alumnus Grant Robertson remembered being introduced to HTML and elementary coding at a summer computer camp Cherry ran in the mid-1990s. "My dad was very into computers at the time, as well," he said, "and between him and Bill Cherry, that enthralled me. So I was hooked in at an early age." In 2021, Robertson wrapped up

Programming one of Heathwood's first computers.

a five-year stint in Amazon's Alexa New Initiatives division to shift into public service as a digital archivist for the South Carolina Department of Archives and History.

As Heathwood's technology program grew, the challenge became how to pay for it. The case for classroom-based computing remained somewhat speculative in the mid-1980s. It was also competing for dollars against a backdrop of mounting expenditures across the school. Shirley had found a donor to catalyze the first phase of digital learning, but it would be many years before the program could count on a dedicated stream of funding from the general budget. "The way we were able to do it," Cherry said, "was the auction."

This annual event was piloted in 1985 by Carol and Jay Popp, who had two sons at Heathwood and were soon to enroll two more.[36] Patterned after a fundraising soiree at Grosse Pointe Academy in Michigan, where they had friends, it brought the charity auction format to a city unfamiliar with it. On the strength of a primitive IBM computer and "absolutely inspirational" volunteerism across the parent body, the Popps assembled an item catalogue that ranged from tickets to the Masters golf tournament, to a new driveway sponsored by former Board chair Bo Tate, to plastic surgeon Bill Campbell's donation of a breast augmentation surgery. Anxiety about whether this black-tie affair would be a hit or a bust dogged them until the moment Ron Long's gavel ended bidding on the first live-auction item: barefoot waterskiing lessons from Yancey McLeod Jr.[37]

"We had no idea what anybody was going to bid for anything," Carol Popp recalled. "The bid for him was $250! And we looked at each other and said, 'We've got it.'"

In its first two years, the auction netted approximately $130,000.[38] "The Heathwood parents and the auction actually funded our technology program for years," said Cherry—who wrote a computer program to add a super-silent auction to the lineup.[39] "Even when we did [classroom] smartboards later on, the auction helped us raise the money. It was a very big part in keeping tech alive."

※

The school's (over)reliance on supplemental funding was symptomatic of a thorny challenge posed by Bob Shirley's ambitions. On one hand, Heathwood was beginning to garner national accolades. In 1984 it became the first private school in the state to win the US Department of Education's Blue Ribbon Award—which no South Carolina private school would win again until 1997, when Heathwood was honored a second time.[40] In 1985 Heathwood was named one of 60 exemplary non-public schools across the country—and one of only two in the Southeast—by the Council for American Private Education.[41] The ambition for a reputation that transcended state and regional boundaries was squarely in line with Susan Robinson's original vision. Determining that there "were no private or independent schools such as we envisioned in Columbia," she and several founding trustees had traveled as far as Atlanta and Baltimore to study schools in those cities. Yet national recognition didn't necessarily translate into a competitive advantage within Columbia.

"We sort of had the philosophy, *If we build it, they'll come*—if we create a great national-level school in Columbia, the parents will like it and there will be a market for it," said then-Board chair Tate Horton. "For the most part that worked out okay. But Columbia isn't Atlanta or Charlotte," he added, referring to cities whose economies sustained significantly larger markets for private education.

"We were always trying to create this market for a school, and sometimes beating our heads against the wall wondering why in the world we weren't successful," he reflected. "It was a slow education process: educating the public about what a school could provide their children—and what our school *would* provide their children—and make them want that enough to pay for it."

Although Heathwood's enrollment grew from 502 to 834 between 1978 and 1987, the pace of annual tuition increases became an increasingly contentious issue within the Board. As the trustees mulled a 16 percent tuition hike in 1987, they had no illusions about the likelihood that some families would leave. The Upper School tuition of $3,755 represented 13.3 percent of the median income of families in the South.[42] The problem, as Perrin DesPortes put it at a December meeting, boiled down to the fact that Heathwood had for too long tried to "run a first class school at a less than first class tuition."[43] Shirley observed that Charlotte Latin and Charlotte Country Day were similar to Heathwood in terms of faculty and SAT performance, but "they are charging what it costs to run their schools and we aren't." From Walter Edgar (who consistently prioritized quality over cost) to Jack McCathern (speaking as "one of the not wealthy members of the Board" for whom the increase would be "difficult"), the trustees unanimously approved another hike. But Ethel Bowman's apprehension that the trustees risked coming off as "a group of wealthy people making decisions for others not so wealthy" was a serious concern.[44]

The stakes transcended social awkwardness. The hike would place Heathwood's average tuition at $3,500 for the 1987-88 school year. Hammond's, even after a 29 percent spike of its own, would be $2,800.[45] That cost differential was no small matter, especially for large families. A three-child family who chose Hammond over Heathwood could save roughly $2,100 per year—equivalent to nearly five months of the median total mortgage payment for single-family houses in the South.[46]

"It was a pivotal moment," Walter Edgar later recalled. "We felt that if we didn't raise the tuition, the school might fold." Although the Board meeting minutes recorded a unanimous vote, Edgar remembered strong opinions on both sides of the question. "It was not an easy decision, and the discussions were heartfelt," he said. "But once it was done, everybody said: 'We've got to pull up our socks and move on.'"

Heathwood was hardly the only independent school grappling with this issue. Private education had been receding from the reach of average American families for some time. As a rising portion of US wealth continued to flow to a narrower group of economic winners, tuition became increasingly daunting for families caught between the middle and the top.[47] So the question for a growing number of parents was what kind of education truly merited a given level of financial sacrifice. Heathwood's future—like that of any other independent school aspiring to prepare students for a world of escalating complexity and competition—depended on its ability to mount a genuinely compelling answer.

In the 1986-87 academic year, Shirley revealed the full extent of his vision. After several years of patient groundwork, Heathwood Hall completed its pivot toward a revitalized conception of progressive education by formally joining the Coalition of Essential Schools.[48]

Founded in 1984 by Ted Sizer, a former headmaster of Phillips Academy Andover who chaired Brown University's education department, this consortium sought to recast the relationship between teachers and students; reorient curricula around individual interests; and reject grading systems based on "credits earned" and "time spent" in favor of "student performance on real tasks." It held that school days should be shaped by "the intellectual and imaginative powers and competencies that the students need, rather than by 'subjects' as conventionally defined." This anti-conventional approach was to be guided by a collection of principles and aphorisms: "less is more"; "student as worker, teacher as coach"; "personalization to the maximum feasible extent." It called upon Coalition members to "model democratic practices that involve all who are directly affected by the school," in part by "deliberately and explicitly challenging all forms of inequity."[49]

At the center of it all would be "demonstrations of mastery" in which students availed themselves of faculty mentorship to carry out projects substantially of their own conception and design. These would culminate in a final requirement for graduation: an "exhibition of mastery" before an audience of family, faculty, peers, and outside experts.

The second decade of the Shirley era would be more adventurous than the first.

chapter six

AN ESSENTIAL SCHOOL

*"Student as worker; teacher as coach"—the marvelous Ms.
Meriwether—brown bags and blackboards—community service—
Johns Island—Mr. Highlander—Femme Fatale, Big Fat Momma,
and a golden age of drama—buzzer beater—DIY soccer—honor
council—Stefan & Tyna—exhibition of mastery—curricular explosion*

[1987-2000]

The Coalition of Essential Schools (CES) meant different things to
different people, and by joining it Heathwood Hall sent a signal
that could be read more than one way.

Some of the CES's Common Principles invited interpretation as educational radicalism. "Schools should not be 'comprehensive' if such a claim is made at the expense of the school's central intellectual purpose," this guiding document declared, scorning traditional efforts to "merely cover content." It insisted instead on a "less is more" doctrine that aimed to foster "student mastery" in a "limited number of essential skills and areas of knowledge." It envisioned schools as sites of democratic deliberation and activism where personalized learning would be guided by the conscious expectation that different kinds and groups of students demanded pedagogical practices "tailor-made" to serve their specific needs. Heathwood also abandoned the traditional A-B-C-D-F grading system in favor of a 4.0 scale ranging from "distinction" to "marginal work."[1]

Yet for Heathwood's parent body much also seemed familiar. "Affiliation with the Coalition gave Heathwood a framework of principles which were similar to its own," Board chair Tate Horton observed. Beyond commitments to low student-teacher ratios and other objectives shared widely by independent schools, the CES envisioned a kind of school culture that broadly resembled the one Heathwood had been fostering already. The Coalition called upon member institutions to "explicitly and self-consciously stress values of unanxious expectation, of trust, and of decency (fairness, generosity, and tolerance)," adding that "families should be key collaborators and vital members of the school community." Rejecting the metaphor of "teacher as deliverer of instructional services," it promoted a vision of generalist "teacher-counselor-managers" charged with "coaching students to learn how to learn and thus to teach themselves."[2]

Of all the CES aphorisms, the one most commonly cited at Heathwood was "student as worker; teacher as coach." The philosophical resonance of this credo was especially evident in the experience of Class of 1990 graduate Josh Lieb, who also exemplified its amplification during the late 1980s.

Lieb came to Heathwood as a sixth grader whose brain endangered his body. He'd been set to follow his older sister to Dent Middle School. But Dent "did not seem welcoming to kids of my size," he recalled. "Especially in middle school, as an undersized but oversmart kid, it was easier for me to get along at Heathwood than at a bigger school where there were bigger kids who weren't so accepting—which I'd already gotten quite a taste of."

His first few months at Heathwood charted a course familiar to many newcomers. It seemed like all of his new classmates had known each other "since they were babies." That was both intimidating and appealing. "The thing that defined Heathwood was that sense of community," he said. "And it didn't take long before I was at least a tangential part of that community."

But he also found an invigorating sense of academic freedom and particularism. For Lieb that translated into the chance to dive so deeply into Latin that he ended up stretching the "teacher as coach" metaphor to its logical extreme. The teacher was Margaret Meriwether, a Yale-trained classicist and Fulbright scholar who came to Heathwood in the mid-1970s after a decade as a university professor.[3] As Lieb entered high school, his cohort of perhaps half a dozen Latin pupils began to dwindle further, having exhausted their appetite for antiquity or decided to pivot to living languages. Extremely small classes were not unheard of at Heathwood at the turn of the 1990s. Dan Venables' ninth-grade Honors Algebra II roster frequently topped out in the single digits; one year Lark Palma ran a four-person AP English class in her administrative office. But Meriwether, at the end of her career, became a truly unique mentor to Lieb.

"I was the only student Ms. Meriwether had," he recalled.

It was an unforgettable relationship. "She was a genius," he marveled. "She was a pure Southern eccentric. She had a crazy hiccupping stutter … and she had something wonky with one of her eyes. But she was the smartest person you'll ever meet in your life."

Lieb's burgeoning love of language found reflection in her own. His progression through high school played out partly in the passenger seat of Meriwether's vintage Buick, which ferried them to Latin declamation contests throughout the state. The awards he racked up were the least memorable things about their partnership. "I would meet her in the Columbia Mall parking lot," he remembered, and their adventure would unfurl against the soundtrack of a bygone century. "Her father had played all the old Gilbert and Sullivan operettas to her as a little girl, and she knew them all by heart," Lieb said. "She was also very thrifty, and she never even had a car radio. So she would sing Gilbert and Sullivan operettas to me the whole way.

"She was hilarious," he said. "But she was brilliant … I've been around the world, and I've met a lot of really brilliant of people. She was as smart as anyone I ever met."

By the time Meriwether retired in 1990, Bob Shirley had stacked the faculty with teachers who had a knack for forging authentic connections with students. One measure was the number of Upper School students who spent their lunch hours in the classroom of a favored mentor. In the early 1990s, math nerds wearing T-shirts emblazoned with multicolor fractals plotted on the Gaussian plane would stream into Daniel Venables' classroom—where they'd play Pente with jam-band fans drawn by the math teacher's weekend avocation as a singer-songwriter.[4]

Similar scenes played out all over campus. "I wasn't in the Dan Venables fraternity," said Class of 1994 alumna Jennifer Coggiola Morgan, but she often eddied out into John Pulford's room at midday. "I remember staying after class, and we'd all kind of be flopped on our desks having these heavy existential conversations. And it would be John Pressley and Yancey McLeod and me and Amelia Edgar… It was such a mix of us!" she remarked, identifying Pulf's hallmark ability to inspire students of widely contrasting scholastic inclinations. "And we'd stay in there through lunch and chew the fat, talk about everything. I just remember being in his presence. It was almost like Robin Williams," in the film *Dead Poets Society*, she added. "That's how I remember it: just hanging on every word, and him challenging and pushing you."

Bob Shirley projected a similar intellectual liveliness and accessibility. "He used to recommend books to me, even in high school," said Morgan, noting that the headmaster served as her Episcopal confirmation mentor. "They were always very challenging adult books. And I appreciated that he actually saw something in me that could handle it. I always felt special in that way. You know: you're 16 and the headmaster says, 'Come over here! I've got a book for you!'"

Class of 1998 graduate Jonathan Danforth said that Shirley and Anne Weston made him feel the same way. "I was not a great student but I was certainly excited about learning, which now I realize can be separate things," he remarked. "And they understood that at the time—even though I didn't. They knew I'd sort of walked a different path and they did their best to accommodate it. I always felt, especially with Dr. Shirley, that there was not quite a peer relationship, but certainly an elevated relationship of knowledge and respect and conversation. It was interactive, not professorial."

At the turn of the decade Shirley moved a few more pieces around the chessboard in an effort to cement the kind of learning community he envisioned. He shifted Bob Haarlow—whose collegial approach to high expectations eclipsed his native interest in pedagogical theory[5]—to head the Middle School. Lark Palma, a progressive fellow traveler in the Ted Sizer mold, replaced Haarlow as Upper School principal. A new hire would prove equally consequential: Shirley recruited Ted Graf from Sizer's CES education shop at Brown University.

Graf started in the Middle School, where Robin McLeod and Sue Swick were the spirit leaders of a curriculum that blended traditional content with project-based learning. It was there that Graf and Dan

Palma formed a humanities teaching partnership that set the template for Heathwood's incarnation as an Essential School. (Both men would eventually teach in the Upper School as well.)

"You walked into the classroom the first day," Palma explained, "and said, 'Okay guys, we're going to give you the exam question today.'" In CES parlance, that was the *essential question.* The main mandate was that it be maximally open-ended. One of Graf and Palma's classes, for instance, revolved around the question *What makes a good society?*

"There was literature about utopian societies, readings in psychology. Almost anything could fit—it was just a matter of sitting down as a teacher and understanding how the literature and the history could inform that question," Palma said. Humanities classes integrated English and history content that was typically taught separately in US schools. "We could be creative, and we could choose material we connected with personally—questions we knew a young person could connect to, and were rich enough so that intellectually they could engage with them at a really high level.

"And when it was exam time, there was no secret: you're going to have say how your answer to this question was informed by the course material—and material you've mined out on your own. There's no right or wrong answer. It's all about intellectually manipulating the information to come up with your own answer. The question was never *yes* or *no.*"

Class of 1993 alumnus Nate Terracio encountered a similar ethos in Francis Broadway's Upper School chemistry class—at least for a handful of students who might have taken AP chemistry had Heathwood offered it at the time.

"About six of us got handed a project that we had to do on our own, with guidance from him," said Terracio. "In second-semester chemistry in college we did the exact same project," he remarked. "Except in Broadway's class, he gave us an overview and we had to *figure out* what experiments to do—whereas in college they gave us an overview and said, 'Here are the experiments you should do.'"

For Class of 1994 graduate Duncan Belser, Broadway exemplified Heathwood's evolving orientation toward community service.

The inwardly focused volunteerism of the late 1970s, centered largely on campus beautification, became more outward-facing in the 1980s. Heathwood's chapter of Key Club International, a student-led service organization, launched during the 1982-83 academic year.[6] A chapter of American Field Service, an international youth exchange organization, was started in 1986.[7] In 1991-92 Amnesty International joined the fold along with Results, a student-organized group dedicated to fighting childhood starvation by working with Harvest Hope food bank and other local organizations.[8] For several years at the turn of the 1990s, Broadway helped Heathwood forge a partnership with the Urban League of Columbia to run a summer day camp on campus that offered math, science, computer, and art instruction alongside outdoor activities for at-risk elementary school students across the city. Belser recalled his stints as a camp counselor as being particularly meaningful. "It was an example of how Heathwood supported a greater Columbia growth vision," he said, "by creating opportunities to share knowledge and create a fun place to learn and grow" for children whose access to extracurricular academic enrichment was otherwise limited.

Francis Broadway, Scott James, Heather Gilmer, Kerri Davis, and Julie Gregg help clear wreckage from Hurricane Hugo from a home in Eastover, SC, in 1989.

It was during this period that Lark Palma launched what would become Heathwood Hall's longest-running and most beloved community-service tradition: an annual senior class trip to Johns Island shortly before graduation. As an alternative to the boozy cruises that had become a school-ending rite for a number of senior classes,[9] the Class of 1988 pioneered a partnership with Rural Mission, a faith-based non-profit that rehabilitated homes for low-income residents on Johns and Wadmalaw Islands near Charleston.

"I believed that there was so much celebrating of the kids' achievements—and endless parties, and drunken proms—I just wanted to help give them an opportunity to give back," explained Palma, whose son Ian Merrill was a senior that year. "It was also a great chance for the kids to have one final big togetherness time."

For more than 30 years, successive graduating classes—joined by a healthy contingent of Heathwood faculty and parent volunteers—followed in their footsteps, repairing hundreds of dwellings for elderly residents.[10]

The urge to look and act beyond the campus boundaries helped fuel a golden age for theatrical productions. Under the direction of Dan Palma, Heathwood thespians dramatically expanded the scope of their ambitions.

The Mary Rainey Belser Auditorium—named for the trustee whose chairmanship of the Board between 1990 and 1994 was pivotal in the school's CES-inspired metamorphosis—became a home base for increasingly adventurous expeditions. Heathwood sent *Oliver*, *The Wizard of Oz*, and a superlative rendition of *One Flew Over the Cuckoo's Nest* on the road to USC-Salkehatchie, mounting them as dinner theater in a part of the state where live performance was a relative rarity.

In 1989, sophomore Charlice Hurst edged out junior Josh Lieb at the Palmetto Dramatic Association Festival's playwriting competition at Furman University, where a steady stream of Highlanders would claim acting awards as the decade progressed. Hurst's one-act, *Femme Fatale*, centered on a Black mother who leaves her white partner before giving

Dan Palma directs Anne Bailey and Chris Wilson in a 1983 production of Mary Chase's Pulitzer-winning "Harvey."

birth to their daughter, whom she raises alone.[11] Lieb's entry showed another side of the bracing intellectual and artistic freedom that was taking root on the east bank of the Congaree. A one-man romp titled *Big Fat Momma*, it was an early step into the risqué terrain that would become the basis for an Emmy-winning career in irreverence.

This liberated energy spilled over in many directions. The early 1990s were the heyday of "Mr. Highlander," an anarchic evening of anything-goes comedy and mock beauty-pageantry that launched in 1986 and could only have thrived in an era predating smartphone cameras and social media. If the stereotypical school administrator's job description is to say *no* a dozen times a day, Heathwood struck a considerable contrast. Some students asked permission, like Class of 1993 alumnus Ryan Waldron, whose hyper-spirited stint as a basketball game announcer left fans of all stripes thunderstruck.[12] Some students begged forgiveness, like Jonathan Danforth, who achieved senior-prank infamy by hacking the school's telephone hold system to replace Muzak with *Monty Python* skits.[13] Either way, the frequency with which students were met with enthusiasm in scholastic endeavors—and toleration in extra-curricular ones—distinguished the school's culture in this era.

"The thing with Heathwood," Lieb reflected, "was not so much that it was organized, but that it was free-wheeling—so we could do these things … If you wanted, intellectually, to give something a try, nobody got in your way."

That freedom proved especially consequential for Nate Terracio, who used it to expand his horizons beyond the formidable reputation he had developed as a budding scientist beginning in Middle School.[14] Bitten by the drama bug in seventh grade, Terracio came to value Heathwood partly for what it encouraged: "'Try something, and if it doesn't turn out great, that's okay.'" But equally important, in his view, was "*not to be told*: 'Oh, you were the guy who did this really great eighth-grade science fair project, so therefore you're going to be a science person.'

Todd Robertson and Selvesta Miller portray Atticus Finch and Tom Robinson in a 1993 production of "To Kill a Mockingbird."

"That is a true mark of an excellent education," he said. "To put people in a position where they feel okay to fail … To be given the freedom to try other things, even though people were pigeonholing you. I'm sure there were teachers who were pigeonholing me. But the *school* did not pigeonhole me—and by me, I mean any of us … It's a real testament to the learning environment that I feel like I'm truly not the only person who took a left turn and actually made a successful career out of it."

After becoming the director of Columbia's Koger Center for the Arts in his mid-40s, Terracio drew a straight line back to Heathwood. "I'm in the arts business," he said. "There is no doubt that I ended up in this career path because of seventh- to twelfth-grade drama."

Lieb offered a similar reflection. "I think Heathwood made my career more likely," he said. Its "high Episcopal roots" and "Anglophilic aspirations" eased his transition to Harvard, where his work for the *Harvard Lampoon* set him on the path to write and produce for TV shows including *The Simpsons*, *NewsRadio*, and *The Daily Show with Jon Stewart*. "Heathwood looked out into the bigger world in a way that the other schools [in Columbia] didn't."

Whatever the merit of that assertion, the hothouse atmosphere of the drama department was undeniable. Its cross-fertilizing, student-driven creativity reached an especially satisfying peak in 1993. Victory in a state drama competition was the least remarkable thing about one Heathwood production students put on that year. Their award-winning one-act play, *Love, Sanity, and Other Impossibilities*, had been written by Class of 1989 alumna Melissa Swick. It featured original music composed by Duncan Belser and his Class of 1994 peer Charles Hedgepath.[15] On the strength of this collaborative endeavor, the performing company accepted an invitation to mount it and another play at the Edinburgh Fringe Festival in Scotland.

Two trends marked Heathwood athletics during the second half of the Shirley era. One was the rise of athletic recruiting, which, albeit very modest in scale, helped to elevate the school's competitive profile. Class of 1993 graduate Terrance Bannister, who was an early example, joined classmates Dixon Woodward and Selvesta Miller as All-State football players. Svetlana Trjeskal (Class of 1995) and Elena Vishniakova (Class of 1997), both of whom entered the 1,000-point club as girls basketball standouts,[16] showcased another side of Shirley's efforts to diversify Heathwood's enrollment via international exchange students.

Bannister was also a core member of a basketball cohort that began to gel under the guidance of Rip Blackstone, who started coaching JV ball at Heathwood not long after having made partner at a Columbia law firm. As a senior, Bannister played a key role on a team, led by class-mates Miller and Hunter Rice, that cruised to a second straight independent-school state championship. But the first title, during his junior year in a supporting role, was the more dramatic of the pair.

"I still cannot describe the feeling," head coach Stan Wood said almost 30 years later. "We had been to the championship game three years earlier, with Jay McCathern and Karl Pundt and those guys," he recalled, but that team had lost a close game they felt they could have won. In 1992 Heathwood made it the final game again, and faced a one-point deficit with three seconds left on the clock. In a timeout, Wood drew up an inbounds play designed to put the ball in the hands of standout senior Jeddie Suddeth. But Suddeth got tangled up in traffic on his way to the mark as the inbounds count wound down, so Rice passed to W.D. Morris at the elbow of the foul line. The senior, who had probably scored 90 percent of his points that season within two steps of the basket, caught the ball 17 feet from the hoop with nothing to do but shoot.

"And he just put it in like he had been shooting that shot all his life," recalled Wood—who happened to know something that few others did in that moment. "One of the cool things I remember about that season is that at the beginning of the year I had the players write down what their strengths and challenges were. And W.D. wrote that he felt one thing he did well was shoot from the corner of the foul line.

"I don't know that I'd ever seen him do that," Wood laughed. "But doggone it if he didn't end up winning the state championship on that very shot."[17]

The next year, the girls varsity clinched a state title of their own. Led by point guard Svetlana Trjeskal, who scored 22 in the championship game against Hammond, a squad featuring five Palmetto Athletic Conference all-stars beat several public schools along with private ones in the first of several seasons to feature talented student-athletes from Russia.[18] Elena Vishniakova graduated in 1997 as a second-team all-American high school center.[19]

A second trend attracted less notice than the marquee varsity teams, but expressed an important aspect of the school's culture. In the mid to late 1980s, the expansion of Heathwood's athletic offerings had been driven substantially by new facilities, like the tennis courts and the Woodward track. In the 1990s it was often driven— like much during this period—by students themselves. One result was the "developmental" Green Wave basketball team, which in truth functioned more like a recreational outlet than a pathway to the varsity. The signature example, however, came thanks to a small but motivated cohort of Upper School girls.

For Class of 1994 alumna Eveleigh Horton Huey, few things about Heathwood eclipsed the eureka moments she experienced in Daniel Venables' AP Calculus class. "He made things pop and just come to life. He got so animated to see the light turn on when somebody got a concept. I remember his hand motions, even, and the noises he would make. His exuberance really was contagious." But what distinguished the school for her was that "you could be a student—and you could play two sports in a season if you wanted to. Or you could play a sport every season ... They gave you the sense that, if there was something you wanted to do, you could do it."

And in tenth grade, when she and several classmates decided that they wanted to play soccer, it didn't matter that Heathwood didn't have a girls soccer program. "Katherine [Juk] Draffin and Jennifer Coggiola Morgan and I went and put one together." They brought their proposal to athletic director Stan Wood, and ended up experiencing a feeling akin to what Clinch Belser had felt almost 40 years before, at the old Heath Mansion, when his query about basketball caused the erection of the school's first hoop. On the strength of student initiative, Heathwood fielded a club soccer team for girls in 1992, and a varsity team the following year.

The mid-1990s also brought a decision to join the SCISA athletic league in most major sports.[20] Heathwood had long resisted affiliation with this organization, which had begun as an alliance of segregated schools. But after a lengthy deliberative process overseen by trustee and Class of 1982 alumnus Jay Hennig, the Board determined that the time was right. Upon the dissolution of the Palmetto Athletic Conference in 1994, Heathwood had landed in the Charlotte Independent Schools Athletic Association, whose drawbacks included long travel times and a dearth of coverage in Columbia newspapers.[21] SCISA had meanwhile shed its original segregationist skin—and Heathwood had already grown accustomed to competing against some of its members in tournaments and non-CISAA contests. So in 1996 Heathwood began that transition.

The story of the 1990s could be told as a series of concerted efforts to turn Heathwood's attention outward. Thespians hit the road. Sports teams reflected a broader spectrum of Columbia society (and, in some cases, international diversity). Winterim trips ranged progressively further afield. Highlanders continued to read Herman Melville and Nathaniel Hawthorne. But Zora Neale Hurston and Maxine Hong Kingston joined the mix as teachers like the Palmas, Ted Graf, and Amy Railsback Graf offered students overdue exposure to African American, feminist, and immigrant literature.

Yet that burgeoning cosmopolitanism was one side of another productive tension that energized the school. For it all played out amid a social atmosphere that resembled an island more than a crossroads. Students from this era recalled campus life as being sheltered above all else, with all the benefits and drawbacks that stemmed from the almost familial intimacy that "Heathwood lifers" felt especially keenly.

Meredith Lanier and Tally Smith brave the rain for a Winterim marine biology expedition.

"We were all in the same classes together year after year after year," Nate Terracio reflected. "So there's some really great lifelong bonding. But you didn't get the opportunity to experience and grow the muscles that it takes to meet people for the first time."

The flip side was that, as a small school with a high level of student retention, Heathwood drew on its Episcopal ethos to emphasize the dignity and value inherent in every member of the school community. In other words, students had to learn to get along with just about everyone—because at the end of the day there was no way to elude peers who turned up your classes over and over again.

"You can call it a family, or not," said Josh Lieb. "But we were all inextricably connected to each other. And that was definitely the best part of the school. Because whether you loved or hated somebody, they were in some ways a brother or sister. You were stuck with them."

Ms. Page near the end of her Heathwood teaching career.

For Jennifer Coggiola Morgan, that registered alternatively as deep comfort and a feeling bordering on claustrophobia. "The kids in my class, they were almost like brothers." Noting a pattern that was widely evident in the romantic life of the school, she added: "Interestingly, I never dated anybody in my class. We'd all seen each other since we were four and five."

But the intense familiarity that constricted some kinds of relationships made it easier to appreciate peers whose talents and interests diverged from hers. "The jocks were as celebrated as the thespians, who were as celebrated as the artists," she said. Compared to other private schools where she had acquaintances, "Heathwood was a much more welcoming environment to a diverse student body.

"But we were very white," she added. "I could probably count on one hand the number of kids I graduated with who were people of color."

That was a common refrain among students from the 1990s, who were in some cases encountering more ethnic diversity in their humanities and English coursework than in the classrooms where they discussed as-signed reading. "If there's only 60 people in a class, there's only so much diversity you can mix in," observed Terracio. "Getting out into the real world and coming face to face with the range of people that live in the United States—you miss out on that by going to a smaller school that is fairly homogeneous."

Bob Shirley's impact on the school could be measured partly by his attempts to make it more heterogeneous. "The purposeful mixing of backgrounds is very important," said Shirley, for whom student body di-versity was part and parcel of a progressive education. "But people don't like to talk about it." His tenure coincided with the ascendency of racial color blindness as a prescription for addressing longstanding disparities in American life. Insofar as blindness to deep-seated societal inequities can easily end up reinforcing them, this ideology may have served better as a commendable aspiration than as a proactive strategy for confront-ing inequality of opportunity. Whatever the case, Shirley favored a more energetic approach.

In 1979, when he came to Heathwood as headmaster, minority stu-dents accounted for 4.4 percent of the school's total enrollment.[22] That remained the status quo though the mid-1980s, at which point numbers began to rise thanks to two main efforts. One was outreach to upwardly mobile Black Columbians, guided largely by longtime Heathwood fam-ilies like the Ponders, the Coopers, and the Jameses. The other was a dramatic expansion of need-based financial aid.

Up to that point, tuition aid had been directed largely toward chil-dren of Heathwood employees and Episcopal clergy. In the recollection of Bob Haarlow, who served in various administrative roles from 1985 to 2000, the parent body did not evince a great deal of agitation to over-turn that status quo. "I don't remember, 'We need more diversity,'" he said. "I just don't remember it. But Bob [Shirley] found ways to get them there through financial aid." Shirley didn't hear widespread clamoring for change, either, but found some important allies who advanced that cause. In 1989, trustee Bob McCoy and former Board chair Bob Royall took charge of a fundraising effort to endow minority scholarships.[23] Shirley identified Jim Reynolds, Bo Tate, Tate Horton, and Mary Belser as particularly effective advocates as his tenure progressed.

By 1992 minority enrollment had roughly tripled in absolute terms and doubled as a proportion of total enrollment, accounting for slightly more than 10 percent of Heathwood's domestic pupils (who were joined that year by five exchange students hailing variously from Germany, Spain, and Brazil).[24] In the late 1990s, a program called Blue Ribbon Scholars used financial aid to attract about 20 to 30 academically gifted pupils, largely at the Middle School level.[25]

Between the 1989-90 and 1999-2000 school years the top tuition rate nearly doubled from $4,480 to $8,550[26]—and Heathwood's annual financial aid budget more than quadrupled, from $230,312 to $990,646. This reflected the increasing burden of private education on families. In 1999, Heathwood's Upper School tuition represented 19 percent of the median annual income of families in the South.[27]

Students at work.

As the financial aid program expanded, its contours shifted. During the 1989-90 academic year 21 percent of Heathwood students received some tuition aid, and 11 percent of the aid budget went to minority students. Ten years later Heathwood provided aid to 25 percent of its students. Minorities, who accounted for 11.7 percent of the student body, received 28 percent of the total aid budget.[28] Compared to peer institutions across the nation, Heathwood enrolled a lower proportion of minorities but was more generous with financial aid across the board. Minority enrollment across 612 NAIS schools stood at 18.1 percent in 1999, and these independent day schools aided approximately 14.1 percent of their total student population.[29]

Enrollment numbers can only say so much about the ways Heathwood served individual students. They say even less about how particular students helped to shape the school in turn. But both of those dynamics were evident in the widely varied experiences of four students who came to Heathwood via quite different paths around this time.

Insofar as Heathwood retained a cloistered atmosphere in the 1990s, the close-knit social fabric had a saving grace that stood out to many students. "It was small enough that everyone was celebrated for their individuality, from the valedictorian down to the person who finished at the bottom of class," in Nate Terracio's view. "Because even if you look from a straight academic point of view, people in the bottom third have a lot to offer," he said. "And I think the school did a great job getting the best out of them—not only for themselves, but for the school as a whole.

"Every school has a bottom third—there's no way to not have a bottom third—and the bottom third at Heathwood would not have been the bottom third had they gone other places. [But] I think celebrating the strengths and differences of everyone helped us *all* to flourish, and be the best versions of ourselves."

In straight academic terms, Terrance Bannister would have placed himself in the bottom third. As a freshman at Columbia's Eau Claire

High School, he felt stuck in a system oriented around the minimal expectation of achieving the 2.0 grade-point average and 700 SAT score
required by the NCAA to play Division I collegiate sports.

"I had mediocre grades, and I just wanted to change myself," he recalled. When Heathwood emerged as an option, his mother and grandmother opposed it, worried that the upper-crust environment would
overwhelm a poor kid from Bluff Road's notoriously crime-ridden
Starlite subdivision. "They were totally against it," Bannister said. "They
were like, 'You're going to be one Black man amongst a bunch of whites.
And you're just going to get smothered.'"

But he was determined—going so far as to forge his mother's signature before Bob Shirley insisted that she be a full participant in the
decision—and entered via summer school before his sophomore year. "It
was definitely good for me," he said. "In a place where my family probably didn't think I was going to excel, I was a captain in three sports. I
was chaplain on all the teams I played on. I was in student government."

Known for nerve-loosening frivolity in the locker room, he gained
a reputation for a deeply rooted altruism outside of it. To judge by the
number of coaches and peers who described him as one of the "most
genuinely good" or "authentically kindhearted" people they ever encountered, it would surprise few that Bannister spent the first year of the
COVID pandemic doing the same thing he'd done for the previous sev-
en: poking around under bridges and homeless encampments offering
mental-health support, social services, and a path to shelter for people
who lacked those things. At Heathwood, he also began an upward academic climb that eventually delivered him to Howard University, the
"Mecca" of international Black intellectual culture. "I came up from a 2.0
to a 2.4. But a 2.4 at Heathwood would probably have been a 3.7 at Eau
Claire!" he laughed. "And there were just different things I was able to
experience. Like going on college tours that were not even for athletics.
Doing community service. It was just a big deal."

Heathwood's student honor code also made a big impression on him.
For honor council members it could entail weighty decisions. Jennifer
Coggiola Morgan would remember the moral responsibility she felt as

a junior when charged with addressing a first-time cheating offense by a freshman. "We had to talk about it, go over the honor code, and give them a sentence. I remember going home, saying to my mom, 'I could have just ended some kid's career. This is heavy stuff.' And we all took it really seriously." Bannister, by contrast, associated it with the regular mentoring sessions he had with Bob Shirley. "He taught me about the honor code. That grew me, because a lot of people don't understand what an honor code is." His appreciation was tightly bound up with a remarkable instance of misplaced property. "I left my wallet with $100 in it and it stayed in Gasque's classroom for a week!"

Racial and gender issues posed particular challenges at the turn of the 1990s, as illuminated by the stories of three students who grappled with them in ways that ultimately influenced Heathwood's culture for the better.

Entering Heathwood as a freshman in 1987, Charlice Hurst was "really optimistic" after having bounced around gifted programs in the public sector. "All that segregation was decades ago, and now color doesn't matter," she remembers thinking. "So I expected people to embrace me just as me."

Reality was not quite so rosy. "There was still such a strong color line," she said. Yet she felt little in common with her new Black classmates, who tended to come from wealthier families. And she had an even harder time adjusting to reigning expectations for feminine comportment. "The first year, the white kids I couldn't relate to. Culturally, it was very different. One of the things I encountered when I got there was that girls were supposed to abide by a certain model of femininity—you were supposed to be delicate, and you weren't supposed to act smart. There were some girls there who were really smart—but you weren't supposed to act like it. You weren't supposed to speak up in class. That was a shock, because at the school I had gone to before, the girls were super vocal—probably more so than the boys—and we'd have all sorts of debates in class. And then I get to Heathwood, and if a girl was vocal in class, she was a 'bitch.'"

By rejecting those terms of engagement, Hurst, whose activist bent occasionally surfaced in newspaper stories and letters to the editor of *The State*,[30] helped expand the boundaries of Heathwood's intellectual culture. "Charlice bucked the dominant system," as Bob Shirley put it, looking back with admiration from the vantage of 2021. "Charlice was very early on saying the kinds of things that we are hearing very loudly now."

What Heathwood gave Hurst was "a level of preparation I don't think I would have gotten anywhere else," she said. "Not just in terms of academic skills, but learning how to learn, and learning how to think. We weren't boxed in by standardized tests and standardized curricula." Adults like Lark Palma, Bob Haarlow, physics teacher George Fox, and Jim Gasque became sources of growth and compassion. "I was extremely prepared for Harvard," said the student who earned a degree there in three years, and eventually became a professor at Notre Dame's Mendoza College of Business, "because Heathwood emphasized writing so much."

What Hurst gave Heathwood was, characteristically, delivered in the form of a critique. Having found the history and literature curriculum lacking in its treatment of Black contributions to American politics and culture,[31] she carried out a senior capstone project drawing on figures like James Baldwin and W.E.B. Du Bois to examine the shortcomings of how African American history, sociology, and literature were taught (or not) within predominantly white educational institutions. This exercise functioned not only as an early template for what would later be rolled out as the senior exhibition of mastery, but as a catalyst for curricular change that took off almost as soon as she finished presenting her project before an audience that included the state superintendent of education.

Stefan Romero came to Heathwood the same year as Hurst, in the sixth grade. At the outset, the New York City native's most powerful impression was that "the North hides its racism better than the South." That conclusion augured trouble for a self-described "strong-willed" Black male who "had a mouth" and a clear idea of what he would and would not tolerate. There was a certain exoticism about landing amidst the soybean fields on a campus where Middle School boys sometimes brandished Polaroid snapshots depicting their faces smeared with the blood of the first deer they had shot. But such rites of passage dovetailed with an adolescent search for selfhood that led some young men to embrace the ready-made identity symbolized by the Confederate battle flag, which flew above the dome of the South Carolina State Capitol between 1961 and 2000.[32]

Romero remembered his sixth grade year as a barrage of unprintable epithets, to which he reacted with such predictable regularity that Heathwood's disciplinary authorities "had a table waiting for me in Dr. Shirley's office."[33] As he progressed through Middle School, participating in organized athletics for the first time in his life, the situation improved. His peers, he felt, increasingly regarded him less as "just this Black kid" than as "my teammate." By high school he had established himself as a football and track standout whose buoyant, mostly good-humored brand of boisterousness had won him plenty of friends.

That is how Tyna Bakir encountered him in 1990, when she landed in South Carolina shortly after the Iraqi Army invaded her home country of Kuwait. Heathwood felt broadly familiar to Bakir, who had attended Charlotte Country Day for four years in elementary school before moving back to Kuwait with her father. The rarity of her background as a Middle Easterner didn't prevent her from finding a social footing at the outset of tenth grade, and the school's soft Episcopalianism posed no particular conflict with her religious affiliation as a Muslim. Socially, both of those facets of her identity "were basically thrown out the window when I went to Heathwood," she remembered, "because I was looked at as white."

She did not view herself that way. In her part of the Middle East, ethnic categorizations and chauvinisms had less to do with skin color than with nationality. In South Carolina, where people were largely regarded as either Black or white, Bakir felt like she was neither. The fact that she had no real control over how others classified her "kind of made me feel lost."

In a sense, Bakir's cultural dislocation had left her with a particular form of racial color blindness. A girly confab during downtime one day revealed the degree to which it put her out of step with the social mainstream. "Do you find anybody cute?" a classmate asked her. Yes, Bakir confessed: Stefan Romero. "But he's Black!" came the reply, in Bakir's recollection.

"I was like, 'Okay...'" Bakir responded. "And she goes, 'You don't care???'

Revisiting the memory 30 years later, Bakir marveled at her own naivety. "I didn't understand. I honestly didn't understand what she was trying to say."

The meaning became clear when the pair started dating about a month later. "All the girls stopped talking to me," Bakir said. "I had the white girls cutting me off because, *How could you do that?* And then I had the Black girls cutting me off," she added, "because they were acting like, *How dare you take one of these few Black guys in the school from us?* So I had absolutely no girlfriends except one," she said, naming Class of 1993 alumna Jennifer Ertter. "She was the only one that would talk to me."

Instead, Romero and Bakir were talked about. Each remembered their relationship both for its intensity—"I definitely did love him," Bakir said—and the dirty looks and snide commentary it inspired. They felt censure not only from classmates, but also some adults at the school.[34] "My mom, too," Romero remembered. "She was like, 'You shouldn't be mixing.'"

To the limited extent that Heathwood students had pursued interracial couplings before, they had done so quietly or clandestinely. Romero and Bakir were uninterested in hiding. For certain people around them, that was "an uncomfortable thing," Romero recollected. "People hadn't dealt with it. I'm trying to remember what teacher made the comment about 'jungle fever,'" he added, alluding to a term whose popularity had been catapulted as the title of a contemporaneous Spike Lee film. But that phrase seemed to be on everyone's lips—and not as a celebration of this unfamiliar brand of romance. "It was new to the school," Romero said. But he and Bakir refused to be shamed.

Despite the difficulties they encountered, each continued to value Heathwood well into middle age. Both praised their scholastic preparation and the holistic nature of the educations they received. Even though it confronted Bakir with her "first ever experience of racism," she regarded it as "an amazing school"—largely on account of experiences it offered beyond the classroom, like a Winterim service trip to build houses and another that took her whitewater rafting. Romero treasured the eventual, if fitful, community embrace that led him to boogie-boarding lake parties and other settings well outside his prior experience.

Their relationship produced many things: prurient gossip, academic distractions, social ostracism, and the heady rush of young love. It was also a public demonstration of what authentic progress in racial relations looked like, modeled with a fearlessness that challenged the Heathwood community to live up to a lofty rhetoric that white and Black people alike had found easier to espouse in the abstract. But in the longest run, it produced something more sublime.

For unrelated reasons, Romero and Bakir finished high school elsewhere: she returned to Kuwait for her senior year, and Romero graduated from Columbia's Spring Valley High School, where he proved himself capable of playing football at the state's top competitive tier.[35] In an era predating email and social media, they lost touch with one another completely. Bakir married a Lebanese man, had three children, and worked in her family's high-end furnishings business. Romero had a wife and kids, too, and found his way into medical IT consulting in New York City, where he also helped to run youth athletics programs for underprivileged kids. As fate would have it, both their marriages ended during the Facebook era, and it was on that platform that Jennifer Ertter brought Romero and Bakir back into contact for the first time in more than two decades. Some time later they came together at a mini-reunion of Heathwood friends.

"I hadn't seen anybody in 26 years," recalled Bakir, who had moved from the Middle East to Toronto in 2010. "And it felt good and happy to see everyone. But when I saw Stefan—it was weird," she said. "It was like we were back at Heathwood. The connection was there, still."

They married in August 2016. She took her husband's name—Tyna Bakir Romero—and their home filled with the joyful noise of a brood they likened to a modern Brady Bunch. It grew in September 2019, when they had a son. Reaching to express the joy of renewed fatherhood, Stefan would channel his inner Jim Gasque to describe Amir at the age of 20 months: "He is the sun which wakes the Earth."

Charlice Hurst's capstone project—along with another, on architecture, by Class of 1990 alumnus and future architect Bret Horton—became a model for the most lasting legacy of the Shirley era. Their success drove a movement to make senior "exhibitions of mastery" a graduation requirement. Ted Graf spearheaded this campaign.

"It was really easy with the Coalition to stay in the idea zone—just to philosophize," Graf recalled. "But to get really practical, we believed that if we didn't change the way we assessed—particularly a culminating assessment—nothing else would change.

"For our school at the time, it was the key to making the rest of it happen," he continued. "If you had to show your research skills, your defense skills, your interest in the topic, your ability to reason and write, your ability to pursue something—if that was the endpoint, then if you planned backwards into the rest of the school, an education had to look different."

Selling trustees, parents, and traditionalist faculty members on this change was a delicate business. "Bob was really smart," Graf reflected about Shirley's strategy. "He didn't need to be the most vocal person, he didn't need to be out in front of it, he didn't need to be the figurehead. In fact," said Graf, who went on to head two other schools as his career progressed, "I'd love to know from him whether he deliberately chose a strategy where I, Daniel [Venables], Lark [Palma], and others pushed it forward more from the classroom than from an administrative level."

By this point in his own career, Shirley had reached a conclusion: "Leadership has to do with how other people behave around you, more than how you behave." In Graf he saw a powerful advocate for a cause they shared, and found subtle ways to cement their alliance while amplifying Graf's administrative clout. One memorable tactic played out when Shirley tapped Graf to accompany him to a CES conference in Chicago—and elected to drive rather than fly. Their 12-hour rap session on the open road, in the headmaster's view, paved the way for much that followed.[36]

Under Lark Palma's guidance as Upper School principal, Graf and Venables created a handbook that laid out expectations and rubrics for assessment. "They had to have some degree of rigor in order to pass," Venables said. The job of ensuring that fell to a nested series of mentors charged with guiding each student. "There were committees, an outside expert from the community, a [faculty] adviser. So we had lots of people helping the student produce something of value."

In the early 1990s exhibitions of mastery were incorporated into humanities classes in ninth through eleventh grades to acclimate students to the challenge.[37] In 1992 the trustees amended Heathwood's diploma requirements to include a senior exhibition of mastery beginning with the Class of 1994.[38]

Duncan Belser's exhibition was an exemplar of the creativity, multi-disciplinarity, and faculty support that characterized these culminating projects. Inspired by his love for Latin and a Winterim trip to Rome and Pompeii, Belser developed his own translation of Book 3 of Virgil's *Aeneid*. "But I had to do something academic," he said, so he incorporated archeological findings from the Uluburun Late Bronze Age shipwreck, whose excavation in Turkish waters was being completed in 1994. To scratch his drama itch, Belser recruited teachers to don costumes and perform video vignettes depicting scenes from the epic poem. Lark Palma wrapped a giant scarf around her head to play Queen Dido. Allison and Daniel Venables portrayed sailors. Bill Cherry had a role—but, more crucially, helped Belser corral what was then a gargantuan amount of data into a Hypercard presentation that knitted all these elements together. At a time when CD burners cost around $10,000,[39] Belser had to solve the challenge of transferring his multimedia presentation onto the machine available for his public demonstration.[40]

"Bill Cherry is best in class," Belser said. "He was always trying to read about and learn about the newest wave." Cherry found a program that allowed him to slice up his presentation "into about 30 floppy discs," from which it could then be reassembled without degradation.

In terms of student assessment, the then-chair of Heathwood's Board offered a memorable one. "Duncan's never done anything that wasn't complicated," in his mother's wry appraisal. "And he just thrived to be able to do that exhibition." Another came by way of an entrepreneur in the audience. Adam Winter, a physician who had younger children at Heathwood, offered Belser a job. "I spent the next three summers," Belser

Bill Cherry shares his vision of the digital future.

said, "and the first three years of my career working for his software company, developing interactive web-based software."

For Daniel Venables, the strength of the exhibitions lay in their integration of multiple fields of scholarship. "One of my advisees did one on fetal alcohol syndrome," he offered by way of example. "You wouldn't put that in any particular bucket when it comes to academic disciplines. Another did one on magazine ads and the psychology driving the use of colors and fonts and pictures." Disparate interests often led students toward the social sciences—fields more typically encountered in college than in high school. "They were looking at stuff like highway fatalities and cell phone usage—all kinds of things that required research."

"They taught me to write and to learn on my own," said Jennifer Coggiola Morgan, who set out to demonstrate the ineffectiveness and unconstitutionality of the death penalty in an exhibition that featured one of her mother's legal clients, who was on death row. "So when I got to college,

Math teacher Daniel Venables.

I was not overwhelmed. I was so confident." She felt more academically engaged and prepared than her peers at the University of Vermont. "There was a curiosity I had about the world that I found a lot of my friends didn't have," she reflected. "Even friends who went to boarding schools in Boston and New York didn't know how to write a research paper. I was blown away. That exhibition, that was a thesis we did when we were 17," said Morgan, who went on to work as a news correspondent for CNN and NBC. "That has served me, genuinely, my entire life."

"We became much more rigorous," Daniel Venables concluded, drawing a characteristically blunt contrast between the exhibition era and what had preceded it. "We went from a private school for rich kids that really didn't do anything but get them into good colleges, to actually offering a good education, where there was rigor and kids were really doing some good academic things."

The establishment of senior exhibitions helped to unleash an energy that many Heathwood faculty members remembered as unique in their careers. "Lark and Bob were really forces for change," said John Pulford, who continued teaching at Heathwood until his retirement in 2016. "We went overboard a little bit with those Coalition principles, but I loved it. That was my favorite time teaching in my whole life. The late '80s and early '90s were, to me, just fascinating."

Seeds planted during that time flowered into a curricular freedom that Ted Graf looked back on with incredulity. "Dan Palma and I were allowed to develop a non-Western cultures class in the 1990s in South Carolina!" he marveled. "We taught two African countries in depth for a semester, and then two Asian countries," he said. "Under Bob, there was a genuine authentic openness to Dan and me learning as much about Nigerian culture and Igbo culture as possible, and then teaching *Things Fall Apart*" by Chinua Achebe.

Heathwood continued to cultivate traditions whose origins went back as far as the old mansion days. Cold weather brought Homecoming, "Lessons and Carols" at Trinity Cathedral, and Jim Gasque's black-tie recitation of "The Night Before Christmas" before an all-school assembly. Hot weather brought the Maypole dance and the Highlander Games. Any weather but all-out rain might find the campus awash in the plangent airs and drone reed harmonies of a kilted Billy DuBose, Heathwood's "official bagpiper."[41] But the school's intellectual life was also opening up in exciting new directions.

"I taught a bunch of books that even today are considered edgy," Graf went on. One was Jean Toomer's *Cane*, a modernist fusion of prose and poetry from the Harlem Renaissance that features a lynching. Graf did "wacky things" with William Faulkner's *Light in August*. He coaxed his AP English students to engage explicitly with the political dimensions of curricular decisions by inviting their parents to play-act the part of a public school board considering which piece of literature best illuminated the Civil War: Mark Twain's *Adventures of Huckleberry Finn*, Toni Morrison's *Beloved*, or *Narrative of the Life of Frederick Douglass, an American Slave*. Student groups were charged with arguing the case for each one. "It was one of my proudest moments," Graf recalled, "because we were having a real conversation about race, and the kids were actually leading it." Two votes culminated the exercise: one in which the parents selected Huck Finn, and one in which the students selected Douglass's memoir-cum-treatise.

"We were really encouraged to try stuff," Graf said. "And I'm not sure I've ever again been in a place that had that much intellectual activity. We didn't agree all the time, but there was a creativity and an intellectual liveliness that's been hard to capture anywhere else I've worked."

Young Will DuBose marches and drums alongside his father, Billy DuBose, Heathwood's "official bagpiper," circa 1998.

The spirit was immediately apparent to Class of 1985 alumnus Marshall James, who joined the faculty between 1993 and 1999.[42] "The focus was really on the exhibition," he said, but that created space for an impressive array of electives. Having spent three years abroad through the Japan Exchange and Teaching Program, James taught basic Japanese, anthropology, and multicultural literature.

Though he emphasized that his own experience as a Heathwood student had been "as positive as could be," James thrilled to the changes the school had undergone. "I was hardly aware that Black people had written novels until I got to college," he said. As a Heathwood teacher, by contrast, "One of the books I taught—and was kind of reluctant to teach, because I didn't know how well it would go—was *The Autobiography of Malcolm X*. And it was the most popular book. Kids loved it."

The kids were another change, and not just because a dozen of them launched a Diversity Council in 1994.[43] "The students were more progressive. There were some gay students who were out—which I was amazed by, because that would have never happened in the early 1980s. There were some interracial relationships, so some students didn't think twice about dating a white student or Black student. So those were positive developments."

They reflected broader social trends. "I attributed it, at the time, to *The Real World*," James reflected, citing MTV's inaugural foray into reality television, which offered a strikingly inclusive depiction of American young adulthood. "People were just more open to different ways of being, and loving, etcetera."

James was one part of a faculty influx that invigorated Class of 1996 alumna Lynn Manning Cooper. "I think we had all been looking at each other for so long," she laughed, alluding to the continuity of Heathwood's familial atmosphere. But suddenly a new kind of role model was becoming ever so slightly more common. "I mean, people did not necessarily love Rebecca Hamm," Manning remarked, about a short-lived northeastern faculty import. "She was hard and difficult, she had super short hair, she was super liberal. She was not afraid to share her ideas in class. And I think it was jarring for some people.

But it was like 'Oh, wow!' It was kind of inspiring to see these people," she said. "It was diversity, and that's what we needed."

Manning came to value Graf partly on account of how different he was from the Southern outdoorsmen who'd set the tone of her upbringing. "I think we all saw what it meant to be a funny, artistic man. Maybe we didn't have many of those in our lives," she mused. "He was a published poet. He would come in and say, 'Oh guys, I started to write this poem, what do you think?' We had a poetry club!"

Yet change rarely visits institutions without provoking countercurrents. As the turn of the millennium drew near, a new tension percolated through the Heathwood community.

"In the 1990s, the parent body became very conservative," said Daniel Venables, one of several teachers who began to feel constricted by what another called a "hard-right turn" in South Carolina in the latter part of the decade. "That was a challenge. Because here we were doing really good, progressive, Bob Shirley education, where kids were really doing amazing things, and then the parent body started to get conservative ... All of a sudden they were questioning everything we were doing that wasn't textbook education."

Heathwood's parent body was not monolithic in terms of political orientation, and faculty impressions of parent-body attitudes were likely skewed by one of the oldest patterns in human affairs—namely the way the objections of a small but noisy group tend to attract more attention than the satisfactions of a large but quiet one. Nevertheless, teachers who registered an atmospheric shift were not imagining things. The tenor of American conservatism changed dramatically in the 1990s. Amid the rise of right-wing radio, partisan religious organizations like the Christian Coalition of America, and the 1996 launch of Fox News, the patrician intellectualism of old Republican standard-bearers like William F. Buckley and George Will gave way to a pugnacious breed of entertainers like Rush Limbaugh and Bill O'Reilly. Parent anxieties were simultaneously being fueled by a nonpartisan development that arguably loomed larger: the rapidly intensifying competitiveness of college admissions.[44] Insofar as parent-body "conservatism" became more conspicuous during the 1990s, it was substantially around questions about how college admissions officers would interpret those elements of Heathwood's curriculum that veered furthest from traditional practices.[45]

Heathwood's implementation of "integrated math" in 1995, for instance, stirred much apprehension. Following an approach more common in Europe, it wrapped multiple branches of mathematics (like geometry, algebra, trigonometry, statistics) into any given grade-level course, rather than presenting them separately as remained the norm in US secondary education.[46] An education committee report presented to Heathwood's trustees in 2000 credited integrated math with elevating Heathwood's average math PSAT scores above students' average verbal schools—a marked contrast to 1980—and noted that 86 percent of the previous year's graduates had completed calculus.[47] Heathwood also stood out from peer institutions by offering seventh graders the chance to take a high-school-credited math course—a testament to Marifred Cilella's work as Lower School head and director of academic administration. Yet integrated math was already on its way out at that point, and worries remained about how other blended courses—like humanities in place of traditional English and history—appeared on college applications.

"I was getting pushback: How is this going to look on the transcript?" Venables recalled. "I had to fight. But I was respected in the parent community; parents were trying to get their kids in my classes. My stock was high. So I got to do some stuff that was off the beaten track, and that was progressive, educationally, and get away with it.[48] But other teachers were having trouble."

"I remember those tensions in the '90s," Marshall James said. "A lot of parents probably suspected Bob was a progressive. And this weird curriculum and weird grading system I think many parents didn't like, and didn't know how colleges were interpreting.

"And I think perhaps there were some issues with all these teachers from the northeast—and on top of that, with the Coalition thing," he continued. A substantial parent contingent seemed "more interested in a standard way of teaching"—which stoked anxiety about the prospect of losing students to other schools.

This dynamic was also apparent to Frank Ellerbe, who joined the board in 1996 and chaired it between 1999 and 2002. "Part of what was going on at the same time, that can't be ignored, is that Hammond was seen as a more conservative alternative—maybe more traditional, and potentially more demanding," he said. "Lark Palma, who was head of the Upper School, was probably too far out there for the community." And although enrollment topped 800 in 1995 for only the second time in Heathwood's history, it ebbed slightly in the late 1990s.

"During the entire time I was on the board," Ellerbe recalled, "we wanted to increase enrollment by 30 or 40 more students—if we could just do that, the finances would work so much better. That was always an issue. And there was definitely a perception that maybe Heathwood was a little bit to the left of where it needed be.

"I thought we were on the right track—I thought we had a better approach than Hammond, and certainly that was our experience with our children," Ellerbe added, singling out the senior exhibition of mastery as an especially valuable preparation for their subsequent studies at Princeton and Stanford. Yet Ellerbe perceived "a little bit of a course-correction," beginning just before he joined the board, "back away from the more progressive extreme."

Lark and Dan Palma left in 1995 for Portland, Oregon, where Lark became headmaster of the Catlin Gabel school. In what would prove a far-sighted move, Shirley soon tapped Anne Weston to lead the Upper School.

"I was worried for Bob," recalled Ted Graf, who departed with Amy Railsback Graf in 2000. "The climate of the state was changing in such a way that Amy and I weren't sure that's where we wanted to be with our two young kids. And we were worried Heathwood would be forced to the right whether Bob wanted it to or not."

Shirley had navigated and largely neutralized these forces for 20 years. "I got a pass from the community," he explained. "Because I had been in a fraternity, I went to the University of South, I went to Furman, I went into the Marine Corps, I got a pass: *Old Bob is okay, he's not going to do anything we don't want.* And that pass allowed me to not have to defend things too much when something got hot, and somebody complained about it."[49] He also drew political capital from his success growing Heathwood's facilities, which culminated in 1996 with the opening of a third building by architect Richard Molten: the Susan Gibbes Robinson Center for Science and Math.

But the landscape was shifting.

"The most interesting time, academically, to me was the period when Tate Horton was chairman of the board, followed by Mary Belser, followed by Boyd Hipp," Shirley reflected, echoing John Pulford's enthusiasm for the years between 1987 and 1994. Many of the initiatives that flowered during that period bore their fullest fruit in the second half of the 1990s. But the energy of a great journey has a way of dissipating at its destination.

Heathwood's founding headmistress celebrates the 1995 groundbreaking of the eponymous Susan Gibbes Robinson Center for Math and Science.

Ted Graf felt that "maybe the school was trying to be too many things to too many people." As college admissions became increasingly competitive—driven by the sheer size of the Millennial generation—parent anxiety mounted across a spectrum that ran the gamut from athletic opportunities to math curricula. Against the backdrop of the 1990s culture wars, literature reading lists came under intensified scrutiny everywhere. These trends transcended Heathwood Hall. The list of things Americans demand from schools may only be rivaled by the list of things they attempt to exclude. Threading the needle was only getting more difficult. "This is true for lots of schools, today, too," said Graf in 2021, during the sixth year of his tenure as headmaster of Headwaters School in Austin, Texas. "I wasn't sure Heathwood had quite the focus it needed. Hammond was presenting itself as a 'world school' at that time. I felt like Heathwood was getting too diffuse."

Shirley wanted to double down on progressive pedagogy. "I wanted to go on with it, making Heathwood more like the University of Chicago Laboratory Schools," he said. "And the Board didn't really want that." Shirley, who had become increasingly involved in efforts to introduce CES principals to public schools in South Carolina,[50] also proposed a summer program whereby Heathwood would train learning-disability teachers for the state "so that LD kids could have a full education at the same time they were having a special education." He found scant support for that idea, either.

In 1999, Heathwood's longest-serving headmaster came to a realization: "I saw the end of my effectiveness." With two years remaining on his contract, he announced that 1999-2000 would be his final school year. Heathwood Hall had undergone a profound metamorphosis under his watch, but charting a course for the 21st century would be the work of another set of leaders.

chapter seven

CAMPUS RENAISSANCE

Anne Weston—Steve Hickman—Raven Tarpley and the Episcopal awakening—September 11—building spree—Wood's PEAK— alumni in the classroom—"Jesus wore a beard"—dress code history— yoga, robotics, math meets, salsa—high scorer—the ACCEPT inflection point

[2000-2008]

A s the trustees carried out a national search for a new head of school in 1999, their thinking began to revolve around someone who did not consider herself a candidate for the job. Anne Weston had come to Heathwood Hall in 1978, the same year as Bob Shirley. Having started out as a 22-year-old science teacher, she remembered when the campus had been a site of raw challenge and potential. Cleaning out the files in her biology classroom one of those first springs, she found a colony of field mice that had chewed a path from the letter R to the end of the alphabet. In the ensuing two decades, there was scarcely any role she had not filled.

"Back in those days," she recalled about the early years, "if you could drive a bus, you were a coach." So Weston coached cheerleading, tennis, and JV basketball. After about ten years of teaching, she got a nudge from Upper School head Bob Haarlow to consider a new kind of role. As the cost of employer-sponsored health care mounted in the 1980s, many US corporations turned to workplace wellness programs to buffer rising expenses. Longtime Heathwood benefactor Gayle Averyt, who had implemented that model as CEO of Colonial Life & Accident Insurance, advocated its adoption at Heathwood. With his support and that of Bob Shirley, Weston took a sabbatical year to begin work on a doctorate in public health. In 1989 she became Heathwood's director of wellness, running programs primarily for staff but also for students. Her administrative roles gradually multiplied to include an all-purpose support position as a flexibly defined "program director," as well as student and faculty counseling as dean. With her 1995 elevation to Upper School head (and assistant head of school), she came into her own as a leader whose genuineness was as apparent to teenagers—who are exquisitely attuned to counterfeits—as it had

Anne Weston (far right) on a community service work site.

long been to colleagues. As Class of 2009 graduate Brice Spires put it: "I don't know any kid that Anne Weston can't connect with."

The Board whittled down the candidates to three finalists. Two of them, in the estimation of then-chair Frank Ellerbe, were "in the mold of Bob Shirley." The third was Stephen Hickman, who had spent the better part of two decades in the financial services sector before working for several years as an administrator, teacher, and coach at Lakeview Academy, an independent K-12 day school in Gainesville, Georgia. Hickman's deepest professional experience was in business development and strategic planning for the Nasdaq Stock Market, whose Silicon Valley office he helped to establish in 1987. He had also served as COO and CEO of a small firm in North Carolina.

Contemplating what Heathwood was likely to need in the coming decade, the trustees rooted their decision partly in what the school already had. "With Anne Weston being so well ensconced as head of the Upper School," Ellerbe said, "and really well-known throughout the community and throughout the school, she would continue to pursue the educational approaches that Bob had inculcated at Heathwood. But boy, wouldn't it be great to get someone who could think more about finances, and get the financial house in order a little bit more. Not that things were that bad or anything," he added, "but I think it was a little bit of a pendulum swing."

※

Nestled in active farmland just a few miles upriver from the primordial cypress swamps of Congaree National Park, Heathwood Hall often struck newcomers as a place apart. Steve Hickman's first visit triggered a small-world epiphany. Passing through the Earl Devanny Gate, he realized that the campus entrance honored his own childhood principal—from the Presbyterian Day School in Memphis, Tennessee, before Devanny came to Heathwood.

Hickman was drawn to Heathwood by three main things. In pedagogical terms, he appreciated its blend of traditional and experiential learning. "Bob [Shirley] and his team had laid a lot of groundwork around some concepts that were important to me: demonstrations of learning, experiential learning opportunities, and hands-on ways for kids to apply their knowledge," he said. "In addition to some of the more traditional ways of education, I thought that the exploration the school was doing was something I believed in, and could get behind."

Hickman also valued the school's longstanding commitment to student diversity—"not only in terms of racial and ethnic diversity, but religious diversity and socio-economic diversity"—and the use of financial aid to bolster it. "I was blessed to go to a school similar to Heathwood," he reflected. "I grew up in a single-parent household, and the only way that I was able to go, at least for the last few years, was because of financial assistance … So I had a little bit of personal experience of this idea of accessibility and affordability. Quite frankly, I'm a firm believer that diversity in all its aspects is a great positive to the community. What's important is finding mission-appropriate kids, regardless of their background. And those many backgrounds," he said, "make the school much stronger."

The third attraction may have been the most consequential, for his dedication to it would rival an ambitious campus expansion as his biggest legacy. Hickman believed deeply in the importance of Heathwood's Episcopal identity, and made it a cornerstone of his stewardship of the school. Over the next eight years, the interplay between some of his more conservative instincts and Weston's enduring commitment to CES progressivism would become a fruitful tension shaping Heathwood's academic evolution. But when it came to the school's spiritual life, the most powerful dynamic was Hickman and Weston's alignment.

Having been founded in 1951 as an explicitly church-centric school where ordained ministers conducted multiple weekly chapels in full liturgical vestments while students memorized dozens of hymns and prayers, Heathwood drifted in a decidedly more secular direction during the last quarter of the 20th century. Bob Shirley was a member of the vestry at Trinity Cathedral, and he took his spiritual commitments seriously enough to occasionally serve as a mentor to adolescents working toward Episcopal confirmation, but as an educator he valued independence from the church more highly than alliance with it. Marketplace branding was also a challenge for a school that aimed to attract students of all creeds amid a competitive educational landscape. Non-Episcopalian newcomers to Columbia had little way of knowing that Heathwood Hall had always welcomed Jews, Roman Catholics, and others just as readily as Episcopalians—and when Hammond finally moved away from segregationist admissions policies in the 1980s, it became a more agile competitor for a wider variety of families, thereby challenging a competitive advantage Heathwood had long enjoyed. These dynamics had bred some uncertainty about how heavily Heathwood should emphasize its Episcopal identity.

"I think we went through phases of what that meant," Weston reflected, "and maybe were apologetic about it at some points, or worried it might detract from our attractiveness to students." She thirsted for a more forthright embrace. "I think it's really important to be able to talk openly and honestly about the spiritual nature of life," she said. "It is so important to address that as you're working with all people, and especially with young people: believing in something that's bigger than yourself. I think faith and hope and mystery are all very, very important in the development of a well-rounded young person. And yes, you can get it other places. But I think it's really powerful when you can get it in the place where you spend a lot of your waking hours, which is at school."

Hickman, who had become an Episcopalian as a compromise between his Presbyterian upbringing and his wife's Catholic one, was a fully committed partner in that mission. "The Episcopal school tradition," as he explained his own approach to it, "is really not about trying to indoctrinate a particular faith tradition, but rather allowing students to grow up in an environment where their spiritual life is important whatever their faith tradition is. Done in the best way, it affirms your faith journey no matter what that faith journey is. It's done through the Episcopal tradition—but I think everyone is committed to allowing a young person to know the importance of their spiritual journey without dictating what that journey is.

"It's about *spiritual* formation," he concluded, "not necessarily *faith* formation."

Heathwood's revitalized commitment to its Episcopal identity took varied forms. Guided in part by a clergy advisory group at the Board level, chapel went from an occasional event to a weekly one, and the Upper School's pre-existing requirement of two half-credit religion electives[1] was bolstered by some new practices. Every class cohort across the school began the day with a prayer and devotional reflection. A new 12-week religion course was implemented in sixth grade. Contemporary Christian music took on a bigger role in Upper and Middle School chapels, where students eventually began consulting prayer books. A weekly Bible study group sprang up as a morning activity for interested Upper Schoolers.[2] Hickman supplemented Heathwood's commencement ceremony by presenting new graduates with Bibles alongside their diplomas.[3]

Nothing revitalized the campus's spiritual life, though, as profoundly as the arrival of Raven Tarpley. When Anne Weston spotted her at a community supper at Trinity Cathedral in 2000, Tarpley was a full-time caterer hungry for a vocational change. Weston coaxed her to Heathwood to teach an Upper School class on the New Testament. By the next year she was teaching a full slate of classes—religion and eighth-grade English—and sliding into a permanent role as a full-time chaplain. A gifted storyteller with a huskily soothing voice and an affinity for freethinking teenagers, Tarpley also treasured Heathwood's place in her own childhood. She had attended school at the mansion between 1959 and 1966. For decades after finishing sixth grade, she received a telephone call each August 19 at the stroke of 2:08 p.m. Every time she picked up the receiver, it was her once-and-forever school headmistress Elsie Lamar, timing her birthday wishes to the exact minute of Tarpley's first breath.

"I was still in school when she started doing that," Tarpley marveled, and Lamar continued every August until her death in 2002.[4] "Years later I discovered that she did that for hundreds of people, and especially students at Heathwood Hall."

Tarpley was hired as a lay chaplain in the summer of 2001 while the Board searched for an ordained chaplain. The steadiness she exhibited that fall was the first of many qualities that would endear her to students and colleagues. On the morning of September 11, 2001, Heathwood was on a delayed-opening schedule to accommodate faculty meetings. At 8:46 a.m. a Boeing 767 collided with the South Tower of the World Trade Center in Manhattan, followed at 9:03 a.m. by another that crashed into the North Tower. By 9:37 a.m., when a Boeing 757 plowed into the Pentagon, many Heathwood children were already en route to

Chaplain Raven Tarpley.

school. As they began arriving, desperate New Yorkers were flinging themselves from the upper stories of the twin towers to escape fires that soon brought each building crashing to the ground.

"The students were coming, and we knew it," Tarpley recalled. "So the question was: How do we respond to this?" Answering it was complicated by the fact that no one knew exactly what was happening. It would take another 12 hours for CIA Director George Tenet to attribute the attacks to the Al Qaeda terrorist network.[5] As the morning unfolded, fear ran rampant among South Carolinians that the Savannah River nuclear plant might be targeted, or the Naval Weapons Station in Charleston, or even Fort Jackson—the largest US Army entry training center in the country. A less speculative concern soon came to Anne Weston's attention: one of her Upper School students was the daughter of a commercial pilot scheduled to fly in and out of the northeast that morning.

Lower and Middle School administrators felt an urge to shelter younger children from the traumatic news. "In the Upper School, however, we decided that it needed to be acknowledged," Tarpley said. So the faculty led the entire Upper School student body onto the grassy expanse separating the Averyt Early Childhood Learning Center from the Robinson Center for Science and Math, where they joined hands in a giant ring of some 250 adults and adolescents, and prayed. As Tarpley later reflected: "A lot of the kids who stood in that circle that day remember that our first response was to be a community of prayer—and to include all the people of United States, and the world, in our prayers."

For physics teacher Timothy McKnight, who was beginning his third year on campus after a five-year stint at Lexington High School, that moment crystallized the value of Heathwood's Episcopal ethos—even though he belonged to a different flock. "As far as my transition from a public to an Episcopal school, being able to have that kind of support for kids—emotionally and spiritually—is something I really appreciated a lot," he said. "The support for the whole student has always been very important. And I do remember that, standing out in that circle."

The place where the Upper School gathered that September morning had once been a far broader clearing. During the first eight years of Heathwood's tenancy on Burwell Manning's gifted land, no permanent structure existed to the west of the original classroom pods. The 1981 opening of the ECLC accentuated how empty that space still remained. It mostly functioned as a giant recess ground, even after the installation of mobile classroom trailers midway through Bob Shirley's tenure turned one edge of it into the least-envied teaching space at Heathwood.[6] Not until the 1996 addition of the Robinson Center did the campus's center of gravity begin to shift. Steve Hickman would supercharge that process.

In May of 2001, less than a year into his tenure, Hickman proposed a $14 million tax-exempt bond issue to refinance $3 million of preexisting debt and underwrite future construction.[7] Taking advantage of interest rates then hovering near a 30-year low, the Board approved the plan and initiated a $13 million capital campaign to go along with it.[8] As the bursting of the dot-com bubble gave way to an economic expansion whose gains, like those of the 1990s, flowed disproportionately to the wealthiest 10 percent of American families,[9] Heathwood's core market opened their wallets in a robust burst of philanthropic giving.

The results were transformational. The Nord Intermediate/Middle School Building opened in 2003, redefining the western edge of campus. In 2005, student-athletes began pounding the hardwood floorboards of a new athletic center, which was elevated above the floodplain next to the original gymnasium over what had previously been the senior-class parking lot. The next year brought the Chapel of the Epiphany, a 300-seat sanctuary nestled beneath the pines west of the ECLC and north of the new Middle School. For Raven Tarpley, who had spent four years trundling around campus with a rolling cart full of candles, crosses and other liturgical paraphernalia, having a sacred space devoted exclusively to worship was an "unbelievable change."

"With each addition of space," Anne Weston reflected, "you defined something new for the students around community: you could provide added opportunities for students to be together, which I think is part of the richness of school."

Head of school Steve Hickman and Bishop Dorsey Henderson prepare to break ground on the Chapel of the Epiphany in 2005.

Still further north and west, a forest clearing that had long ago held a football field became the center of an increasingly ambitious outdoor education and leadership initiative pioneered by Stan Wood.

In the late 1990s, having coached sports for something like 36 seasons and directed Heathwood's athletics department for eight years, Wood felt a little like a chipmunk who'd strayed too far from the forest. "I was probably the only athletic director in Columbia who had never played golf," recalled the lifelong outdoors enthusiast. "I'd rather go on a camping trip, or go backpacking, or get on my bike." As he took stock of Heathwood's sports programs, he felt surrounded by energetic leaders. "We had John Daye on the football staff. Missy Lawhorne was still here—she was really capable of doing a lot of things. Debbie Bray was here. We had a really good athletic staff ... And I just felt like it was time for me to do something different."

So in 1997, he approached Bob Shirley with a proposal for an outdoor education program modeled partly after the old Project Adventure ropes course, which had been dismantled in the 1980s to make way for the Woodward Track. With Shirley's blessing, what eventually became known as the PEAK program (Pursuit of Environmental Adventure and Knowledge) started that year with the installation of a climbing wall in the original gymnasium—and, more importantly, an urge to get outside the classroom and the campus.

"One thing that was interesting," Wood recalled, "is that when we decided to do this, I really didn't know how to get on the river in Columbia and paddle. I didn't know where the bike parks were. I didn't know where we could take a group hiking—until we decided to do this. And then all of these things sprang up out of nowhere," he said. "There's a landing right down the road on the Congaree. Pisgah [National Forest] is right down the road. There were all kinds of things that became apparent that we were able to take advantage of. And once we discovered those, all of a sudden we had kids on buses." They didn't necessarily need to travel far. For 25 years students had been driving past the sweet gum swamp near the base of Heathwood Road. Now Lower Schoolers plunged in, grade after grade, to investigate beaver dam systems that may have been older than their own classrooms.

Wood's ambitions grew in three directions. One arm of the program focused on wilderness adventures: rock-climbing, hiking, camping, canoeing, kayaking. Another focused on environmental stewardship through a recycling program and community-service initiatives like river and beach cleanups. "And then we had an environmental education piece that we would talk about in classes," Wood said. "I could talk about climate change, temperate zones versus tropical areas versus polar areas—things that helped people understand how the Earth's environment works."

In 2000, Class of 1995 alumnus Dunbar Lyles was hired as the program's first full-time associate. For Hickman, PEAK dovetailed with Heathwood's commitment to experiential learning and its focus on developing the whole child. "We doubled down on it," he said. An Alpine

Tower ropes course went up in 2003. Three years later a boathouse was built next to the pond, whose surface filled up with kayaks. The 2005 debut of the PEAK Student Leadership (PSL) program turned the outdoor-adventure piece into a leadership-training vehicle that also drove a renewed commitment to all-ages camaraderie.

"I had a great education in the Lower School at Heathwood," reflected Brice Spires, who retained vivid memories of reciting math facts for principal Mary Ann Hoffman in a rite of passage known as Ribbit, where success brought a commemorative toy frog from the Lower School head—along with the right to join the student chorus yelling "ribbit!" to proclaim their achievement in division assemblies. "But the stuff that sticks out is all the extra stuff," he said, "like campouts with Coach Wood: all the things that are outside the classroom, the other experiences you get."[10]

Spires was in Middle School when the Alpine Tower was erected in the forest clearing where a previous generation had run tackling drills. "When that went up, everybody was like, 'This is the coolest thing that's ever happened out here!'" he recalled. "I was actually scared to death of it. The first two years, I refused. I wasn't going to do that." But gradually he overcame his fear, and then set about helping smaller children do the same as a PEAK Student Leader.

"We'd work with Lower School groups right after school ... I would help second and third graders on the Alpine Tower," he said. "I fell in love with it." The PSL knit together Upper, Middle, and Lower School students in much the same way as the Highlander Games had done, only on a year-round basis.

"I remember sitting in my office in the Robinson Center in the afternoon," Anne Weston said, "and watching these high school kids helping little kids learn to ride bikes. I mean, what a rich opportunity for *both* of them."

Yet PEAK Student Leaders did more than become role models for little kids in Heathwood's after-school program. On weekends, "I'd come help run a four-hour program with full-grown adults," said Spires. "So it would be Coach Wood and four or five high school students—and a bunch of guys in their 30s and 40s there to do communication leadership training with us on a ropes course.

Navigating the PEAK ropes courses.

"They're looking at you when you're up there like you're in charge. And you're 17 years old," he went on. Afterward Spires would sometimes marvel at the way he and his peers managed to command confidence and authority 50 feet above the ground, directing white-collar managers in exercises designed to promote risk-taking initiative. "I think that's a testament to Stan, the way he scaffolds responsibility on kids as they get older and more experienced," he said. "By the time you're out there doing it, it's almost second nature ... He helps you grow into something—yet, at the time, you're not even realizing that that's what you're doing."

It is hard to imagine a use of Heathwood's campus and surroundings that would have brought greater satisfaction to Burwell Manning, who had the good fortune to witness it before his death on February 4, 2005. "He believed that being outside was good for children," said his daughter Lynn Manning Cooper. That so many children discovered and nurtured a love of the outdoors on land he had given was a fact whose significance might be gleaned from the manner of his burial. After a funeral service at Trinity Cathedral, Manning's family accompanied the hearse to the Brown Chapel African Methodist Church in the Arthurtown section of Bluff Road.[11] The cemetery of that modest 1850 sanctuary lay half a mile by the flight of the dove from Heathwood Hall, making it the closest consecrated ground to the fields, forests, and wetland bottoms that constituted the spiritual center of Burwell Manning's life.

Sunday mornings may be the most segregated hour in American life, as Martin Luther King Jr. lamented, and the same might be said of afternoon burials. When the funeral procession rolled up to Brown Chapel, an elderly parishioner emerged from the redbrick structure in apparent bewilderment. "Are y'all protesting, or something?" she asked. But as the initial surprise gave way to spiritual sympathy, Burwell Manning's mourners made their way down a grassy track to his gravesite, where the church's choir joined them in song.[12]

When Brice Spires graduated in 2009, Wood hired him as a PEAK summer associate, which morphed into a side job for the duration of Spires' undergraduate studies at University of South Carolina, where, inspired by John Pulford and Bill Russell, he majored in history. In this way he became part of another group that began to grow in the 2000s: Heathwood alumni who returned to teach, coach, or fill other roles at the school.

After graduating from Furman University, Class of 1990 alumna Suzanne Jackson Nagy was lured back to campus by a job opening for an administrative assistant in the Middle School. Before long she was coaching tennis and teaching seventh grade. In the classroom, Nagy extended the influence of teachers who had steered her own intellectual growth. Her memory of Debbie Lamm, who served as Middle School principal in the 1980s, was especially vivid.

"She read *To Kill a Mockingbird* out loud to our class," Nagy said. "I just remember sitting for days on end watching her read [Harper Lee's classic novel], and thinking about Jem in that book. That was the first seed planted about civil rights.

"I went to Winterim my senior year in Washington, DC, for Presidential Classroom, and I met John Lewis," she added, referring to the Georgia statesman who helped organize the 1963 March on Washington and led the first Selma-to-Montgomery nonviolent march to protest the disenfranchisement of African American citizens in 1965. "I grew up in a family that didn't really talk about civil rights," Nagy reflected, attributing that less to antipathy than inattention. "But when you meet John Lewis, holy cow! Civil rights became this passion that drives the way that I interact with other people in lots of ways."

By the time Nagy became assistant head of the Middle School in 2008 (after a hiatus of several years during which her family moved to Little Rock, Arkansas), she had internalized the classroom craft and wisdom of a teacher who had galvanized a younger generation of students. Sue Swick, who taught in the Middle School from 1989 through 2007 before returning for a second stint from 2011–2020, became a lodestar for Nagy.

"Sue was the quintessential teacher, in that she integrated everything," Nagy recalled. "She would play piano. She would do plays. She would craft art projects. If we were studying the Middle East, the students would have to be able to draw maps of the whole Middle East from memory. We would study the Holocaust, which was a hugely impactful thing for me, as a person, having to teach that: The whole idea of empathy, and the power of words, and the negative power of doing nothing.

"She would set up a Seder meal," Nagy elaborated. "She was Catholic, but she would go to any length to make it interesting for a kid."

For Nagy, Swick embodied the best part of Heathwood's Episcopal identity—and stood as a model for how it could figure into the education of 12- and 13-year-olds. "You've got to figure out who you are when you're in seventh grade," Nagy reflected. "You have to think about power, and social justice, and the treatment of other people. Her content was deliberately chosen to shape the people we were teaching."

Lynn Cooper remembered taking part in Swick's signature Book Buddies project as a seventh grader. Like longtime Upper School science department chair Jim Morris's Biology Buddies initiative, which paired eleventh graders and four year-olds to grow plants in the Robinson Center's greenhouse, Book Buddies was a deliberate effort to foster connections across the age spectrum. Seventh graders would write and illustrate a book for first-grade partners—a personalized Christmas-themed story in one permutation, and later an adventure-style story keyed to the seventh grade's heroic mythology unit. After joining the Middle School faculty in 2004, Cooper helped carry that tradition forward as Swick's colleague.

Such interclass collaborations, together with the PEAK program, enhanced the K-12 experience for self-described "Heathwood lifers" in the 2000s. "I feel blessed that I started out at Heathwood at an early age," reflected Amanda Finney, a Class of 2009 graduate who began as a pre-schooler riding the school bus from Sumter in a carseat. "The Lower School was transformational," she continued, naming Patty Lamar, Jennifer Caballero, and Sharon Shirley as formative teachers.[13] By the time she reached fourth grade, Finney thrilled to projects like Marsie Pulford's create-a-country assignment. "You studied all of these countries around the world, and then you had to create one," Finney recalled. "You had to figure out the type of government, and who was going to lead it, and what the people look like, what do they eat, what is their currency ... It really got kids to think outside the box."

As an Upper Schooler, Finney found a further level of intellectual adventure in the tenth-grade English class of Lynn Cooper—who bounced between the Middle and Upper schools carrying a richly varied set of influences. Cooper would eventually take over the literary aspects of Jim Gasque's class, teaching *Macbeth*, Homer's "Odyssey," and Flannery O'Connor when the iconic English teacher downshifted to focus exclusively on composition. Yet she also bore the intellectual imprint of Ted Graf's humanities classes, where students would read George Orwell's *Animal Farm* alongside the history of the Russian Revolution, and Graf would coax them to draw their own insights from the juxtaposition. "He would never tell you what he wanted you to know," she recalled. "He would hint at it, and he would give you just enough, and tell you to go look for it."

The legacy of Graf and Dan Palma's cosmopolitan curricula lived on in Cooper's reading lists, which ran from Mary Shelley to Franz Kafka. "We read *Frankenstein* and whatever—the usual ones—but I also remember reading 'The Yellow Wallpaper' with her," Finney enthused, referring to the social reformer Charlotte Perkins Gilman's semi-autobiographical 1892 feminist allegory about a woman confined by a husband seeking to cure what he deems her "slight hysterical tendency."

Some other academic traditions continued to flower. In the 2000s Rip Blackstone wielded the gavel in the mock trial of Billy Budd, an initiative originally developed by Lark Palma. Having begun as way to engage with Herman Melville's classic novella about a sailor court-martialed for mutiny aboard a British warship, the exercise migrated from Amy Railsback Graf's humanities classroom to John Pulford's American history curriculum. Pulford then partnered with a University of South Carolina program that used the mock trial as training for new US Department of Justice prosecutors and USC Law students; Heathwood juniors served as the jurors to cap off a unit on Constitutional law.[14]

Yet the Shirley era's hallmark progressive experimentation also came in for a measure of discipline under Steve Hickman. In John Pulford's estimation, Hickman's attitude boiled down to *Let's stop experimenting, and see what works.* "It was a totally different style," the longtime history teacher said, "but I think it was something we really needed at that time."

The result was not so much an about-face as a synthesis. Heathwood scaled back its participation in the Coalition of Essential Schools network, for instance, but retained the senior exhibition as an academic cornerstone—underscoring a continued commitment to qualitative, mastery-focused student assessment. Along a more conventional track, the Upper School bolstered its college-preparatory focus by offering more AP and honors classes. Hickman organized professional development around the Schools Attuned to All Kinds of Minds program, whose neurodevelopmental framework emphasized the varied learning styles of students with diverse strengths and weaknesses.[15] At the same time, Heathwood reverted to the traditional ABCDF grading system and made concessions to the broader national trend toward quantitative student assessment and data-driven digital "learning management systems."

"We didn't have our first learning management system until partway through Steve Hickman's tenure," said English teacher George Scouten, who came in 1998 at a time when teachers were still recording effort grades in a paper book. "And there was a lot of pushback about it being antithetical to the philosophy of our school ... there was a lot of concern that this would shift us—and it probably did—to a place that was more concerned about metrics."

Yet even as Hickman insisted on the value of such tools—including email—as a means to keep parents maximally informed about their children's scholastic progress, he left matters of pedagogical philosophy largely to faculty. "I gave a lot of autonomy to my division directors," he said. "We would sit down as a senior team and create some goals, but my feeling was that you let that division director not only do what he or she thinks is the best way to go about their work, but also, they need to pick their team."

"I was an old point guard," he said: "Get the ball to the person who needs the ball."

As part of an effort to improve the school's external marketing, Hickman also pushed to get top teachers recognition he felt was overdue. To that end, Heathwood began submitting faculty members for SCISA Teacher of the Year Awards. Lower School teacher Sharon Shirley was the first winner in 2001, followed by a six-year stretch during which Heathwood had a near monopoly on the Upper School category. Daniel Venables, Jimmy Gasque, Louisa Gonzalez, and John Pulford claimed four in a row, followed by Jim Morris after a one-year hiatus. Class of 1987 alumna Peyton Bruner Sasnett was named SCISA Middle School Teacher of the Year in 2008.

Scouten credited Hickman as a savvy administrator who was "very good at seeing talent and finding ways to keep talent here." And like many colleagues, he considered Weston to be the indispensable partner the trustees had hoped she would be. "She carried the pedagogical torch that Bob Shirley lit," said Scouten, who named longtime administrator and counselor Jim Robinson as another crucial guardian of Heathwood's relationship-driven approach to educating the whole child. "We were philosophically, I think, doing a lot of the same type things."

"I felt very lucky to have learned a lot from Bob and tried to continue a lot of those things," said Weston. Yet "there was always a little bit of uneasiness around some of the new things that Bob Shirley would explore," she continued. "There is always fear when you do something different in an academic environment. People are worried: *Don't experiment with my children.* I think Steve felt that to compete with Hammond, we wanted to look a little more traditional."

Looking more traditional was partly a matter of literal appearances: Hickman introduced a more conservative dress code, beginning with a requirement for students to wear Heathwood-logo collared shirts on chapel day. That gradually became mandatory on an everyday basis, and by mid-decade additional rules were implemented governing bottom wear (khaki or navy pants, skirts and shorts, and no jeans allowed). The "prescribed dress code" subsequently evolved to permit plaid bottoms, and Heathwood-logo dresses were introduced in 2016.

The regulation of student appearance has a long history in American schools—as does pushback from pupils bristling at restrictions. Heathwood is no exception.[16] Perhaps the most memorable response to Hickman's dress code concerned its prohibition of facial hair. As grumbles percolated through the Upper School, Grant Robertson donned a fake beard over his real one and hung a sign around his neck reading JESUS WORE A BEARD. "I did that for about a week," the Class of 2002 alumnus recalled.[17] The Class of 2001's Kent Ureda held out in protest until the cusp of a disciplinary suspension, at which point he parted with his whiskers in what Anne Weston remembered as a "public shaving party" in the Robinson Center.

"The facial hair interpretation of the dress code was not well received by the students," contemporaneous Board meeting minutes dryly noted, "but everyone is now in compliance."[18]

The International Studies Diploma Program (ISDP), which Scouten developed in the late 2000s, typified the synthesis between forward-looking faculty members and Hickman's entrepreneurial approach to school leadership. An optional diploma "specifically designed to prepare our young people for an increasingly crowded, connected, and diverse global community,"[19] the ISDP offered a rigorous track for ambitious students—and a market response to both Hammond's rebranding as a "world school" and the implementation of International Baccalaureate programs at public schools like A.C. Flora and Lexington High.[20]

Toward the end of his tenure Hickman also proposed the development of a residential program for international students and a merger with Columbia's Sandhills school for children with learning differences. He couched both proposals in language reminiscent of Warren Buffet's investment philosophy as CEO of Berkshire Hathaway: "They would support the school's mission, would help diversify revenue, and would create high barriers of entry making duplication more difficult."[21] Although neither plan was enacted, both contained seeds that eventually germinated in slightly different forms: Heathwood would soon expand the enrollment of international students using a host-family model rather than on-campus boarding; and although the Board deemed a merger with Sandhills too risky,[22] it continued to expand the capacity of the Academic Achievement Center (formerly known as the Learning Center) to support students with learning differences.

A certain marketplace savvy was also evident in the way Hickman, Weston, and Tarpley framed Heathwood's renewed emphasis on spiritual education. "We very deliberately have never called ourselves a Christian school," Tarpley observed. "Because that sets off a lot of bad bells in people's heads—especially in the South, where so many 'Christian academies' got started because of white flight.

"A lot of people, especially from other areas of the country and other faith backgrounds, are so afraid of Christian fundamentalism as practiced in the South," she continued, "that just the mention of us being Christian-affiliated at all is like, *Whoa boy, that's bad*. And that's always been a struggling point, I believe, for admissions at Heathwood."

The job of projecting an expansive, nondogmatic vision of what Heathwood *did* call itself could hardly have fallen to a person more authentically suited to it. Tarpley offered a class in world religions, and her New and Old Testament classes were oriented more around equipping students to appreciate the literary allusions of Milton and Dante than advancing a doctrinal mission in the manner of Columbia's evangelical Ben Lippen School, which grew into a multi-campus private K-12 institution during the 1990s and 2000s.[23] She loved nothing quite so much as conversations with teenagers proclaiming their atheism. "That's exactly where you need to be!" she would think to herself—and tell them in so many words. "Because that means that you are thinking about your relationship with God—what God is, and if God matters, and all that. You're thinking about it!"

"I wasn't really into the whole spiritual thing," said Amanda Finney. "But I just felt such a connection to her," she went on, reminiscing about Tarpley's classroom and a Winterim service trip to the Dominican Republic, where the chaplain joined students building latrines for an under-resourced school. "She always made you think. Even about the Old Testament or New Testament, she would push: *Why do you think that?* Well, I don't know! And she'd push you."

For Hickman, the ultimate value of Heathwood's Episcopal affiliation was the way it formed a basis for leadership. He came to appreciate that dynamic even more deeply as his career continued in other places. "I've led three schools. Two were Episcopal and one was not. And I enjoyed my experience at all three," he reflected. "But I think having that grounding as an Episcopal school really helps decision-making. I relied on that idea of respecting dignity and worth. If you play that out, it helps you make decisions around tough issues. For instance, as a cultural hot button, sexual orientation can really get people off the rails. Or transgender—especially in schools. And I really come back to this core idea of respecting dignity: it helps you make decisions around, *We need to take care of our kids.* This is all about taking care of each kid that we have."

For students in the 2000s, Heathwood Hall continued to be a place shaped most profoundly by the intimacy of student-teacher relationships and the profusion of opportunities to grow and learn beyond the classroom.

It also rewarded student initiative. When William Ellerbe faced a junior-year schedule choice between a Bible class and a study hall period, for instance, he expressed his disinterest in those options by designing an individualized course in Shakespeare's tragedies instead. With Cindy Yarberry as a faculty mentor, the Class of 2004 alumnus matched five plays with film adaptations and scholarly articles, and wrote a paper examining each one. Then he spent part of the next summer writing a play of his own, inspired by a 1966 Bob Dylan song (and a personal quest to write better dialogue than the *Dawson's Creek* re-runs that his younger sister, like millions of American teens and tweens, was then lapping up).

"The school really supported me," he recalled. *Fourth Time Around* won first place in the Palmetto Dramatic Association's state playwriting competition,[24] and Heathwood mounted a production of it under drama department director Melissa Swick Ellington—the same Class of 1989 alumna whose own prize-winning one-act had taken Heathwood thespians to the Edinburgh Fringe Festival a decade before.

In a school whose size meant that coaches and teachers were perennially looking for enough participants to sustain teams and clubs, students who needed a push to venture outside their comfort zones often got one.

"I never felt pigeonholed into anything," said Brice Spires, who'd found an early niche as a PEAK student leader. "We have a lot of kids that play, say, a club sport—and so they think: *I'm just going to do this, because I'm good at it, and I don't want to try something else because I might not be good at it.* But we have a lot of great teachers and coaches who are able to say, 'You know, you'd actually be good at this other thing, too!'

"I was not a great public speaker," he said, by way of example. "I hated giving presentations in class. I didn't think I was very good at it. And one day, Dr. Scouten—who was head of the English department at the time and was in charge of Model UN—came to me and said, 'Hey, Mr. So-and-So said you'd be really good at this.'"

All Spires knew about Model UN was that it sounded like something he would never want to do. But suddenly he wondered if his teachers might have seen something in him that he'd been ignoring. So he gave it a spin. In his very first competition, as it happened, his team won first place. "I was like, *You know, maybe I'm not too bad at this!*" he remembers thinking. "I could be comfortable being up in front of other people." That revelation helped pave the way for a career in teaching. Spires would eventually join Heathwood's Middle School faculty as a history teacher in 2015—and run summer camp sessions on public speaking.

"Heathwood was so small that you could do anything and everything," reflected Amanda Finney. "People and teachers were like, *Try this! Do this!*—and were always pushing you to try new things and challenge yourself."

For her senior exhibition Finney made a documentary film exploring contemporary Native American culture. Drawing from a summer internship at the Turtle Mountain Chippewa Indian Reservation in North Dakota, as well as interviews with Heathwood lacrosse coach Marty Ward—a member of the Cherokee and Onondaga nations—she took her place in the long line of students to seek assistance from Bill Cherry, who by this time was an old hand with the real-time video editor that had been the most cutting-edge technology incorporated into the Robinson Center.

"It was very hard," Finney recalled. "I would have to call him and be like, 'Mr. Cherry, you have to let me into the computer lab! I get it—it's nine o'clock at night—but my basketball game is over and I've got to do this thing!'" And Cherry, who "had known me since age five," always seemed ready to facilitate.

Heathwood's school culture also reflected a broader generational shift, as the probing skepticism and deflective nonchalance of Generation X gave way to a Millennial cohort at greater ease with earnest engagement and meritocratic striving. "It was certainly cooler to be smart than I feel like it had been in the 1990s," said Lynn Cooper, commenting on how campus life felt different when she returned in the mid-2000s to teach. "It was cool to be motivated."

For Finney, thriving at Heathwood meant being motivated on as many fronts as possible. "It was cool to be smart," she mused, "but you also needed to go to the Friday night party as well—you needed to be smart, *also* play soccer, and *also* go to the Friday night party." She played basketball, tried lacrosse and tennis, dabbled in drama as the backstage

Stan Wood (far right) and Anne Weston (fourth from left) lead a Winterim trip.

manager of *Into the Woods*, served on the honor council, and attended national independent-school diversity conferences in places like Seattle and Boston. She felt liberated, not pressured, by that maximalist approach to a well-rounded education—and credited it with fostering a certain fearlessness that would serve her well in adulthood.

"I was hustling, and I didn't know what I was hustling for," she reflected. "I wanted to be a TV anchor, I wanted to be a lawyer, who knows what I wanted to be—I'm still trying to figure it out. But I was hustling, and Heathwood was a great environment to do that, because it allowed you to try so many things.

"I learned how to wet-exit from a kayak in the pond with Coach Wood!" she exclaimed. "All of those things: You just try it! A lot of people aren't able to try. They feel like it's risky, or they're going to lose or fail.

"I've been unemployed," she continued. "I've left many jobs, and done many political campaigns. You kind of have to just take risks and try it. And I think I learned that at an early age." Those lessons culminated—if that verb may be used for someone barely 30 years of age—in 2021, when Finney became chief of staff of the White House press office under President Joe Biden.

※

An expanding extracurricular menu gave students much to choose from. The decade's outset saw Daniel Venables stepping out of his math classroom to lead Friday yoga sessions.[25] Science department chair Jim Morris oversaw a Middle and Upper School robotics club along with Tim McKnight, who later added an astronomy club to the mix.[26] Class of 2009 alumnus Pierce Jones exemplified the growth of science, engineering, and math at Heathwood. After making Lego robots as a Middle Schooler,[27] joining classmate Jeghang Wee in back-to-back victories at the SCISA state math meet as part of Heathwood's Upper School math team,[28] and earning a degree in biomedical engineering from Vanderbilt, he joined Teach for America and then became a Middle School science teacher and debate coach.[29]

While a mid-decade dance team "combined jazz, hip hop, modern, tap, and ballet," the Ultimate Frisbee Club claimed the "record for the most club meetings, which is every day."[30] The Coffee House club, a venue for student singer/songwriters started by Ted Graf in the mid-1990s, eventually fell into the enthusiastic hands of McKnight—who hung a choral microphone from his physics classroom to record a demo for the Class of 2009's Colleen Francis: the first step on a path leading to Nashville to ply that trade.

Some traditions fell away, victims in one way or another of changing times. So the rowdy and edgy Mr. Highlander pageant met the same fate in the mid-2000s that had befallen the prim "Merry England" nostalgia of the Maypole Dance in the late 1990s.[31] But other interests percolated. As members of the French Club took to their stovetops to produce dessert-heavy Mardi Gras soirées, the Spanish Club held salsa eating and flamenco dancing contests.[32] Meanwhile, the approach of the 2008 presidential election found Heathwood's Young Democrats and Young Republicans debating in morning meeting ahead of a mock election in the Upper School. On the strength of a 75 percent student turnout rate, the McCain/Palin ticket edged out Obama/Biden by a 55 to 45 percent margin[33]—almost exactly mirroring South Carolina's statewide popular vote, though departing dramatically from Obama's 29-point victory in Richland County.[34]

As campus facilities and programming grew, so did enrollment, which rose to an all-time high of 876 in Hickman's final year. That powered a financial aid budget that consistently surpassed that of every other NAIS member school in South Carolina.[35] Combined with community outreach efforts directed by teacher, coach, and administrator Willis Ware, the result was a student body that reflected the headmaster's emphasis on diversity in all its forms. A high-water mark in that regard came in 2011-12, when racial and ethnic minority students accounted for more than 20 percent of total enrollment.[36]

When it came to enrollment growth, the old point guard got an assist from Heathwood's athletics department. "He lucked out," said John Pulford of Hickman's fortuitous timing on the sporting front. "He had some great coaches and they started winning games.

"I hate to say this, but sports are big," the history teacher went on. "It charges the whole school. People want to go to games … recent grads want to get involved. Winners attract people. Teams that continually lose, really don't." And in the 2000s, there was an awful lot of winning.

One seed of Heathwood's 21st-century sports success was sown in 1996, with the arrival of John Daye as head football coach.

"When I think about great teachers who taught me how to write, I think about Marshall James," reflected Class of 1997 football standout Freeman Belser. Daniel Venables, he added, was to credit for his success on the AP Calculus exam. "There were so many great teachers and people who cared about me, even when I screwed up," Belser continued. "Anne Weston watched out for me, and really cared about me. But in terms of what impacted the trajectory of my life after Heathwood the most, it's probably Coach Daye."

Demanding and encouraging, Daye schooled his players in the art of maximizing their strengths, minimizing their weaknesses, and above all, embracing accountability to the team. There was no such thing as a minor assignment, no matter how far it might be from the ball or a play's desti-nation for it. Class of 2006 wide receiver Rhodes Amaker, who retained a vivid memory of being upbraided for dilly-dallying on a decoy route—not even in a game but a mere practice—attributed almost mystical powers to the all-seeing head coach. "You didn't want to be caught doing something wrong under the Raven's watch," he laughed. "It was just the fear of God when Coach Daye singled you out on the football field."

For Belser, who anchored the defense on Daye's first Heathwood squad, it was an education above all in attention to detail and time-man-agement skills. He credited Daye for his subsequent success as stu-dent-athlete at Davidson College, where he played football while pursu-ing an education that pointed toward an eventual career in the law.

Daye also amassed more gridiron wins during his 11 seasons than any other coach in school history. Heathwood claimed state championships in SCISA's AAA division in 2001 and 2004, and twice finished as runner-up.[37]

The football titles were two of 26 state championships claimed by various teams under athletic director Jeff Whalen, who helmed the pro-gram from 1998 to 2021. Girls' track-and-field was especially successful, racking up six championships while their male counterparts won two. Whalen's own varsity boys basketball squad advanced to the state final three years in a row between 2010 and 2012, winning once.

Whalen's tenure was also marked by a broad expansion of athletic opportunities. A swimming team formed in 1999, followed by boys la-crosse and wrestling the next year. The year 2007 brought sporting clay shooting, girls golf, and boys and girls bowling. The latter teams, whose home lanes were eventually located at the increasingly well-developed intersection of Bluff Road and South Beltline Boulevard, would go on to win five state titles under coaches Bill Cherry and Jim Robinson. The short-lived or on-and-off nature of several other teams—including girls lacrosse, equestrian, and softball (both hard- and slow-pitch)—attested to Whalen's willingness to give anything a try as long as there was suffi-cient student interest in a given year.

Heathwood's sports success came despite a decision to step back from athletic recruiting during the 2000s. "It's tough for some kids to come in here, academically, in their junior year—and get through that and get ready for the senior exhibition," Whalen explained. "So the biggest thing for us is to find people who are younger, and then develop them," he said. High school remained a natural entry point for students of all varieties, including athletically gifted ones, but Heathwood shied away from actively recruiting sports prospects. "The highest-profile athletes," Whalen said at the end of his tenure in 2021, "have for most part been here since Lower and Middle School."

In the first decade of the 2000s, none achieved a higher profile than Class of 2005 graduate Brionna Dickerson Zimmerman, who came to Heathwood in sixth grade. Named to *The State*'s all-region basketball team as an eighth grader,[38] Zimmerman scored points not so much by the basket as by the bushel. She cemented her legendary status with performances like a 63-62 victory against Cardinal Newman in which she scored 61 points. ("Good thing that other girl made both of her free throws!" Whalen would quip.)

"Brionna was a revelation," said Rhodes Amaker, who would watch varsity girls games before playing with the boys.[39] "She could shoot. She could get to the hoop. She could do it all," he remembered. "Teams would triple-team her, and they just couldn't get it done." In the nearly half-century history of Heathwood Hall basketball, 16 Highlanders have earned a coveted place in the 1,000-point club. It is hard to determine what makes Zimmerman's 3,351 career point total more remarkable: her record's resilience to the 2,943-point haul of future WNBA MVP A'ja Wilson,[40] or the fact that Zimmerman amassed all those points despite missing her entire senior season with an injury.

Zimmerman went on to play for the University of South Carolina, where she became the first African American women's basketball player to earn degrees from both the Honors College and the master's program in international business. Marquee Division I collegiate sports programs tend to recruit high schoolers who have focused on a single sport to the virtual exclusion of any other activity. Yet at Heathwood Zimmerman found the freedom and encouragement to try all kinds of things. She ran track and discovered a passion for volleyball that lasted well into adulthood. Spanish teacher Louisa Gonzalez fired her enthusiasm for Hispanic cultures—both in the classroom and through a Winterim trip to Costa Rica. In Clare Scurry's art studio she found "the one thing outside of athletics that I thrived in—she expanded my knowledge of so many different techniques and art forms." Yet Zimmerman also played trombone in the school band for a couple years, and auditioned for plays—even if casting turned out to be another story.

"Heathwood gave me so many opportunities to try everything—and I wasn't expected to be great at everything," she said. "Maybe because I was good at basketball they gave me some grace for everything else," she laughed. "But I was excited for the opportunity to try a lot of things that I probably wouldn't have tried otherwise." So it is fitting that Zimmerman's most lasting legacy at Heathwood came away from the hardwood. It grew out of a series of conversations with Brandon Gantt and Rhodes Amaker, fellow athletes one class ahead of her who yearned for a more authentically inclusive social atmosphere on campus—and set out to create one.

"There was such diversity within our community in terms of socio-economic background, racial background, or in terms of interests," Zimmerman said. "People were coming from so many different angles."

But as Amaker saw it, "There wasn't always a social place for different parts of the community: minority, or religious, or any sort of differing opinion. At Heathwood you get a lot of white, affluent kids with conservative parents," he said, counting himself as precisely that sort of "classic Heathwood student." But someone like Gantt, a three-year all-state quarterback who lived in Gilbert and was saddled with the assumptions that often shadow exceptional Black athletes, faced an uphill battle to gain purchase in a social milieu dominated by kids from exclusive enclaves like Lake Katherine and Kings Grant.

"We realized that we needed a diverse space for people to ask questions about other people," Zimmerman recalled. "Especially back then, we were so cliqued-up in high school. But one of the things I prided myself on was not having a clique. I wanted to be friends with everybody, or at least be able to interact with everybody.

"There are questions about backgrounds, or about religion, about race, about stereotypes, that people did not feel safe asking," she continued. She wanted to create a social space where students could try to "understand other people without feeling they were going be judged or made fun of—or didn't want to come off as being racist."

With guidance from Willis Ware and English teacher Sally Plowden, Gantt, Amaker and Zimmerman investigated initiatives at peer institutions, and made a research trip to the Ravenscroft School in Raleigh, North Carolina. In 2003, they established the ACCEPT Club: Ambassadors Celebrating Cultures and Embracing Pluralism & Togetherness. It pursued an ambitious aspiration via modest tactics—acts as simple as joining a new table at the lunch hour.

"We would do just little things just to interact with more people," Zimmerman said. "We encouraged members to get to know new people, to step outside of your friend groups. That was really big for us." Club meetings provided a venue to extend "rich conversations we were already having as friends" to a "wider community."

Amaker came in for some light ribbing from bemused friends whose club affiliations ran more toward the Young Republicans. "Just come to a meeting," he would encourage them. "You don't have to join the club. But come and hang out and listen to what these students have to say."

"We could all get in a room and have such a great conversation," Zimmerman said. "There were times we would argue and fuss, but it made us closer. Because it gave everybody a platform to be able to express how they felt, without judgment, and be heard."

For Amaker, what distinguished ACCEPT was the "innocent and naive" spirit that animated it. It wasn't about burnishing résumés for college applications. It was born of the realization that "you just don't have the forum unless you create something."

"It allowed me to forge meaningful relationships with a lot of different types of people," he said. "By the time we finished, we had 15 or 20 kids. And it wasn't just African Americans, Asians, Indians—it was also white kids as well."

The club did not "finish," however, with the graduation of its founders. And by the time Amanda Finney was leading it in 2009, the culture-shift Zimmerman, Gantt, and Amaker had been aiming for was increasingly evident. Efforts like theirs, in combination with a diversifying admissions pool, helped bring Heathwood to an inflection point. In pointed contrast to their 20th-century antecedents, minority students who graduated in the latter 2000s—especially those who had started in Lower School, and hence entered the cliquey thickets of adolescence with a secure sense of social belonging—were increasingly likely to discount their ethnicity as a significant factor in their personal experience of Heathwood.[41] Whatever circumstances they faced away from campus, African American students were more inclined to eschew being labeled as "Black" Highlanders. (Their preferences are reflected in this and subsequent chapters.)

Anne Weston, who likewise dated this shift to the late 2000s, situated it within a longer arc of Heathwood's efforts to cultivate a truly open and inclusive school culture.

"Bob Shirley was very forward-thinking in how to create scholarships and make funding able for people who otherwise couldn't afford to come to school," she said. "That was the banker in him. And he started very early with conversations, particularly around race with our Black families, about how could we attract and be a place that Black families would want to send their children," she continued. "I remember sitting in on some tough conversations. Hearing the hurt—*challenges* is maybe a better word, but that had hurt in it—that Black families faced coming to a predominantly white school ... where they didn't necessarily feel they belonged in the same way that others did."

By the conclusion of Steve Hickman's tenure, she felt that the school had reached a "critical mass—where more diverse people saw themselves at Heathwood, and so that attracted more."

Meanwhile Heathwood's intellectual diversity found reflection in the exhibition of mastery topics with which each graduating class capped off their secondary education. William Ellerbe explored the failure of party-based Communism to gain a foothold in US politics the way it had done in the parliamentary democracies of Europe. Geopolitical tensions between Taiwan and mainland China sparked Rhodes Amaker to explore the potential global ramifications of reunification. Inspired by his family's country-music roots and his grandfather's incipient Alzheimer's, Brice Spires explored music-based modalities of memory therapy.

Yet this culminating exercise was the endpoint of a journey that had unfolded over the course of many years. "From an early age, we were doing so much writing—and presentations," said Amanda Finney. "Even going back to that fourth-grade create-a-country project: We had to have a country fair, and every teacher would come around and quiz you and grade you, and you would have to stand there and talk about it.

"I know a lot of people talk about Gasque, but it started way earlier," she continued, reflecting on her own maturation as a writer and communicator. "Because of Heathwood's small classes, and intimate relationships with teachers, you get hand-in-hand experience of how to do a presentation, how to speak.

"A lot of people credit their college" for their professional success, remarked Finney, who attended Wake Forest and earned a master's degree from Syracuse University's Newhouse School of Public Communications. "But singlehandedly, Heathwood Hall is why I'm standing in the West Wing right now. I just feel very lucky."

chapter eight

ADVERSITY

*The Great Recession—Chuck Jones—Michael Eanes—Michael
Heath—scientific revolution—exhibitions and entrepreneurship—
edible forest—buzzer beater—faculty power*

[2008-2015]

S teve Hickman left Heathwood Hall alongside the Class of 2008, taking a head of school job in Little Rock, Arkansas. The swiftness and timing of his departure—which was motivated partly by family considerations and occurred just as the Great Recession was tightening its grip—left some turbulence in its wake. After a three-decade stretch that had featured only one leadership change, Heathwood cycled through five heads of school in the course of seven years.

Lacking time to conduct a proper search for Hickman's successor, the Board named Anne Weston and Steve Mandell, then the assistant head for admissions and student services, as interim co-heads of school for the 2008-2009 academic year. Mandell was a skilled administrator who "made the trains run on time," as then-Board chair Leighton Lord put it. "Anne had the academic part." The pair had an important partner in assistant head Liz Summers, who had served as director of finance and operations since 2001; her financial savvy would become even more essential after Hickman's departure. By the time Chuck Jones arrived as a permanent head of school in February 2009, dark clouds were piling up on the economic horizon.

Youthful and broad-shouldered, Jones had played football at Princeton University, where he earned a bachelor's degree in religion before pursuing a career in education and coaching. He came to Heathwood from a position as provost and middle school director at Forsythe Country Day School, near Winston-Salem, North Carolina. On the day of his very first Board meeting, Jones felt compelled to inform Heathwood's faculty that uncertainty about the coming year would delay their contract renewals, which would not include pay raises.[1] A report by admissions director Jane Beach underlined the challenges. Although the academic year had started with the second-biggest student body in school history at 869, springtime re-enrollment was down from the year before. New enrollment was also down. New inquiries were down. The percentage of admitted applicants who enrolled was "way down." She attributed these trends to a pair of mutually reinforcing dynamics: "Families continue to cite the worsening economy and the availability of church pre-schools and [public] magnet schools as the reason for non-matriculation."[2]

The Great Recession bruised independent schools everywhere. Tuition rates at top-tier institutions continued to outpace inflation. In 2009-10, Heathwood's annual cost of $14,905 represented 27 percent of the median income of Southern families.[3] (That ratio would remain stable over the subsequent decade.) As job losses mounted and real-estate values dropped, families faced tough choices. The National Association of Independent Schools reported that more than half its members experienced declining applications during the recession—and that numbers remained depressed more than decade later.[4]

Yet although the recession was an unmistakable hardship, it was not the only economic development that posed a challenge for Heathwood. The nature of US economic expansion from the 1980s through the first decades of the 21st century posed additional challenges. Successive waves of mergers and acquisitions consolidated Columbia's banking sector, eroding white-collar jobs in that realm.[5] Small businesses lost ground in the competition with Wal-Mart and other big conglomerates, exacting a toll on the city's entrepreneurial class. The fate of Kline Iron & Steel, a downtown business long owned and operated by a Heathwood family, illustrated these changes. In 1997 the company sold a third of itself to American Tower, a Boston-based corporation that acquired the remainder in 2000 and shuttered the Gervais Street plant in 2004.[6] Columbia's vibrant healthcare and legal sectors remained a steady source of doctors and attorneys capable of paying full tuition, which helped support financial aid for lower-income students. But other trends narrowed the school's constituency.

"The price tag has priced a lot of people—what I would call the middle-income families—out of the market," noted Jay Hennig, a Class of 1982 alumnus and longtime trustee who chaired the Board in 2014-15.

"Frankly, when I was a student there, it looked to me like there was a more diverse socio-economic group that could be students."

Meanwhile, Columbia's patterns of economic growth were difficult for the school to capitalize on. "We have businesses that come to Columbia, and a lot of times they bring new people," Hennig observed. "But a lot of those new residents to Columbia have settled not in the city limits, but in places like Lexington, Irmo, and Chapin"—drawn in part by well-regarded public schools in those areas.

Jones "appeared to be the absolute perfect head," said Leighton Lord, who was succeeded as Board chair by Class of 1986 alumnus Wade Mullins soon after Jones assumed the helm. But the timing was cruel for a first-time school leader.

"When I got to campus there was great belief in the mission of the school," Jones said. "And great fear, not about the future of the school, but about the immediate financial picture." Even in the short span between his hiring and his start date, the sands had shifted. He had been interviewed by a search committee animated by "a lot of very noble, progressive ideas," he recalled.

"People were asking me, *What can Heathwood do to have more of an effect on the quality of education broadly in South Carolina?*—along the lines of the Corridor of Shame," he said, using the shorthand term for poorly resourced schools in the rural areas lining Interstate 95.[7] "*What can we do, vis-a-vis the mission of the school, to reach the underrepresented and the unfortunate and lift them up?*"

By the spring of 2009, practical concerns were encroaching on lofty ones. A "pall" hung over worried faculty and staff, Jones recalled. A Board full of "very strong personalities" exhibited a diversity of opinion about what to prioritize. Some focused on balancing the budget while others advocated growing particular programs. Aspirations about further bolstering Heathwood's support for children with learning differences—which Jones, like Hickman and Shirley before him, considered a mission-consistent strength that merited expansion—rubbed up against anxieties about the reputational costs such initiatives could have if they were viewed as "dumbing our education down."[8] Dissatisfaction in some quarters brought

The Goodall Bell Tower marks the campus entrance.

Heathwood's athletics program under scrutiny, which dented staff morale.[9] Hickman-era plans for a new dining commons had mostly been funded, but opinion was split about how aggressively to pursue the remainder.[10] (That effort resumed after a prudent pause, and meanwhile the Goodall Bell Tower transformed the entry to campus in 2011.)

"When I came in, I thought the Board was more tightly aligned than it was," said Jones, who cited his own "immaturity" as an impediment to navigating the trustees and winning the confidence of a restive faculty.[11] "It was hubris on my part—there are a couple examples of hubris with me—where I just figured I'd always been able to pull people together and I could do it again. And I don't think I was successful in that regard."

Every leader faces hard choices about how to marshal limited resources while balancing competing priorities. Not every leader comes into office during the most severe economic crisis in three generations. "There were a lot of very practical and a lot of very noble, aspirational ideas—all of which I thought were tenable," Jones said. "I don't think I realized how difficult the circumstances were going to be."

In the summer of 2011, the trustees replaced Jones with an interim head of school, Michael Eanes, who specialized in limited engagements. Before coming to Heathwood he had served as interim head of seven schools, most recently at the Phillips Brooks School in Menlo Park, California. Eanes occupies a strange place in Heathwood's history. He inspired virtually universal acclaim from trustees and faculty, and equally widespread disappointment over his unwavering determination to spend just a single year in the job. A high point came in January 2012 with the opening of the new Dining Commons.[12]

The search for a permanent head was tough, recalled Leighton Lord, who helped conduct it. "We'd just had this quick turnover of a headmaster, and nobody wants to jump in on that because it sounds like there are problems at the school." One candidate, however, emerged as a clear favorite among faculty and parent representatives: Michael Heath. He was the head of the upper school at Catlin Gabel in Portland, Oregon, which Lark Palma had led since the conclusion of her nearly 20-year tenure at Heathwood in 1995.

Heath came across as almost the antithesis of Chuck Jones, from his body type to his manner of speech. Evincing little native interest in sports, he was engaged most readily by high-level questions pertaining to curricula and pedagogy. In both areas his pole star was Catlin Gabel, a bastion of student-directed experiential learning and progressive politics where pupils called teachers by their first names. The new head had a former English and philosophy teacher's fondness for cerebral colloquies carried out with Socratic subtlety. Asked to name the most satisfying achievements of his tenure, he summoned memories of faculty "in-service work articulating the essential questions of a Heathwood education—getting clarity around those."

He was "fascinated" by the Coalition of Essential Schools chapter of Heathwood's history, and encouraged the faculty to revive its driving spirit.[13] "They had moved away from that pretty significantly, so one of the things I wanted to do was reclaim some of that," he said, calling the senior exhibition of mastery an important "remnant" of that era. "Not necessarily blindly follow the Coalition, but ask questions about what were the good things about that focus," he elaborated. "I deliberately couched that in terms of a reclamation, or reestablishment of certain tenets."

Whatever the merits of Heath's appreciation of Bob Shirley and Lark Palma's educational vision, they meshed awkwardly with some of the ways Heathwood had evolved in the meantime. "It was clear within the first month that this was probably not going to work," said Margaret McLeod Willcox, a Class of 1992 alumna and Heathwood parent who served on the Board. "He came in wanting to assert himself, and so he started trying to make a lot of changes—but hadn't really taken the time to learn who we were."

Heath's interpersonal skills also seemed better suited to the class-room than the captain's chair.[14] He made a "great impression during the [search] process," Lord observed, but struggled to "endear himself to the faculty or parents after he came in." If clarity is what the new head sought in faculty meetings, it proved elusive. Many teachers remembered them as tortuous, anxiety-stoking exercises from which participants emerged scratching their heads.

Colleagues who lauded Heath's intellectual acuity lamented his ap-proach to personnel management and executive leadership. "He was a great guy," said longtime history teacher John Pulford. "He would have been a good principal, but not a headmaster." Some teachers, trustees, and parents bemoaned what they saw as a lack of decisiveness. Others read his book-ish orientation as aloofness—a contrast that was perhaps sharpened by the warm personality of his wife, Dido.

Pulford saw a cultural mismatch at play. "He tried to make Heathwood like Catlin Gabel," the Upper School veteran said. "Those are two different cultures. And he didn't know where else to turn. He was totally out of his league. And of course when people see that, they start going for the jugular: whether it was the Board, or the teachers, or whatever. He had a real hard time."

Whatever the case, Heath's situation mirrored that of Jones before him: the relationship did not click. Yet though there was nothing imaginary about the mounting consternation, the life of a school encompasses a great deal more than its figurehead. So it should not be surprising that students experienced this turbulent phase, between 2008 and 2015, quite differently than faculty and trustees. Their Heathwood journeys were shaped much more deeply by their relationships with teachers and one another, and an academic program that continued to advance on several fronts.

Class of 2011 alumna Eliza Nixon Thorne came to Heathwood halfway through sixth grade during a year of personal upheaval. The Augusta, Georgia, native had abruptly moved to Cameron, South Carolina, a "452-person town" where her new stepfather farmed cotton and peanuts.[15] The road got bumpier with her enrollment at Orangeburg Prep. Thorne pined for her old school and her old friends. "I remember very distinctly being like, 'Nothing can be as good as my life was in fifth grade. How could you take this away from me?'"

She transferred to Heathwood in January. "I remember being pretty intimidated," she said. Her new classmates seemed nice, but "there was definitely that strange, middle school, *who-is-this-girl-coming-into-our-world?* kind of thing."

By June she was getting invited to sleepovers. But adolescence had another blow in store. Club soccer, which had been a steadying force during her transition to a new home and school, was becoming increasingly central to Thorne's sense of self. She had set her sights on the Olympic Development Program, and eighth grade was shaping up to be a pivotal year. But the summer before that season began, a single false step—onto a razor-edged oyster on Edisto Island—slashed her aspirations. A bacterial infection led to surgery, and soon it became clear that Thorne was not going to dash through the midfield quite the way she'd done before.

Freshman year was hard. Thorne was searching for a new realm where she could excel, and overwhelmed by the academic demands of Upper School. Then, as a sophomore, she had an experience familiar to many Heathwood students over the years.

"Jeff Whalen came up to me at school one day and asked, 'Have you ever thought about playing volleyball?'" No, Thorne replied. "'I think you would like it,'" the athletic director said—no doubt doing his usual foot-work on behalf of teams in need of fresh recruits.

"So my sophomore year I picked up this sport that I'd never remotely played, and I absolutely loved it," Thorne recalled. "And had it not been for Jeff coming up and asking, I never would have found it."

An academic turning point quickly followed. After taking biology with Jim Morris and chemistry with Sondra Wieland, Thorne came un-der the wing of Lisa Norman, whose anatomy and physiology instruction cemented a junior-year love affair with the natural sciences. That led her to Peyton Bruner Sasnett, a Class of 1987 alumna and 2007 Richland County Conservation Teacher of the Year,[16] who served as an advisor for Thorne's senior exhibition of mastery: an analysis of the ecological and economic impacts of sea turtle nesting grounds in developing countries.

Sasnett's unusual path to the teaching profession also proved influen-tial for Thorne. After earning a doctorate in wildlife and fisheries biology, Sasnett spent eight years as an aquatic biologist conducting environmen-tal impact assessments for the Environmental Quality Control Division of South Carolina's Department of Health and Environmental Control (DHEC).[17] Her résumé became something of a blueprint for Thorne, who interned with the SC Department of Natural Resources during high school—supporting a genetic study of nesting sea turtles—and after col-lege began her career at DHEC, where she coordinated the state's Adopt-a-Stream program and served as the Savannah Watershed manager before joining Heathwood's Middle School science faculty in 2020.

"Heathwood did not force me to fit a mold," Thorne reflected. "It helped guide me to find my own mold.

"It allowed me to pursue opportunities I couldn't have in a bigger setting," she continued. "I ended up being friends with people I didn't think I would be friends with … and Heathwood made me more trusting of other people.

"We always used to joke about how we'd just leave our book bags out and around," she laughed. "When I got to University of Georgia, I real-ized I couldn't just leave my stuff in the library and expect it to be there when I got back." But Heathwood, to her, was a protected place where students could forge meaningful relationships with peers and adults alike.

"Anne Weston was my advisor," Thorne remarked. "I invited her to my wedding."

Thorne's experience of science education at Heathwood was one case among many that reflected the school's growing sophistication in that subject area. Starting in the early 2000s, Highlanders became increasingly active participants in the South Carolina Junior Academy of Science. Honors science classes required pupils to present research projects at SCJAS annual meetings. In 2011, Heathwood students took first-place prizes in areas ranging from microbiology ("Comparison of The Effectiveness of Silver Nano-particle Bandages, Neosporin Bandages, and Adhesive Bandages on Growth Inhibition of *Staphylococcus epidermis*," by Akida Lebby and Will Norris) to environmental science ("The effect of circulating water using various styles of diversion across a steel roof on the internal temperature of a model house," by Chris Metzger and Fripp Prioleau) to cell and molecular biology ("The Effect of Different Concentrations of Alpha Hydroxy Acid in Water on the Regeneration of *Brachydanio rerio* Caudal Fins, by Brook Grice and Elise McKelvey).[18]

Exploring campus flora with teacher Natalie Ashenfelter.

Class of 2011 alumnus Scott Harriford was another exemplar of Heathwood's improvement in the natural sciences, which was bolstered by a growing menu of elective courses. Harriford, a three-season athlete who also competed on the mock trial team, got fired up by Anne Weston's elective in public health. When it came time to choose a senior exhibition topic, he gravitated toward the intersection of diet and entrepreneurship to design a hydroponic farming system. Harriford turned it into a business proposal that was accepted into a business incubator program at University of South Carolina, where he refined it into a small firm that sold lettuce to restaurants.

By twists, turns, and shifting interests, Harriford found his way from entrepreneurship to politics. A position as a page for the South Carolina legislature's Ways and Means committee led to a job assisting a state representative, and then campaign work for US Representative Joe Cunningham and 2020 presidential candidate Joe Biden. In January 2021, Harriford became the White House liaison for the US Small Business Administration.

Harriford characterized his early career journey as both a winding road and a "direct line" from his senior exhibition.

"I don't think I would have started a business if didn't have to do that extensive research and build my own system. I wouldn't have had that initiative on my own" in high school and as a beginning college student, he reflected. "One of the things you also learn, doing that exhibition, is the need for outside resources. You had to have a board of advisors that could review your documents, and that you could use as a sounding board ... and I had a similar model when I started my business." In a more general way, the exhibition instilled a disciplined approach to assessing his prospects and making decisions. "I didn't [ultimately] want to do hydroponics," he said. "But it helped me figure out another core thing that interested me, which was politics."

In 2011, a group of faculty and parents came together under the leadership of Middle School science teacher Todd Beasley to form an environmental education and stewardship initiative called SEED. One of its signature projects was the planting of an "edible forest." This orchard of more than 100 fruit-bearing trees—heirloom and other varietals ranging from Saijo persimmons to Larkin pomegranates to tropic snow peaches—was one of a dozen thematic gardens created on campus that annually produced enough food to contribute roughly 200 pounds of donations to Columbia's Harvest Hope Food Bank.[19]

For Class of 2019 alumnus Davis Buchanan, those initiatives seemed seamlessly integrated with both the PEAK program and Beasley's fifth grade class on environmental science. "There was a big emphasis on the environment, but we were not only learning in the classroom—we were exploring nature through the campus."

Student activities and clubs ranged from throwback traditions to freshly minted enthusiasms. In 2012, the sophomore girls upset their senior counterparts in Powder Puff Football before falling to the juniors. The a capella contagion continued to spread far beyond its old Ivy League haunts—*Pitch Perfect* hit movie theaters in 2012—registering at Heathwood in the form of Men in Plaid (boys) and Pretty in Plaid (girls), both of which performed at New York's Carnegie Hall in the spring of 2012. More Highlanders sang in 2012 than participated in any other single activity; Heathwood's choir counted some 273 Middle and Upper Schoolers as members.[20] But small groups had little trouble carving out space, from Poetry Out Loud and the strategy game club,[21] to the ping pong and culinary clubs.[22]

The student honor council was dissolved after the 2013-14 year. There was some diversity of opinion about this move, but on balance administrators felt uneasy about continuing to subject students to the judgment of their peers. For reasons ranging from reasonable expectations of privacy to a perceived overzealousness of student tribunals, the honor council was reconstituted as a faculty committee. The first day of Upper School was devoted partially to explanation of the honor code— including attempts to clarify plagiarism and intellectual property violations that were not always intuitive to a generational cohort conditioned by the decidedly nonacademic standards of digital and social media— culminating in a written pledge each student affirmed with a signature.

A giant wave of school spirit crested during the winter of 2013-14, when a varsity girls basketball team led by perhaps the strongest senior class cohort in Heathwood sports history began blazing their way through the regular season. A 93-18 December victory against Orangeburg Prep set the tone for a campaign that would earn four players All-State honors: Class of 2014 teammates Victoria Dickerson, Chelsea Joseph, Gadson Lefft, and A'ja Wilson.[23]

Wilson, a Heathwood "lifer" who'd left a trail of affectionate memories going all way back to a time when her teachers were still taller than she was,[24] dominated the paint. The top-ranked college recruit in the nation averaged 34.4 points, 13.9 rebounds, 5 blocks, and 3 steals per game.[25] The only losses in the Highlanders' 23-4 season came in two contests against North Carolina's New Hope Christian Academy, a national powerhouse; a two-point overtime loss to Columbia's Dreher High School; and a three-point loss to a West Virginia team in a holiday tournament. Conference play was another matter. John O'Cain and Jerome Dickerson's squad rolled over Hammond by 31- and 43-point margins, and posted a 55-point victory over Cardinal Newman.

The SCISA state championship game, however, featured a daunting foe: Charleston's Northwood Academy, whom Heathwood had beaten by just three points in their last regular-season meeting. Exactly one month later, the Highlanders entered the fourth quarter of the title bout trailing by two points. Seven minutes and 53 seconds after that, the deficit had grown to three.

With seven seconds remaining on the game clock, Wilson inbounded the ball to Victoria Dickerson about 80 feet from the hoop. Dickerson flew up the left side of the court toward senior guard Erin Ress, drawing three defenders as she pulled up a couple steps outside the three-point arc. Dickerson rose up with the ball, whipped a crosscourt pass to a trailing Wilson, and watched as the future WNBA MVP launched a 21-foot jumper with a pure left-handed stroke. The buzzer sounded as the shot reached its apex, and pandemonium rocked one half of the packed Sumter County Civic Center as the ball rippled through the net to force overtime.[26]

Leading the break alongside Gadson Lefft, A'ja Wilson seals an overtime victory in the 2013-14 championship final.

Heathwood took over in the extra period. Wilson made a tremendous block at the basket and retained possession to complete an early defensive stop. Ress bounced a clinical, coach's dream of a backdoor pass to a streaking Joseph for a left-handed layup. Lefft barreled down the court for a right-hand finish through a hard foul. Outscoring Northwood 11-3 in the final frame, the 2013-2014 Highlander girls claimed an indelible place in the annals of Heathwood Hall sports.

By the beginning of Michael Heath's third year, travails in the top office were threatening to spin out of control. Despite an economic recovery that had driven US stock indices to record levels[27] and, like previous expansions, delivered disproportional gains to the wealthiest Americans,[28] Heathwood's enrollment continued to drop. From 869 at the outset of 2008-2009, the student body had shrunk to 705 as the 2014-15 school year began. And the worries went beyond student attrition.

"We had a number of faculty who didn't return," recalled Willcox, one of several trustees who had grown increasingly alarmed. "I felt the school was unraveling."

Heath's most controversial decision had come during the summer of 2014. Having shifted Anne Weston from Upper School head to director of advancement the prior year, he informed her that her contract would not be renewed after 2014-15.[29] It was perhaps the most dramatic personnel move in the school's living memory, and came close to touching off a faculty revolt. Teachers who had gone three decades without bringing a complaint to the trustees wrote letters and vented outrage. But the Board was in a bind. To dismiss another permanent head of school even more quickly than the last risked turning six years of instability into full-blown panic. So as they waited out the year of 2014-15, Heathwood relied on the persistence and loyalty of its most precious resource: the school's senior teaching and coaching corps.

The list of teachers and coaches who did *not* walk away from Heathwood in its hour of hardship doubles as a roll call of the school's

Jim Gasque leads a faculty procession, trailed by Luisa Gonzalez, John Pulford, Rip Blackstone, and Stan Wood.

saviors. Among those who stayed through at least 2015 were Marsie and John Pulford; Anne Weston; Bill Cherry; Sue Swick; Middle School science teacher Pam Bulak; music and drama teacher Barbara Bryan; and beloved administrator, teacher, coach, and college counselor Jim Robinson—all of whose service dated back deep into the Bob Shirley era. The tenure of librarian Nancy Reeder, who did not retire until 2017, went all the way back to the mansion and Earl Devanny.

Stan Wood, who had overseen the addition of a second high-elevation ropes course in 2010 and expanded the PEAK Student Leadership Program to roughly 75 students by 2015, paddled into his fourth decade with the spryness of a man who'd found his own secret fountain of youth. Sarah Roth and Lynn Humphrey, whose tenure rivaled Wood's, likewise steamed ahead—making athletic director Jeff Whalen look like the junior member of his department even if you counted his initial stint at Heathwood in the late 1980s. Willis Ware spearheaded the school's community service programming and diversity initiatives while teaching and coaching girls track and cross country.

The staying power of a slightly younger cohort was equally critical, especially considering that mid-career teachers generally face lower hurdles to leaving a school than late-career ones. Science department head Jim Morris soldiered on, as did French teacher Nadege Vaultier Keller—who was fresh off being honored as the 2011 SCISA Upper School Teacher of the Year. Raven Tarpley continued to foster Heathwood's spiritual life with programs like multilingual chapel services, which started off as a way to expand foreign language instruction but gained another dimension in the mid-2010s as international students began matriculating into the Upper School in greater numbers.

Class of 1990 alumna Suzanne Jackson Nagy remained a Middle School fixture who also coached tennis and basketball. Pamela Reed Pope, a Class of 1988 alumna who started teaching Latin in 1994, kept conjugating. Class of 1994 alumna Katherine Juk Draffin, who had joined the Lower School faculty in 2002—consciously modeling her teaching after that of Marsie Pulford—returned in 2013 after a childrearing hiatus. Class of 1996 alumna Lynn Manning Cooper, having also taken some time to raise her young children, returned in 2009.

In 2011, declining health brought an end to Jim Gasque's nearly half-century teaching career.[30] But Rip Blackstone and Sally Plowden emerged as Heathwood icons for a new generation of Upper School students.

Blackstone, who had coached two generations of Highlanders on the basketball court and gridiron, was by now the soul of Heathwood's mathematics program. Having started as a fifth- and sixth-grade teacher in 1992, he moved into the Upper School around the time Daniel Venables left in 2004. Teaching every math class in the course catalog at one point or another, Blackstone also expanded the curriculum, launching BC Calculus in 2014. The former attorney also led the math team and served as Upper School dean of students. Students knew him as an intense competitor in everything from red-zone defense to the American Crossword Puzzle Tournament—where he established himself in the mid-2010s as Top 20 puzzler in the South region.[31] They also

Lack of regulation equipment can't keep Rip Blackstone from competing.

knew him as a ready source of mood-lightening humor who installed a "That Was Easy!" button in his classroom for pupils to press when turning in a test, and wasn't above stretching a novelty net over classroom desks for a ping-pong throwdown against his students. Blackstone would go on to win SCISA's Upper School Teacher of the Year award in 2016.

Plowden, who would claim that honor in 2017, came to Heathwood in 2000 after spending the early part of her career teaching at the collegiate level. Literature lived and breathed in her classroom, where a writer could be just about anything—white male, Southern feminist, Harlem Renaissance poet, Afghan-American novelist—but was never, ever "dead." Whether she was tracing the thread of influence from Paul Lawrence Dunbar to Maya Angelou to an Alicia Keys performance on *Def Poetry Jam*, or connecting the existential questing of *Moby-Dick* to the big questions that hound contemporary adolescents, Plowden made it vivid. And students carried it into their off hours, as evidenced by one instance that was particularly satisfying to a woman who'd done her doctoral dissertation on F. Scott Fitzgerald. When Baz Luhrmann's film adaptation of *The Great Gatsby* hit theaters in 2013, some Columbia moviegoers experienced

English teacher Sally Plowden leads a class.

the ending in more than digital surround-sound, for at least one showing featured a chorus of Plowden's students reciting the book's final paragraphs along with lead actor Tobey Maguire.

Credit is also due to Chuck Jones and Michael Heath for some excellent faculty hires. Math teacher Liza Johnson came in 2010, and three years later won SCISA's Middle School Teacher of the Year award. History teacher John Adams, whose 15-year career was already studded with state and national teaching honors, joined the Upper School in 2010. Standouts who arrived during the Heath era included Upper School English teacher Elisha Sircy and Middle School civics teacher Chris McDuffie, who would go on to win a SCISA Teacher of the Year award in 2021. (As of 2021, Heathwood teachers had won more SCISA teaching awards than any other school in the state.)

Heath also brought back George Scouten, who had left Heathwood in 2010 (after winning a SCISA Teacher of the Year award of his own) for what proved to be a three-year stint as assistant head of school and dean of students at the Linden Hall School for Girls in Pennsylvania.

Yet Scouten returned to an uneasy campus.

"We had this period of time where we didn't have a strong vision coming from the top, or even the ability to focus on implementing a vision," he said. Individual teachers retreated into their shells, bunkering down in their classrooms at the expense of schoolwide cohesion. "There was a fair amount of siloing. The divisions were functioning on autopilot based on the quality of teachers."

The trustees accepted Michael Heath's resignation at the conclusion of the 2014-15 school year.[32] They lost no time naming a replacement. In a move that blended circumstantial duress, calculated risk, and a recognition of the outgoing head of school's keen eye for talent, the Board appointed Upper School head Chris Hinchey as permanent head of school.

chapter nine

REVIVAL

*Chris Hinchey—the 2015 flood—flag friction—college admissions—
enrollment trends—Episcopal School for All—school in the time of
social media—exhibition explosion—international students—Junior
Ninja Course—Makerspace—Ode to a Microbe—trench warfare—
podcasts—mind and body—family ties*

[2015-2020]

Before taking the reins of Heathwood's Upper School in 2013, Chris Hinchey had spent 19 years teaching life sciences at the Salisbury School, an Episcopal boys boarding school in Connecticut where he also served as dean of students and dean of faculty. His intellectual curiosity extended well beyond biology and physiology. Hinchey loved thinking about complex systems of all kinds, from urban watersheds to the evolution of Columbia's neighborhoods. He could hardly walk his dog around town without mulling everything from the history of the old South Carolina Lunatic Asylum on Bull Street, to the local planning of Interstate highways, to University of South Carolina real-estate development initiatives, to the legacy of residential segregation.[1]

Heathwood appealed to him partly on account of Shirley-era academic legacies like Winterim and the exhibition of mastery, partly by dint of the Episcopal schools tradition, but mostly because of the sense of community he felt on campus.[2]

"Adults were interacting with kids in authentic and mature ways. The academic program seemed high-level, but at the same time it seemed that relationships were at the core of the experience," he reflected. As he saw it, Heathwood was aiming to strike a harmony that distinguished the best schools he'd been a part of: "It hasn't just been about rigor, and it hasn't been just about kumbaya. There's been this nice balance."

To Jay Hennig, who chaired the Board at the time, Hinchey was a "known quantity" who offered a better chance of being the natural fit that had lately been elusive in the top office. "He had shown a lot of ability as head of the Upper School. He was well liked by the faculty. He was well liked by Upper School parents," Hennig said. "That made a huge difference. We needed some stability."

Head of school Chris Hinchey.

Hinchey was also keenly attuned to a fundamental tension that had come to govern 21st-century independent schools, which pitted "whole child" educational aspirations against a college-admissions gauntlet whose vanishing margin for error limited parental appetites for experimentation. "The best schools embrace tradition and innovation at the same time," he felt. "If you can do that, I think you have a healthy school. If you do too much of one or the other, I think it tips the apple cart: either you're too stagnant, or you're on the bleeding edge—and most independent schools have a tough time being on the bleeding edge."

Hinchey's approach to school leadership drew deeply from one of his first job titles. He'd initially come to Salisbury to coach varsity basketball, which he kept up for a dozen years. Athletics had occupied a central role in his own education—he played collegiate basketball at Hartford's Trinity College—and many of his Heathwood colleagues saw that legacy in his management approach.

"He was a coach, and I think that carries over into his leadership style," said Sally Plowden. "He has high expectations, so you always try to live up to those, but I have found him always to be encouraging on a personal level. He's also very organized, and he very much stresses community."

In short order Hinchey earned a reputation as an attentive listener who projected a genuine commitment to understanding and honoring the pluralism of Heathwood's varied constituencies. He went about it in big ways and small ones. Through his open office door teachers and students could readily spy a large bowl he kept full of chocolate candies: an unspoken invitation whose significance was not lost on them.

"Chris came in with an understanding of: *Yes, I have ideas about what a school needs to be.* But he also recognized: *This is not my home turf,*" observed English teacher Elisa Sircy, expressing a widely shared appreciation for Hinchey's collaborative approach. "It was more of an Aristotelian democracy and less of a Platonic philosopher king."

Hinchey's grace period did not last long. Barely a month into his first semester as head of school, more than 20 inches of rain inundated the South Carolina Midlands, triggering a 1,000-year flood that swelled the Congaree River to its highest level since 1936.[3] To reach campus, Stan Wood hauled a canoe to the intersection of Bluff Road and South Beltline Boulevard. Brice Spires met him near the first rise of Heathwood Road, and the PEAK veterans stroked their way to the Devanny Gate. Dipping a paddle straight down to test the water's depth at one point, Spires plunged his entire forearm beneath the surface before he felt the paddle blade hit asphalt.

As in 1976, the worst of the October 2015 flooding occurred around the perimeter of campus, which became an island cut off from automobile access for about four days. But Columbia's Forest Acres section, which was home to many Heathwood families, suffered extraordinary damages. The Lake Katherine neighborhood sustained losses that effectively depopulated entire streets, which became eerie provinces patrolled by the National Guard while demolition crews carted away the wreckage.

"Thirty of our families were impacted," Hinchey recalled. "We were out for a week—and even when we came back, we had no fresh water." Trucking in bottled water, Hinchey and Heathwood's staff managed to return students to classrooms almost as soon as the road to campus became navigable again.

The following year brought a test that in many respects proved more daunting. In April of 2016, a Heathwood parent angered by South Carolina Governor Nikki Haley's 2015 removal of the Confederate battle flag from the State House grounds elected to pick up his children from school in a pickup truck in which he had erected a giant version of that divisive banner.[4] In combination with a smaller rebel flag attached to his sideview mirror on a more regular basis, this provocative display sent shock waves through the campus.

"It was bigger than my dining room table," recalled Margaret McLeod Willcox, who named this incident as one of the hardest challenges she faced in eight years as a trustee[5]—not least because the flag-waver's children were beloved throughout the school. But despite being asked to refrain from reprising this display, their father repeated it on "Confederate Memorial Day" the following April.

Further entreaties from Hinchey and Class of 1997 trustee Freeman Belser were met with righteous defiance. And the giant flag was not the only provocation.

"He would come through the carpool line in his scary truck, and he would have weapons mounted in the back window," recalled Lynn Manning Cooper. "The children were afraid of him. I had to stand in the carpool line, and you're standing there with a 10-year-old Black boy who's watching this armed vehicle pull into the carpool circle."

Adults attentive to social media found additional reasons for concern. In March 2017 he had posted to Facebook a portrait of William "Bloody Bill" Anderson, a Confederate guerrilla leader best known for carrying out a massacre of 150 men and boys in Kansas in 1863. Superimposed on the portrait were the words: "I will hunt you down like wolves and murder you." Later that summer he made another post, three days after a "Unite the Right" rally set off violent clashes in Charlottesville, Virginia.

Naming a Black woman who had helped to remove a Confederate statue in Durham, North Carolina, this post expressed a menacing wish: "I hope a rope goes around your neck!"[6]

For Hinchey, one concern stood above all others: "All of our families need to feel safe and comfortable on campus."

In the aftermath of Charlottesville, Hinchey and the Board felt an imperative to act. In September they passed a policy limiting the display of flags on campus to the banners of the United States, South Carolina, the Episcopal Church, and accredited independent schools (such as those visiting for sporting events). Firearm restrictions were also imposed. The leadership group was both confident in their decision and cognizant of the blowback it might bring.

"I knew it was the right thing for the school," Hinchey recalled. "The school has always been at the forefront of making good decisions about what equality means." He drew guidance from the legacy of Susan Gibbes Robinson. "Heathwood is based off its founding, which was somewhat egalitarian and somewhat open—within the parameters of 1951 in Columbia, South Carolina. But even in 1965, when there was this shift change," he said, referring to the year of Heathwood's integration, "it was on the *front* of that change."

Yet that did not make the present decision easy. "I was worried about doing the right thing but putting kids at risk—because in the age of social media, somebody from Ohio could get upset about this, somebody in Florida could get upset about this. And they did. I had people personally threaten me via social media. And then you feel like your family is on the line."

Willcox recalled the "incredibly tense" atmosphere: "We had to hire a lawyer. We had to hire extra highway patrols to be on campus. We had to take Chris and Heather's home address out of our parent directory for their safety. There were threats. We were fearful."

During this time Hinchey came to especially value the presence of alumni among Heathwood's trustees and faculty. "I worked very closely with Suzanne Nagy," he said. "Rox Pollard was the Board chair, and he was great.[7] Margaret McLeod Willcox, Freeman Belser, Kirby Shealy

[Class of 1989], Alison Woodward Gonzales [Class of 1991]: all of them were really involved. To have those alums—who were also longtime Columbia community members—feel like I did, made me feel better that I was shepherding and stewarding the school in a way that was consistent with its founding and its history."

In the end, Heathwood's leadership navigated delicately to bring about a peaceful denouement that concluded with the father's unilateral decision to withdraw his children from the school. It was a mournful episode for many of their teachers, as well as for trustees and faculty who lamented the fractious tenor of US racial relations in the late 2010s. Yet Heathwood's approach to resolving it gave many alumni cause to feel pride in their alma mater—perhaps especially those whose 20th-century student experiences bore a residue of unfinished business.

"I was proud of our community," Lynn Manning Cooper said. "I've never been more proud."

For college preparatory schools in the second decade of the 21st century, perhaps no challenge loomed larger than the increasing competitiveness of university admissions. It was no longer just a story about the Ivy League. Consider a 40-year synopsis of admissions to Clemson University, which had long been a destination for Heathwood graduates.

Between 1980 and 1990, applications to Clemson nearly doubled from 5,437 to 9,786 while the acceptance rate dropped from 70 percent to 65 percent. In 1980, 77 percent of Clemson freshmen came from South Carolina. That ratio dropped to 68 percent in 1990, when 34.5 percent of incoming freshmen ranked in the top 10 percent of their high school class. In 2010, 16,865 high schoolers applied for Clemson's freshman class. In 2020, some 28,600 applied. Roughly 60 percent were accepted, but the applicant pool was quite competitive: 57 percent of that year's freshman class ranked in the top 10 percent of their high school class, and nearly half came from outside the state.[8]

"Think about how that changes the dynamic," said Hinchey. "Before, you were going through Heathwood, growing as a person and figuring out your grades, but maybe you were a B student—albeit with a rigorous curriculum. Well, that might make it harder to get into Clemson now. It's not as much of a layup anymore, because you're competing with kids from California, Oregon, Michigan, Indiana…"

American families have responded to that dynamic, combined with the high cost of private education, in ways that have repercussions for independent K-12 schools. In broad terms, the 2010s saw rising or steady demand for upper and middle school admissions, but shrinking demand and higher attrition rates at the lower school and early childhood levels.[9] Parents navigated complex tradeoffs.

"It's one thing to say, 'Alright, I can handle four years of tuition,'" said George Scouten, who became head of the Upper School upon Hinchey's promotion. "And it's another thing to say, 'I'm going to bite off 16 years of tuition.'

"Another national trend that certainly affects us is that people are less trusting of institutions," he observed. "When I first came, I think the feeling in the admissions office was that if you won over a family, you had them for life. Increasingly we feel like we have to re-win over our own families to move from the Middle School to the Upper School, or from the Lower School to the Middle School … There's more of a willingness to shop around."

That willingness was especially plain to faculty navigating the same decisions for their own children. "Most middle- and high-schoolers are now choosing their schools," said Lynn Manning Cooper. "If a kid says, 'I don't like my English teacher,' they might leave. That's just how the modern family works."

Hinchey approached that reality by trying to develop and emphasize competitive advantages particular to each of the school's divisions. Enrollment began to recover after his first year, and stabilized at approximately 725 students during the late 2010s.

In the Lower School, where small class sizes and a balanced academic curriculum remained central priorities, he set about "trying to mimic the very successful Bob Shirley programs in the Upper School, with experiential learning opportunities." In 2018, the Lower School introduced a LEAP week,[10] inspired by and running concurrently with Upper School Winterim. Kindergartners through fourth graders could opt for courses ranging from "Claymation Studio" and "History of Photography," to "Robotics" and "Math Playground," to "Birdwatching" and "Healthy Cooking."[11]

Hinchey also viewed the chapel program as something that distinguished Heathwood from competitors, particularly in the public realm. "The Episcopal schools tradition seems to have a lot of space for believers and non-believers, Christians and non-Christians, and that appeals to me. To me it affects the soul of the school. Sportsmanship is important, hospitality is important, respect is important … seeing grace and the dignity of God in every person.

"I also like that it undergirds the curricular experience," he continued, "We're asking big questions, we're seeking truth, and we're thinking about things beyond the mortal realm." Hinchey's mantra evoked the Steve Hickman and Susan Robinson eras in equal measure: Heathwood was "an Episcopal school for all." In the Lower School, he said, "the chapel program influences the way we think about how we treat others, and how we like to serve, and how we can be good citizens."

In the spring of 2017, third graders Henry Morris and Turner Rice provided one example of Lower School citizenship in action. For a unit in persuasive writing, they wrote a letter to Hinchey making the case for expanding the dress code to include gray collared shirts. The head of school was sold, and the next year the Plaid Peddler campus store began selling Under Armour shirts that met the boys' approval: "Gray doesn't show dirt when we play at recess!" they told the 2018 yearbook editors.[12]

In 2016-17, Heathwood also expanded the Early Childhood program to include 2-year-olds.[13]

Middle School provided a setting where academic, extracurricular, and spiritual pursuits could be integrated with a greater degree of sophistication. A particularly compelling example came in 2018, when the eighth grade marked the 50th anniversary of the Orangeburg Massacre with a symposium featuring Reverend Simon Bouie and Sister Willie Bouie. They spoke about their own involvement in nonviolent protests for racial justice, including Simon's arrest for sitting at the lunch counter of an Eckerd's drugstore in Columbia in 1960, which prompted a lawsuit decided in his favor by the US Supreme Court in 1964.[14] Assistant US Attorney (and Heathwood parent) Jay Richardson joined the proceedings to detail his experience prosecuting Dylann Roof, who was convicted of murdering nine Black parishioners in Charleston's Emanuel AME Church in 2015. Chaplain Raven Tarpley rounded out the program with a lecture about the Biblical and spiritual components of the civil rights movement.

Middle School clubs, which typically met once per month, ranged from chess and cornhole to news broadcasting and photography.[15] Intramural co-ed flag football was launched for Middle Schoolers in 2020.[16]

Hinchey also envisioned Heathwood's Middle School as a respite from the frenetic pace and accelerating competitiveness that has often characterized the transition from childhood to adolescent school environments.

"We're thinking about child development and lowering stress and anxiety—or helping them recognize stress and anxiety through our mindfulness program," he said. One of the most profound sources of adolescent anxiety—not to mention parent anxiety—was as obvious as it was unavoidable: social media. Heathwood partnered with the Social Institute, whose interactive online platform aimed to help students navigate cyber bullying, ethical dilemmas, and other thorny issues.[17]

"A phone in the hands of a sixth grader," Hinchey remarked, "is a dangerous proposition—for getting in lots of trouble, or for body image issues, or for fear of being left out. Or kids that age are starting to play around with language and sexuality. And playing with it publicly, taken out of context, can create lots of difficulty for little people and their parents ... Kids can make kid decisions, but social media vaults them into the adult world."

The impact of smartphones and social media on contemporary school settings became a central preoccupation of Heathwood faculty and students in the late 2010s. One measure of it could be found in senior exhibitions like Beverly Hennig's "The Role of Social Media in Anxiety Between Genders" (2019) and Emily Putnam's "The Consequences of Social and Traditional Media Posting as a Toxic Mirror for the Female Body as it Leads to Eating Disorders, Self-Harm, and Suicidal Ideation"

(2018). Another was evident in rules governing the use of smartphones, which varied by grade level but broadly kept the devices out of students' hands during class periods.

The senior exhibition remained the hallmark differentiator of Heathwood's Upper School. Students pursued a remarkable variety of topics, and many used their capstone project as an opportunity to apply academic rigor to issues of contemporary social relevance. In 2018 alone, these public presentations ranged from Caroline Bunch's examination of the regional impacts of the 2010-11 Tunisian revolution, to Graham Kemper's critical evaluation of return-to-play concussion protocols in sports, to Nadia Deas's analysis of media portrayals of African American women between 1960 and the present day. Athreya Murali presented "A Study of Cutting Sequences of Eigenvector Trajectories on the Square Grid Under Repeated Linear Maps by a Hyperbolic Transformation Matrix." Daisy McLeod explored the potential economic costs of climate-change-induced sea-level rise in coastal South Carolina. Coco Yuan undertook a comparative study of the role of economic deregulation in Japanese and US recessions. Jackson Scott examined the effects of landfills and municipal waste centers on low-income neighborhoods. Crystal Pusey studied the business implications of Bitcoin and blockchain ledgers.[18]

Heathwood graduates continued to cite the exhibition as critical preparation for college, and in some cases career advancement. Personal reasons partly spurred Class of 2019 graduate Davis Buchanan to study the influence of pharmaceutical lobbying and insurance co-pay policies on the affordability of Gleevac, a chemotherapy drug his grandmother had been prescribed. But that wasn't his only motivation. "The economics behind it wasn't something I had direct exposure to in a class," he explained. "I felt like there were plenty of teachers knowledgeable about that, but no class I could take, so that was something I could independently study and learn on my own."

Two years later, as a rising junior at the University of Pennsylvania, he credited that experience for helping him secure a summer internship at Johnson & Johnson's deal desk. "It was tremendously influential in pursuing internships," he said. "It came up in every round of interviews I had."

The year after Buchanan used his capstone project as a vehicle for deeper engagement with economics, the Upper School introduced AP Microeconomics to the course catalog. The addition brought Heathwood's Advanced Placement offerings to 19 classes, ranging from Biology to Computer Science to US Government and Politics. A more conventional route to curricular improvement, AP courses doubled as a primary means of attracting international students to Heathwood.

Class of 2018 alumnus Ray Wang and Class of 2020 alumna Cassie Guo exemplified that trend, which gained momentum in the 2010s. Both hailed from China, both learned about Heathwood through study-abroad organizations that emphasized AP course selection, and both attended Heathwood all four years of Upper School with the express goal of gaining admission to American universities. (Heathwood was also a destination for a modest number of European students, but they usually spent just one year on campus; students from China and South Korea typically stayed from ninth grade through graduation. In the late 2010s, about a dozen international students attended Heathwood in any given year.)

Wang, the son of a civil engineer and an electrical engineer in Harbin, found a natural kinship with Rip Blackstone and physics teacher Tim McKnight. He amassed enough AP credits to enter Purdue University eligible to earn an engineering degree in three years. Yet he came to appreciate Heathwood for other reasons, as well. As a member of the varsity bowling team, he gained both camaraderie and a deeper fluency in "humor, sarcasm, and understanding idioms." In downtime conversation with history teacher John Adams, he found himself making a stimulating journey from atheism to agnosticism. Despite enduring more friction and turnover with host families than he would have liked—which emerged as a somewhat common experience for international students, who for the most part boarded with non-Heathwood families—Wang graduated from Heathwood much as any other Highlander: with a sense of accomplishment and surrounded by friends.

Guo, who cheekily acknowledged that Heathwood's school colors suited her sartorial style better than Hammond's or Ben Lippen's,[19] was also attracted largely by AP offerings. But her experience likewise led in unexpected directions. She played volleyball and joined the International Culture Club,[20] which she led during her senior year. "It definitely helped me to become a better person," said the UCLA matriculant of her experience as a Highlander. "I learned more things than I would have if I'd gone to a traditional Chinese school—academically and athletically.

History teacher John Adams rocks some plaid.

"Also I spent a lot of time volunteering," she added. "That had a lot of meaning." For her senior exhibition, Guo performed a comparative analysis of the effectiveness of two hunger-related nonprofit organizations in Columbia: Harvest Hope Food Bank and Souper Bowl of Caring.

Although national trends in independent school enrollment demanded somewhat different strategies for each school division, Heathwood remained committed to a cohesive K-12 experience. Cross-class collaborations like Book Buddies and Biology Buddies continued in the late 2010s. As Stan Wood tried to reinvigorate the Highlander Games, new traditions also sprang up. In 2016, for instance, members of the Upper School International Culture Club debuted a weekly Chinese Culture Club for Lower Schoolers.[21] The PEAK program entered its third decade as a community-wide activity hub, adding a ground-level Junior Ninja Course.

A revitalized spirit of experimentation coursed through the campus. Eighth graders competed in a statewide stock market simulation, studied independent documentary films, and spent a quarter learning the fundamentals of video editing. Middle and Upper Schoolers hit up the 3D printers, laser cutter, and heat press in Heathwood's Makerspace to create all kinds of things.

In 2014-15, John Adams' Upper School history students started digging ditches in a scruffy clearing in the pine forest separating campus from the Congaree River. Reinforced with wood planks, these waist-deep excavations grew into a trench complex modeled after the Western front of the First World War. As an exercise in experiential learning, it gave students firsthand knowledge of the hard and often dispiriting labor required of soldiers simply seeking to maintain earthen pits every time rain turned them to mud (which remained a given on Heathwood's floodplain). The project also blossomed into an annual re-enactment of the 1914 Christmas truce, in which German and French soldiers laid down their arms during the war's first winter to mark the

The Highlander Games.

holiday together. The historical verisimilitude extended from vintage food tins and helmeted infantry, to fake rats and a Francophone refugee encampment presided over by French teacher Nadege Vaultier Keller.

In 2017, Sally Plowden's Upper School creative writing students partnered with Kim Bain's third graders to write and publish a children's book titled *Sally Salamander: The Adventure Begins*. Keyed to a self-guided walking tour of downtown Columbia named after South Carolina's official state amphibian—the spotted salamander—the book was illustrated by Class of 2020 alumna Briana Stanley. Julie Firetag's Upper School state and local government class partnered with the mayor's office to expand the original walking tour from 10 destinations to 20, placing new bronze salamander statues at sites ranging from the Nickelodeon Theatre to *Hanging*, a 2014 public art installation on Main Street by Eileen Blyth and Mark Finley.[22]

Interdisciplinary collaborations blossomed in the Upper School.

Laura Slocum, who introduced an upper-level class in organic chemistry in 2017, partnered with English teacher Elisha Sircy in a project that asked their students to write scientific verse. "We have this sort of post-Romantic view of poetry—it always has to be about an inner feeling," Sircy explained. "But poetry is a way of writing about something that isn't necessarily emotional. It can be something intellectual, or even mathematical." So he would explore different poetic forms and genres, students would attempt to set some principle of chemistry into verse, and Slocum would preside over the scientific accuracy of their expressions. The result was apparently contagious: soon enough, Sally Plowden and biology teacher Madison Richardson were pressing their students to compose an Ode to a Microbe.

Students reenact the World War I Christmas Truce of 1914.

When ninth graders came around to medieval warfare in their world history course, Tim McKnight's physics classroom would transform into a trebuchet production line. George Scouten and Upper School government teacher Julie Firetag co-taught an honors class on leadership and applied journalism. In 2021, their students produced a podcast that was honored by National Public Radio as one of 15 finalists in a competition that had drawn more than 2,600 submissions. It was titled "Shoot Again, You Coward," after the last words of Narciso Gonzales, an editor-in-chief of *The State* newspaper who was fatally shot in broad daylight in 1903 by South Carolina Lieutenant Governor James Hammond Tillman over the murderer's displeasure with the news coverage of his administration.[23]

That class exemplified the growth of the Upper School's elective offerings, which stood at 46 courses at the turn of 2020. Depending on student interest, in any given semester they ranged from 3D Computer Design to Dystopian Literature, Genetics to Forensic Science, Studio Art to Urban Planning. Especially for seniors, who were encouraged to take four electives per semester along with English and mathematics while they concentrated much of their energy on the exhibition of mastery, the breadth of Heathwood's curriculum bore more than a passing resemblance to the lower echelons of a collegiate course catalog.[24]

The Class of 2018 featured the first three seniors to earn a Visual Art Concentration Diploma of Distinction, a program launched three years before. Ruth Dibble, Christina Altman, and Genevieve Altman completed 120 hours of artwork annually outside of the classroom, and each held exhibitions with the guidance of Upper School art teacher Scotty Peek.[25] In 2019, Columbia's Still Hopes Retirement Community featured the art of 34 Heathwood students and seven alumni in an exhibition that marked the first time high schoolers had been selected for the Still Hopes gallery.[26]

Meanwhile, intellectual and athletic exploration unfurled beyond the bounds of the academic year. By the late 2010s, the campus buzzed during much of the summer. Outdoor day camps ranged from PEAK activities to the "Amazing Race" while Lower and Middle School classrooms turned into Minecraft design studios and chess training grounds.

Upper Schoolers could take credit-bearing courses in subjects ranging from 3D animation to the geography of the Bible.[27] The turn of the decade brought "Heathwood Rereadables," a summer book podcast hosted by English faculty. Starting with *The Hunger Games*—"the novel that launched 1,000 archers"—Elisha Sircy, Sally Plowden, James Hane, Elise Hagstette, and Timothy Sebring welcomed the occasional special guest to gab about authors ranging from Cormac McCarthy to Shakespeare. Class of 2020 alumnus Pritish Das—whose senior exhibition had explored "Postmodernism and the New Sincerity" through the lens of David Foster Wallace and the NBC sitcom *Parks and Recreation*—crashed the party early on to tackle Toni Morrison's *The Bluest Eye*.

۞

A good school can be measured by what happens between 8 a.m. and 3 p.m. The mark of a great school, in Hinchey's view, lay in what happened between 3 p.m. and 8 p.m. "With the arts or athletics," he reflected, "kids have authentic successes and failures, and they feel more like they own those. So I think it impacts them in a different way than successes and failures in the classroom."

Student experiences bore that out in the late 2010s.

"I can definitely credit a lot of my coaches—Andrew Richardson and Danny Lewis in particular—with helping me to get where I am today," said Davis Buchanan. The varsity football and soccer captain rolled into his senior year eyeing the Universities of South Carolina, Georgia, and Virginia. His coaches, urging him to consider collegiate athletics as a path to the Ivy League, introduced him to a sport he'd never heard of: sprint football, which is differentiated from the standard sport by a 178-pound weight limit.

"I would never have explored Penn if not for their pushing and encouragement," said Buchanan, who joined the Quakers' defensive unit while pursuing a degree in economics. "A lot of great coaches pushed me in that capacity—and also made me a better student. I think that's what I took away from Heathwood: a well-rounded development of mind and body."

Heathwood brass.

Had Yale not dropped its own sprint football program many years before, Buchanan might have been able to face his old teammate Jaelen King, who was majoring in molecular, cellular, and developmental biology there. The Class of 2018 alumnus likewise credited soccer coach Andrew Richardson, along with strength coach Jay Spearman, as formative influences at Heathwood. But the three-season sportsman didn't feel pigeonholed as an athlete. "I never felt like there was something I couldn't pursue," said the Spanish Club member and ACCEPT Club vice president. "For example, I did the math team. That wasn't something I ever thought of doing. But someone said, 'You should come and do this!' And it was a fun experience, from my sophomore to senior year. It was an experience I don't think I would have done in other places."

For Caroline Tinch, who was a junior during the 2020-21 school year, Heathwood had been an extracurricular smorgasbord going back at least to the day Middle School teacher Brice Spires pitched her on the PEAK program. Community service gradually emerged as a central part of her experience, but Tinch bounced from volleyball to basketball to soccer with a confidence born of relationships stretching back to pre-kindergarten.

"It's such a small school, and such a close-knit community, that you can explore and try new things," she said. "I started playing tennis in eighth grade. I had never picked up a racket! But it's Heathwood, so you can just do it, and your teammates are your best friends … Everybody's going to be supportive and helpful, so there's a lot of freedom to do whatever you want."

Extracurricular offerings in the second half of the 2010s remained varied. Membership swelled for the PEAK Student Leaders and the Science Club, whose participants could barely fit into the yearbook photo frame some years. But most groups hovered around a dozen members, whether they were devoted to Spanish, French, books, yoga, tech, gaming, the stock market, quiz bowl, or fantasy football.

The Key Club, one of Heathwood's longest running student organizations, lost ground and eventually folded in the 2010s. It was a victim of its own success. When the chapter was founded in 1982, members committed to performing a certain amount of community service during the school year. By the 2010s, community service was so thoroughly integrated into Heathwood's mission that the Key Club became extraneous. All Upper Schoolers were required to perform 20 hours annually in order to be promoted to the next grade. Middle Schoolers did service learning projects with Columbia's Harvest Hope Food Bank—for which they also raised over $170,000 in 15 years via the annual Turkey Trot[28]—and Lower Schoolers partnered with the Epworth Children's Home. Occasionally students from across the K-12 spectrum would come together, staging events like the 2015 Dance-a-thon, which raised over $29,000 for Palmetto Children's Hospital.[29] In 2019, seven Highlanders ranging from fifth to twelfth grade earned certification as South Carolina Adopt-a-Stream Volunteer Water Quality Monitors—trained by Class of 2011 alumna Eliza Nixon Thorne—in preparation for a year testing the water quality of Gills Creek near campus.[30] And Upper Schoolers who performed 100 years of community service in a given year won special recognition.

Heathwood's mission statement has gone through various iterations over the years, but the version it promoted in the late 2010s was explicit about the school's service orientation: "Heathwood Hall Episcopal School cultivates creative and critical thinking, develops leadership and social skills, and promotes service to others over the pursuit of self-interest through a rich academic and extracurricular program in a supportive community of talented educators and engaged students."[31]

It's a tall order for students to reflect on their education while they're still in the thick of it. But as Class of 1994 alumna Katherine Juk Draffin considered Heathwood's impact on her own children, the overarching theme she noticed was continuity with her own experience.

"I have three very different learners. My oldest and youngest need to be challenged, and I feel like Heathwood challenges them," Draffin reflected. "For my middle child, school is a little bit harder. She has to work a little bit harder." But the relationships she had formed with her teachers, from first grade through Upper School, had made all the difference. "She can self-advocate," Draffin said. "She feels comfortable asking for help, asking questions."

So perhaps it should have surprised no one, least of all her mother, when as a freshman Ellie Draffin joined forces with Adelaide and Adair Wood in a mission to reboot a varsity sports team that had fallen by the wayside some years before. "She emailed Coach Whalen, and George Scouten, and Chris Hinchey," Katherine said, "about organizing a girls lacrosse team." So in a historical echo of Katherine's own early-1990s effort to launch girls soccer with her classmates Jennifer Coggiola Morgan and Eveleigh Horton Huey, athletic director Jeff Whalen soon posted a part-time job opening for a girls varsity lacrosse coach for the fall of 2020.

Schools are complex organisms. Their fortunes rise and fall, but are hard to measure. Energy comes in and out of them. A campus that fizzes one year may flag the next, awaiting some subtle change to rekindle its spirit.

One the first day of Chris Hinchey's tenure as head of school, Heathwood's enrollment had dropped to a 35-year low of 650, across an age spectrum spanning from three-year-olds to Upper School seniors. By the end of 2020 the student body had recovered to its approximate historical average during the Congaree campus era, topping 750 and showing signs of further expansion.[32]

But that is not the only way to judge the school's revival. Over the course of 70 years, the people who have come together to form Heathwood's learning community have rarely thought to gauge its strength by a headcount. Noble Cooper, a Class of 1980 alumnus who experienced the modern campus when enrollment had dwindled to 502 students, talked about Heathwood in terms that mirrored the reflections of Brice Spires and Amanda Finney, whose Class of 2009 was twice as big as Cooper's. Which is to say, still pretty small: closer to the intimacy of the Heath Mansion's old bedroom classrooms, really, than to the 300-person graduating cohorts of Columbia's Dreher High School or the 500-person cohorts at Spring Valley High School.

In terms of its campus facilities, its academic curriculum, its fine arts opportunities and athletics success, Heathwood Hall has passed through enough phases that a Highlander magically plucked from one era and dropped into another would have ample cause for disorientation. As the Board planned for the addition of a high school in the early

1970s, its education committee mulled the possible necessity of offering mathematics courses as advanced as trigonometry for students ambitious enough to apply to engineering schools.[33] In 1982, the math catalogue topped out with "enriched algebra and geometry" and a class splitting the difference between pre-calculus and calculus.[34] Four decades later, some students were taking Calculus BC as sophomores. Alumni who collected their diplomas in the early 1990s, upon returning to campus 20 years later, found that new buildings had shifted the school's entire center of gravity 200 yards toward the river.

Yet as the 2010s drew to a close, Highlanders reflecting on their recent or current experience of Heathwood reprised themes familiar to seven decades' worth of their predecessors. Most of all they talked about the school's familial atmosphere—and the ways that it could inspire comforting security, constricting claustrophobia, and liberating intimacy from one hour to the next.

Jeff Whalen and Rip Blackstone contemplate the sporting life.

Chris Hinchey and George Scouten lead a Homecoming parade.

Jaelen King, who came in fifth grade and acknowledged frustration over how insular Heathwood's socioeconomic demography could sometimes feel, nevertheless valued his exposure to a milieu not commonly experienced by military families like his. And, pointing out that "high schools are a natural place for cliques and groups to form," he felt that, for its small size, Heathwood had struck a reasonably healthy balance.

"Everybody kind of had their group of people," he said. "Whether it was the Black kids who hung together, or the guys who played football or went hunting who hung together, there were a lot of groups." But various groups overlapped with one another, and there was also space for those who didn't to intermingle.

"I came into Heathwood with a good enough sense of self that I wasn't going to be shaped by things that others were doing around me," he reflected. "But I could pick and choose," he said, "what I wanted to learn. And I think Heathwood provided a good opportunity to really get to know people.

"There were some people who had been there from kindergarten to graduation," he went on. "Being able to grow up alongside them, in a small and close-knit community, was an interesting and unique experience that helped me to develop as a person."

Davis Buchanan's view reflected a campus tenure that stretched all the way back to nursery school. "Having had classes with every individual in my grade—having spent at least some time, whether it be in the classroom, or playing sports, or being involved in PEAK in Middle School—there was never a person I didn't feel comfortable approaching, or wouldn't want to have included.

"Partially because of the size, it's somewhat forced on you," he observed, adding that he had never known an alternative to the sheltered atmosphere he found at Heathwood. "But I do think that generally there was a culture of respect and decency and open-mindedness. And that's something I appreciate."

For King and Buchanan—and Wang and Guo and Tinch—who offered their ruminations without the benefit of having acquired much in the way of hindsight wisdom, it was perhaps too early to render a verdict about Heathwood's impact on their lives. But Class of 2011 alumna Eliza Nixon Thorne, who returned as a Middle School teacher in 2020, had had more time to think about it.

"You wonder about being sheltered," mused Thorne, who spent her entire time as a Heathwood student nursing a desire to become one of 30,000 undergraduates at the University of Georgia. Being sheltered "gets such a negative connotation," she went on. "But is it really that bad of a stigma? Because it just means that you were fostered in a place of love."

EPILOGUE
Pandemic Coda

On Friday, January 24, 2020, members of Heathwood's International Culture Club welcomed classmates and other guests to the spring gala they hosted annually to celebrate the Chinese Lunar New Year. Chinese food, music, dance, and other entertainments traditionally marked this festive occasion, but this year's organizers wondered if they should be doing it at all.

With encouragement from Upper School head George Scouten, they decided to move ahead with the gathering. But the mood they struck took their peers and teachers by surprise. "We tried to include some information about how you could protect yourself from the virus," recalled ICC president Cassie Guo, "like washing your hands with hand sanitizer, and wearing a mask."

It was a puzzling spectacle. Not quite three weeks had passed since the World Health Organization had issued a bulletin, little-noticed in the United States, titled "Pneumonia of unknown cause—China."[1] *The State* newspaper had yet to print the words "coronavirus" or "COVID" on its first three pages, and earlier that week US President Donald Trump had assured Americans, "We have it totally under control. It's one person coming in from China. It's going to be just fine."[2]

But Guo, a senior in the Class of 2020, had recently returned from a winter break visit to her parents in Wuhan, China, where hospitals had begun admitting patients with an unknown respiratory illness in December.[3] And she and other ICC clubbers had lately been hearing a very different story from their families—especially after Zhong Nanshan, a respected former president of the Chinese Medical Association, visited Wuhan on January 20 and issued a public warning that the disease appeared to be more transmissible than local authorities had let on.[4] The day before the

Heathwood gala, Guo's parents had been put under a lockdown along with 11 million fellow citizens of Wuhan, where demand for surgical masks and rubber gloves soared as train, plane and bus transport ground to a halt.[5] The virus had by this time spread to seven other countries, including the United States, where the Centers for Disease Control (CDC) confirmed a case in Washington state on January 20.[6]

"I made the gala a little bit emotional," Guo said. "I think I cried, or somebody else cried. Because we were worried about our families."

Onlookers didn't know quite what to make of it. "They didn't take me that seriously," Guo recalled. "Some people asked if I was okay ... They were being sympathetic about my situation, but they didn't really understand how scary the virus was."

꽃

"The outbreak in Wuhan seemed so far away," Chris Hinchey recalled about the progression of minor headlines in US media during the month of January. "Then, all of a sudden, February came." Outbreaks in Germany and Italy prompted the cancellation of Winterim trips to both countries. "Ironically, we sent them to New York," Hinchey said. "But they got out of there before the explosion."[7]

By the time students returned from Winterim on March 10, the head of school was staring down a challenge to beat any crisis he had ever faced. The administration had made substantial preparations for a worst-case scenario, including planning for augmented digital capabilities to support remote instruction. Yet the situation still seemed unreal. Depending on where people were seeking information, and how anxious or laidback they tended to be as a matter of course, reality seemed to be dawning across campus at a differential pace.

Upper School French teacher Nadege Vaultier Keller printed out thick packets for her pupils to take home. Sophomore Caroline Tinch recalled the hilarity with which she and her classmates received them. "She was passing out these giant packets. And we were cracking up: 'This is too funny! You are *so* overreacting!'"

That Friday they went home for a weekend hiatus from classroom instruction that would stretch into 157 days.

On Sunday, March 15, Hinchey sent an email to Heathwood parents. "I write to share that effective Monday, March 16th, Heathwood will suspend all regularly scheduled events, including all classes, extracurricular activities, childcare and extended day care," it began. "Our teachers, staff, and administrators will utilize Monday and Tuesday as remote learning preparation days, and actual remote learning engagement will begin on Wednesday, March 18th."

By executive order, South Carolina Governor Henry McMaster closed state public schools effective the same date.[8] When it came to implementing remote instruction, Columbia public schools faced hurdles that would take considerably longer than two business days to overcome.

"When the pandemic hit, and we had to switch over to doing virtual stuff, we were ready," said Bill Cherry. "Kids had either a computer or an iPad. The system for getting information to kids, for how to grade papers, etcetera—we'd been using it for 10 years. We were a Google school ... we were one of the first."

Heathwood initially anticipated a three-week closure. The school approached remote instruction with an eye toward balancing synchronous activities (watching or interacting with a live teacher at the same time as classmates) with asynchronous work that would give students respite from their screens and a chance to work at their own pace. Three weeks of online learning became six, and eventually lasted to the end of the school year. In May, some students returned briefly to clear out their lockers.[9]

Two things may be said with confidence about the final two and a half months of Heathwood's 2019-2020 academic year: the experience was significantly better than what public school students endured in Columbia and across the country; and virtually no one wanted to go through remote learning again.

If great schools distinguish themselves from good ones by what happens outside the classroom and after hours, however, Heathwood could point to some considerable creativity on the part of faculty and students. On behalf of the PEAK program, Stan Wood, Brice Spires, and Kelly Turbeville organized a virtual campout. The only way to see your neighbor's tent was through a Google Meets window, but some of the lodgings were inspired. First-grade student Hamp Blackwell roasted marshmallows over a patio fire. Lower Schoolers Robin and Evelyn Eddy hung hammocks from a swing set. Sixth grader Nadia Howard peered out of a pillow fort. Turbeville, a Class of 2013 alumna who became a PEAK associate director in 2017, set up camp in the PEAK classroom, in front of a roaring smartboard fire.[10]

When the 2020 yearbooks came out, the student publishing staff split up 425 copies and delivered them as far afield as Orangeburg and Newberry. Junior Addie-Grace Cook zip-tied a stereo speaker to her bicycle handlebars and pedaled books around her neighborhood. Class of 2020 alumna Emma McIntosh used a car—which was a good thing to have when she encountered junior Nebeyou Sneath's pet lynx. Yearbook advisor Cindy Scannella braved 500 miles and an eight-firetruck road jam during a 72-hour odyssey to deliver just two copies.[11]

April, as ever, brought elections for student council. Celia Deese campaigned for sophomore secretary by scoring a mother lode of a precious pandemic necessity—toilet paper—and delivering a roll to every member of her class. Her slogan: "You need me like you need this TP!"[12]

The road to graduation included a drive-by parade for departing seniors, who flogged cowbells to overcome the social distancing doldrums. Commencement exercises took place on the grass in front the Goodall Bell Tower, where the Class of 2020 assembled in folding chairs placed more than six feet apart. Barred from crowding into a group picture wearing their college T-shirts, they posed one by one, and Bill Cherry Photoshopped all of them into a single frame.[13]

In the summer Heathwood's staff pulled out their tape measures and went room to room, measuring six-foot radiuses around student desks in preparation for a return to in-person learning in the fall. Suzanne Jackson Nagy placed an order at Lowe's: 200 old-fashioned picnic tables, to be deployed underneath the Smith-Shirley Campus Center and other buildings that had been raised above the flood plain on concrete piles in the years since. It had cost a pretty penny to build everything up in the air, but the investment would pay unexpected dividends in 2020-2021, when public health guidelines favored the free-flowing outdoor air that students could enjoy beneath these structures.

Yet Heathwood's ability to weather the pandemic was anything but assured.

"It was tricky," said Board chair Margaret McLeod Willcox. "When this thing first broke out, we had no idea if we could even stay afloat." As students endured two-and-a-half months of virtual learning in the spring, it was anybody's guess whether families would risk paying tuition for another year that might bring more of the same. "We didn't know if our Early Childhood program was going to have to fold," Willcox continued. "Because you can't do remote learning for 2-, 3- and 4-year-olds. And last spring those families were having to pay tuition—plus, if they were working from home, pay somebody for childcare. We expected we might have huge attrition."

It was a monumental challenge that encompassed everything from outfitting classrooms with video cameras to livestream class sessions for quarantined students, to mass purchases of face masks and disinfectants, to hiring extra staff to reduce student-teacher ratios even further than they had been before. To keep teachers and students safe, school leaders felt, average class sizes in the Lower School would have to drop from about 20 to 14.[14] The federal Paycheck Protection Program helped the school accomplish these goals.[15] But that left questions about what would happen with sports, clubs, trips, and all the other ways Heathwood tried to foster personal growth and community connection beyond the blackboard.

The tireless board of trustees charged with navigating this test could not have picked a Board chair with a deeper emotional investment in the school. Apart from being a Class of 1992 alumna and current Heathwood parent, Margaret Willcox was the daughter of Robin McLeod—who had been a pillar of the Middle School faculty for more than 20 years before her passing in 2017—and the granddaughter of Nancy Boyle, who had infused the school with her own grace-giving spirit during Heathwood's transition from the mansion to the Congaree River campus.

In a series of emails reflecting CDC guidance and local conditions, Hinchey outlined a plan to welcome all students back to campus five days per week. It had four pillars: mandatory face masking indoors and out, physical distancing within classrooms, an emphasis on frequent hand-washing, and an intensive sanitization sweep through campus every evening after children went home. "The fifth pillar," Hinchey wrote in a July email, "is represented by the responsible and thoughtful behavior of our students and our Heathwood families when they are away from campus."

Daily school schedules were rejiggered, providing for staggered lunches, which would be delivered to the classrooms of younger children and served on a grab-and-go basis to older ones. Whenever possible, students would eat outside, or at the picnic tables beneath raised buildings. Early childhood staff would measure each child's temperature upon arrival; anyone exceeding 100.4 degrees Fahrenheit would be sent back home. Families of older children were asked to perform daily fever checks on their own. A "Connected Learning" platform, deliberately pitched in the middle ground between in-person instruction and the fully remote learning of the previous spring, would serve as a bridge for any students asked to undergo a quarantine in the wake of a positive COVID test, diagnosis, or known exposure.[16]

Governed by protocols that would soon become second-nature, some student-athletes returned to campus in mid-summer to begin training: volleyball, football, cross-country, and tennis players.[17] The first day of classes was August 19. Seniors decorated their cars to mark the occasion.

Columbia public schools, lacking the space, resources, and administrative agility of an independent school blessed with 122 acres of land, prepared for a fully virtual start to the year on August 31. Richland County School District One planned to bring its 24,000 students back to school on staggered two-day-a-week schedules beginning October 12 and phasing in fully by October 26.[18] The divergence of public- and private-school plans created an immediate competitive advantage for Heathwood, which welcomed 78 new students in a school year that saw the Upper School reach its maximum capacity of 260 under COVID protocols.

As COVID case counts rose in the state heading into the winter holidays, the Richland One and Two districts announced a return to fully virtual learning for "at least two weeks" following the holiday break.[19] The districts' 50,000 students would have to wait until March to fully return to five-day-a-week in-person instruction.[20]

※

It is hard to say what made Heathwood's 2020-21 school year more remarkable: the ways it looked completely different from any that had come before, or all the respects in which it remained utterly familiar.

To walk around campus on a pretty day was to gaze over athletic fields where students had once planted grass by hand, stroll past live oaks Jim Gasque had once worried over like babies, and wander through shaded pine groves that now rang out with the happy noise of masked children scrambling after balls and one another at recess. From the first day of school until the last, Highlanders of all ages abided by the school's face-covering requirements with an even-keeled agreeability and lack of drama all the more noteworthy given the politicization of face masks among their elders across the state and country.

Raven Tarpley had retired in 2020 after two decades as Heathwood's chaplain, and public health guidelines forced a hiatus on chapel gatherings in their traditional form. But a new chaplain, Jill Williams, recorded weekly video chapels for each division of the school.

Lynn Manning Cooper went back to teaching "mindful reading" to eighth graders, who had been cultivating deliberate reading habits since entering Middle School. But Cooper often sported a $5 fabric mask from the cottage business of sophomore Webb Hodges. And Ray Bradbury's science fiction stories took on another dimension of meaning against a pandemic backdrop. "They're mostly set in outer space, but tons of them have to do with the emotional ramifications of social distancing," Cooper reflected. "So we might be reading a short story from the 1950s, but it's particularly important this year."

The deepest joys of returning to campus were often less a matter of scholastic inquiry than relationship revival. Nadege Vaultier Keller could have churned out take-home exercises until the printer ran dry the previous March. But it was really only in her classroom—where life-size cardboard cutouts of Brad Pitt and Danny DeVito stood in one corner, playful gifts from students past—that French became a means of building relationships as well as knowledge. Rip Blackstone, either giddy or punch drunk after the soul-sapping trials of virtual teaching, set his students loose on a madcap mission to erect a giant wall of junk food packages within the window mullions of his Robinson Center classroom: a kaleidoscopic color clash to lighten any mood.

Highlanders also returned to sports. "At first it was mind-boggling," recalled athletic director Jeff Whalen. "To figure out all these protocols, and make sure our coaches were following all those protocols, and testing every day.

"I was amazed by the students," he said. "I know it had to be frustrating ... But the students were great about it."

Game days did not look exactly the same, especially at the beginning. As football season got under way, the athletics staff taped off bleacher sections so that players' parents could watch them compete. There were separate entrances for home and away teams, hand sanitizer dispensers everywhere, and the limited spectators had to wear masks. But as the season progressed without any serious incident or outbreak, Friday nights regained at least part of their function as a community event. "We were able to set up portable bleachers in the end zone, and allow our seniors to come," Whalen said.

A similar progression played out for other sports. Outdoor competition proved easier to manage than indoor winter sports. "Only two teams did not get to finish their seasons," Whalen said: "The B-team girls basketball and my varsity boys basketball team." Although neither team had a COVID diagnosis traced to a campus transmission, infections and household-member exposures stemming from other sources forced too many quarantines and game cancellations.

Student and staff exposures were inevitable, especially during the wave of infections that crested in January 2021. For much of that month, Richland County averaged more than 300 confirmed cases per day.[21] But the Heathwood community worked together to accomplish an uninterrupted year of fully in-person education. "[O]ur protocols and guidelines have proven effective," Hinchey wrote in an email to parents as graduation approached. "If you have friends in other parts of the country, you know that our experience has been an anomaly."

✻

Nine months of in-person learning during the worst global disease outbreak in a century was a substantial achievement. But the convulsions of 2020 and 2021 went far beyond the public health crisis. In the United States, the pandemic era also featured waves of civil rights protest, backlash, and violent social discord of a scope and intensity unlike anything the country had experienced for 50 years. As Black Lives Matter demonstrations gripped and galvanized Americans with hope and fear, Heathwood faculty and students pressed forward with efforts to answer a question that went all the way back to the school's beginning.

What did it mean to be an "Episcopal school for all"?

From Susan Gibbes Robinson to Bob Shirley, from Steve Hickman to Chris Hinchey, every steward in the school's history had faced that essential question amid the social circumstances and political realities particular to her or his time. As Hinchey confronted the moment in Heathwood's 70th year, he set about building on a set of initiatives his administration had started laying out before COVID hit.

"We've had a director of diversity since 2005. And last winter, I was thinking that we weren't doing enough," Hinchey said in April 2021. "So I sat down with Willis Ware."

Ware convened student and parent focus groups to gather community feedback about how Heathwood could live into its mission circa 2020. While director of enrollment management Suzanne Jackson Nagy rolled out an admissions initiative focused on outreach to African Methodist Episcopal churches, Ware oversaw the establishment of two Upper School "student affinity groups"—a Black Students Union and a Queer-Straight Alliance—along with a push to revive Heathwood's ACCEPT Club, which had flagged in the mid-2010s.

Christian Pearson, a track and cross-country standout who counted Elise Hagstette's unit on Dante's "Inferno" as an educational high point, joined the BSU as a senior. For him it provided a protected setting for discussions that frequently encompassed issues, feelings, and challenges in the world beyond Heathwood's campus. Part of the value proposition lay in having physical interactions instead of virtual ones.

"On the internet, if you voice frustration anybody can respond. But it might not be the response that you hoped to gain," the Class of 2021 alumnus said. "It's easy for things to be taken out of context, or it's easy for people to misinterpret what you mean to say." Indeed, willful misinterpretation seemed like the reigning artform on some social media platforms. "When you're in a safe space—especially in person, with other people who are likeminded—it's easier to speak your mind. And it's easier for them to understand what you mean to say."

For Yana Johnson, who as a freshman became one of seven winners of the 2021 *New York Times* Teen Personal Narrative Contest,[22] the presence of a BSU was one aspect of a campus culture that set Heathwood apart from other SCISA schools. She had attended two others, and felt subjected to "intentional and unintentional" prejudice within their walls. Coming to Heathwood as a new student in eighth grade, Johnson said she had a reasonably smooth time finding her social footing. The BSU was not the only club that fortified her sense of social belonging—she belonged to the Young Democrats too, and was eyeing James Hane's student magazine club for her sophomore year—but it served as a reaffirming shelter.

Heathwood "is still a predominantly white institution," she said. "But I think there's actual community here, and the administration is respectful and understanding."

Like many terms that wound their way into the national lexicon during the 2010s, "safe space" had the capacity to evoke reactions ranging from automatic embrace to emphatic aversion. Even among adults who shared a view of the world as a rough-and-tumble place that required the cultivation of resiliency above all else, the utility of providing young people with "safe spaces" as a means to that end remained a subject of considerable debate. Yet as current Highlanders ruminated about the value of safe spaces during spring of 2021, many unconsciously echoed the reflections of men and women who had passed through the school many decades before. One of the most common observations by early Heathwood students—especially those from the mansion era—was that the school was a "protected place." From Gayle Boineau Darby and Will Prioleau to Michael Perry and Noble Cooper, no other attribute stood out as more fundamental to the ethos of Heathwood Hall.

For Willis Ware—and the parents and students the school consulted—ever-shifting social circumstances required shifting solutions. "Young people want to be heard, whether they admit it or not, or recognize it or not," Ware said. "I think sometimes students see social media as an easy, seemingly nonthreatening way to put yourself out there. And yet often students find that it's not nearly as safe as you thought it would be. But when you're in a group where you've got community norms that have been communicated, and there's a fairly clear understanding of the purpose of the group, and what we're trying to accomplish in terms of providing support and encouragement to build up the *whole* community, that's a completely different dynamic."

Class of 2005 alumna Brionna Dickerson Zimmerman, who took over Heathwood's girls basketball program in 2020, elaborated on how she viewed her administrative role supporting the school's diversity, equity, and inclusion efforts:

"Our number one goal is to give every student the best experience we can give them while they are on campus. And part of that is giving every student a voice, a support system, and the reasonable freedom to experience who they are. And although we want to help mold who they are, we cannot dictate who they are," she said. Lamenting the swift politicization of seemingly any initiative that explicitly acknowledges the existence of racism in contemporary American society, Dickerson acknowledged that Heathwood invites criticism with any action it takes.

"Being able to be in a group of people that are likeminded—that's okay," said the co-founder of Heathwood's ACCEPT Club. "Because you want to be able to feel heard, you want to have people who can relate to what you're experiencing, no matter what your affinity group is. Above that, our goal for the ACCEPT Club is to bring those affinity groups together, and be able to share experiences and share voices. It's amazing to have your own group that's related to your passion or background. But it's an elevated experience to take that support and comfort and bring it to a group that may not align as much with you. That, for me, is the ultimate goal.

"What we preach with our community is understanding and grace," she concluded. "You don't have to like what other people have to say, but there is so much value in just listening … We have to extend that level of grace and understanding and show a level of love to everyone."

Heathwood Hall's Class of 2021 collected their diplomas on May 28. In lieu of the traditional service trip to Johns Island, the seniors partnered with Homeworks of America to clean, paint, and carry out light construction projects for families in need at four sites in Columbia.

Commencement exercises took place, as they had the year before, on the lawn in front of the Goodall Bell Tower. This time around, the seats were placed closed enough to permit the occasional whisper between classmates. The rite of passage culminated a year whose turmoil and dislocations had galvanized Heathwood's graduating class like few others. Their senior exhibitions of mastery served as a collective testament to an educational experience very much alive to the world they were about to enter as young adults.

Jackson Meriwether examined the impacts of politics on the transmission of COVID-19 in South Carolina. Jack Taylor explored the spread of misinformation through social media. Jackson Byrd analyzed the journey of QAnon conspiracy theories from the fringe to the mainstream.

William Lamar studied the effects of climate change and metropolitan development on duck migration over the past century. Hanna Jacobson evaluated the relationship between climate change and harmful algal blooms.

Lexi Singletary investigated the possibilities for improving American policing through the lens of use-of-force policies. Emily Kahn presented a study of gentrification, environmental racism, and institutional racism in Columbia's Ward One. Clara Wilson scrutinized the causes of America's opioid crisis. While Jack Cook focused on the yield curve as a recession predictor, A.J. Kuse charted the evolution of government interventions as a response to economic crises over the past 20 years.

Which is not to say that every senior exhibition was ripped from the headlines. Lilly Abernathy explored collaborations between doctors and midwives to improve the birth experience. Morgan Iseman asked: "Is franchising a safer investment than starting an independent business"? Van Clark evaluated the case for legalizing sports betting in South Carolina. Johannamarie Nwanagu made a bid for the most creative exhibition title in school history: "Jellyfish is the New Black: Afrofuturist Couture."

As another summer approached, Heathwood's faculty looked ahead to the semester on the far side of it.

Upper School English teacher Elisha Sircy and government teacher Julie Firetag planned a collaborative unit on the history of political violence—a topic given renewed relevance by the US Capitol invasion of January 6, 2021. "What does patriotism look like, and what are the ways that it can spill over?" Sircy asked, posing the essential question. Among other angles, he intended to introduce students to various historical representations of Julius Caesar and Brutus. "Obviously Dante was not a big fan of Brutus," he laughed; the "Inferno" places the Roman dictator's assassin in one of Satan's three mouths, to be masticated in perpetuity. "But John Wilkes Booth? Big fan of Brutus!"

Rip Blackstone developed a syllabus for multivariable calculus, which he planned to offer for the first time in 2021-22. He also plotted out another addition to the Upper School's elective course catalog: Introduction to Finance.

As the whoops and cheers of summer campers rang out from the PEAK ropes courses, renovation crews descended on the Robinson Center to carry out a 25-year upgrade. Administrators looked forward to welcoming close to 800 pupils on the first day of classes. Heathwood Hall had closed the book on its 70th year, and a new one was coming.

It was time to begin again.

APPENDIX

HEATHWOOD HALL EPISCOPAL SCHOOL: HEADS OF SCHOOL

1951-1955: Susan Gibbes Woodward Robinson

1956-1960: Mary Anderson

1960-1969: Elsie Lamar

1969-1971: Rev. Richard Nevius

1971-1972: Frank S. Morris (interim)

1972-1977: Earl Devanny

1977-1978: Jimmy Walker (interim)

1978-2000: James Robert Shirley

2000-2008: Stephen Hickman

2008-2009: Anne Weston and Steve Mandell (interim)

2009-2011: Chuck Jones

2011-2012: Michael Eanes (interim)

2012-2015: Michael Heath

2015- : Chris Hinchey

BOARD OF TRUSTEES CHAIRS

Author's Note: Gaps in the documentary record, including missing Board Meeting Minutes for much of the 1950s and 1965-1970, preclude a definitive list of Board of Trustees leaders. The 1951-1973 period is reconstructed here to the best of the author's ability, but some years remain unaccounted for. The Board was reconstituted in 1973, and surviving records permit a more confident list from that point on—though occasional gaps in the record for that period may also introduce discrepancies.

1951-?: R. Hoke Robinson

1958: Walter Sims

1958-1960: Mrs. W. Bedford Moore, Jr.

1960-1964: James A. Morris

1964-?: Joseph Faulk

1967-1968: Rev. Joseph E. Sturtevant

1969: Rev. James Stirling

1970-1972: Rev. Henry Barton

1972-1973: Tabb Heyward

1973-1975: Robert Royall

1975-1977: Bob Burg

1977-1981: Julian Walker

1981-1983: James Smith

1983-1985: James Reynolds

1985-1987: Bo Tate

1987-1990: Tate Horton

1990-1994: Mary Rainey Belser

1994-1995: Boyd Hipp

1995-1998: Jim Gray

1998-2002: Frank Ellerbe

2002-2006: Tobin Cassels

2006-2009: Leighton Lord

2009-2011: Wade Mullins

2011-2013: David Sojourner

2013-2015: Jay Hennig

2015-2017: Julie Hicks

2017-2019: Rox Pollard

2019-2021: Margaret McLeod Willcox

2021- : Freeman Belser

CAMPUS DEVELOPMENT

HEATH MANSION

1914: Heath Mansion originally built

1951: Heathwood Hall begins operation in the mansion

1954: Little Red Schoolhouse added to campus grounds

1971: Chapel and classroom annex (later moved to the Congaree River Campus, where it became classroom space and a dining commons)

CONGAREE RIVER CAMPUS

1974: Classroom pods, Gymnasium, Dining Commons, Administrative/Library Mobile Trailers

1981: Averyt Early Childhood Learning Center

1984: Wells-Roberts Tennis Courts

1985: Smith-Shirley Campus Center (including the Mary Rainey Belser Auditorium and the Dorothy and Chalmers Poston Library)

1988: Henry Woodward Track

1996: Susan Gibbes Robinson Center for Science and Math

2003: Nord Intermediate/Middle School Building

2003: PEAK Alpine Tower

2005: Athletic Center

2006: Chapel of the Epiphany

2006: PEAK Boathouse

2010: PEAK Odyssey ropes course

2011: Goodall Bell Tower

2012: Dining Commons

2017: Averyt Tennis Center & Pavillion (expansion)

NOTES

Introduction: NINETY CANDLES

1. The others are New Hampshire's Levi Woodbury (1789-1851) and Ohio's Salmon P. Chase (1808-1873). Byrnes was the only American to achieve that distinction in the 20th century.

2. Information about James Byrnes drawn from: Robertson, David. *Sly and Able: A Political Biography of James F. Byrnes.*

3. Excerpts of thank-you letters written to the Byrneses by Mrs. L. W. Heriot's second-grade section were printed in *The State*, May 28, 1969, p. 9. The children were identified by first name only, but according to the 1969 Heathwood yearbook, the only second graders bearing these names were Karen Ibach, Penelope Jones, Anne Witten, and Frank McCrory, all of whom were in Mrs. Heriot's section.

4. "The Columbia Visit By Nixons Leaves Lasting Impressions," *Columbia Record*, May 5, 1969, p. 13.

5. Richard Nixon's Daily Diary, May 1, 1969 – May 15, 1969. WHCF: SMOF: Office of Presidential Papers and Archives, Box RC-2, Richard Nixon Presidential Library.

6. In the photograph that would later appear in newspapers, the poster was held by Will Prioleau—but only because its original bearer had bent down to tie his shoes. "But at that moment the limo pulled up," Prioleau later recalled, "and Nixon came right over to me."

7. The tally in Ward 16 was: Nixon, 791; Humphrey, 148; Wallace, 48. *Supplemental Report of the Secretary of State to the General Assembly of South Carolina, Election November 5, 1968.*

8. Robertson, p. 532.

9. *African American* and *Black* are used interchangeably in this book, with the understanding that these racial descriptors reflect socially constructed identities, not biologically or naturally determined categories.

10. Robertson, p. 535.

11. Gallup Organization. Accessed at https://news.gallup.com/poll/110548/gallup-presidential-election-trial-heat-trends.aspx

12. "Gallup Poll Finds Nixon Is Maintaining a Large Lead," *New York Times*, Oct. 10, 1968, p. 51.

13. Report of Election Simulation based on Gallup poll of Sept. 20-22. Nixon Presidential Library, White House Special Files collection, Box 36, Folder 14.

14. That outcome would have thrown the election to the House of Representatives, where Wallace hoped to extract concessions against civil rights by playing the role of kingmaker.

15. Robertson, p. 198. This was a delicate and sometimes unsavory dance. Byrnes' sympathetic biographer David Robertson credits him with delivering "one of the most inflammatory speeches on race ever read into the Congressional Record" in 1919. (Robertson, p. 85.) Yet the only time Byrnes ever lost an election was when the Catholic-born convert to Episcopalianism refused covert membership in—and the powerful electioneering support of—the Ku Klux Klan in his 1924 Senate campaign. (ibid, p. 91.)

16. Robertson, p. 539.

17. *Brown v. Board of Education* II, 349 U.S. 294

18. *Briggs v. Elliott*, 342 U.S. 350 (1952) was the first of five cases combined into *Brown v. Board of Education of Topeka*, 347 U.S. 483. Among the facts surfaced in *Briggs* were the revelations that the 600 Negro students in one Clarendon County school shared two outdoor toilet stalls, and that another school lacked faucets, requiring drinking water to be brought in buckets from the home of a neighboring minister. (Quint, p. 12.)

19. The lawyer was John W. Davis, who "had personally argued or participated in the writing of more cases before the US Supreme Court—more than 250—than any other attorney of the 20th century." (Robertson, p. 514.)

20. Robertson, p. 517.

21. Speech by James Byrnes' to the South Carolina Education Association, March 16, 1951. Cited in Ball, p. 140.

22. At Byrnes' request, the SC legislature approved a ballot referendum permitting the abolishment of the constitutional requirement that the state provide a system of public education. Voters approved the measure, by a 68 percent to 32 percent margin, in the 1952 election. ("South Carolina Voters Back Byrnes School Clause," *Christian Science Monitor*, Nov. 6, 1952, p. 17.)

23. *Gantt v. Clemson Agricultural College of SC* went all the way to the US Court of Appeals, Fourth Circuit. (320 F.2d 611)

24. *Millicent Brown et al v. Charleston County School Board, District 20,* 226 F. Supp. 819 (E.D.S.C. 1963)

25. McNeill, p. 39. Richland County began admitting small numbers of African Americans to white schools in 1964, but five years later nearly 80 percent of African American students in the county still attended fully segregated schools. ("Columbia, S.C., Follows Nixon's Ideas on Integration," *New York Times*, Sep. 2, 1970, p. 26.)

26. Hawkins p. 238.

27. Edgar 1992, p. 128.

28. "Private Schools in Columbia Filling in Wake of New Plan," *Index Journal* (Greenwood, SC), July 25, 1968, p. 15. In the first four business days after the plan was announced, Hammond Academy received 80 applications for enrollment, pushing the school to capacity. By 1971, Hammond's enrollment had grown from 239 at its founding to approximately 700 ("Dixie's 'Segregation Academies' Filling Fast," *Montgomery Advertiser*, July 12, 1971, p. 1. [Associated Press])

29. In 1966 federal funding was terminated to two South Carolina districts under this initiative, and in 1968 HEW listed 21 SC districts as in probable non-compliance, including Columbia City Schools. In 1968 HEW established guidelines more forcefully requiring a unitary school system rather than dual race-based systems between which students could opt via "freedom-of-choice" plans; HEW specified that there were to be "no Negro or other minority group schools and white schools—just schools." The amount of federal funds at risk to SC districts was significant, totaling $33 million annually by 1968. (McNeill, p. 48-56.)

30. "Nixon Raps HEW on Schools, Favors 'Freedom of Choice,'" *Charlotte Observer*, Sept 13, 1968, p. 1.

31. *Brown v. Board of Education II*, 349 US 294 (1955). Dent then distributed a tape and transcript of the interview for rebroadcast across the South—defying the liberal Republican leaders in the campaign's national headquarters. (Robertson, p. 539.) In this the campaign was hewing more closely to the assurances with which Strom Thurmond had whipped Southern votes for Nixon at the Republican National Convention, where Ronald Reagan and Nelson Rockefeller initially controlled enough delegates to make a play for the nomination. "I know you want to vote for Reagan, the true conservative," the South Carolina senator told his colleagues, as one of them later recalled, "but if Nixon becomes president, he has promised that he won't enforce either the Civil Rights or the Voting Rights Acts. Stick with him." (Maxwell and Shields, p. 6, citing the eyewitness account of former Congressman Pete McCloskey.) After speaking with Byrnes in early October, Nixon then doubled down on his attack against HEW—but not before promising to pay the former governor a visit in Columbia should he win the White House. (Robertson, p. 539.)

32. As it happens, the eight Electoral College electors pledged to Wallace included James H. Hammond, a descendent of Hammond Academy's namesake. *Supplemental Report of the Secretary of State to the General Assembly of South Carolina, Election November 5, 1968.*

33. "Gas Routs Whites Who Upset Buses at South Carolina School," *New York Times*, March 4, 1970. p. 1. In response, Richland County Representative Heyward Belser delivered an acclaimed speech in the SC House of Representatives lamenting that "dark hour in the history of South Carolina" and calling for "orderly obedience to the law of school desegregation." (McNeill, 92.) Belser's son Clinch attended Heathwood

in the 1950s and his daughter-in-law Mary Belser would later chair Heathwood's board, as would his grandson Freeman Belser.

34. "Trustees Plan for Opening Of Elementary Church School," *The State*, April 1, 1951, p. F-1.

35. For example see "Heathwood Hall School Study," Dec. 19, 1960. Heathwood Hall Archive.

36. Speech by Richard Nevius provisionally dated 1969, Heathwood Hall Archive. "One of the strongest reasons" for joining NAIS, Nevius emphasized, was that it would help distinguish Heathwood from the segregation academies served by the South Carolina Association of Independent Schools (SCISA).

37. The first private school to welcome children of all races was St. Anne's Roman Catholic School in Rock Hill, which admitted its first Black students in 1954. (Edgar 1992, p. 128.)

38. Two sources inform this estimate. The first is Heathwood's 1968-69 annual yearbook, which is imperfect insofar as ascribing racial identification on the basis of skin color, especially as represented in faded black-and-white photographs, is a fraught endeavor. The second source is a document conveyed by the school administration to Board of Trustees Chairman Rev. J. E. Sturtevant on February 1, 1967, summarizing the enrollment of African American students by grade for the academic years beginning 1965-66, including projections through 1969-70. (Heathwood Hall Archive)

39. These were two of many state institutions—schools, colleges, hospitals, parks, golf courses, restaurants, beaches—Matthew Perry Jr. helped to desegregate via his legal work with the NAACP. In 1979 he became South Carolina's first Black federal judge, appointed by Jimmy Carter, and in 2004 the federal courthouse in Columbia was named after him. ("M.J. Perry Jr., Legal Pioneer, Dies at 89," *New York Times*, Aug. 5, 2011, p. A-22.)

40. This was in fact the second time USC had been desegregated; from 1873-1877, during Reconstruction, African-Americans were admitted to the university, whose tuition was at that time free. (South Carolina Encyclopedia, www.scencyclopedia.org/sce/entries/segregation/)

41. Heathwood Hall Newsletter, Mar. 23, 1973. Heathwood Hall Archive.

42. Interview of Robert Royall by Margaret Clarkson.

One: THE MANSION AND THE MATRIARCHS

1. "Family Income in the United States: 1951," US Department of Commerce, Bureau of the Census, Series P-60, No. 12.

2. Inflation conversions are per Friedman's inflation calculator at westegg.com/inflation

3.   Plowden C. J. Weston enjoyed tremendous wealth. At the time of the Civil War, he was the only American to own more than 1,000 slaves. (Edgar 1999, p. 311.)

4.   At Weston's death his estate was valued at $478,266.56, of which enslaved "Negroes" accounted for $133,850. Weston's estate represented approximately $13.5 million in 2020 terms. (Inventory of Francis Marion Weston, January 1855. Heathwood Hall Archive.)

5.   Female schools were also to be established in Georgia and Tennessee. (Last Will and Testament of Francis Marion Weston, Heathwood Hall Archive.)

6.   Worth about $130,000 in 2020 dollars.

7.   Lucas, p. 128.

8.   Steeley, p. 46-70.

9.   Federal forces caused most but not all of this damage, some of which was wrought by Confederate forces, local civilians, and accidental fires. (Report on the Committee of the Destruction of Churches, Episcopal Diocese of South Carolina, 1868, p. 1-16.)

10. Journal of the 104th Annual Conference of the Protestant Episcopal Church, South Carolina Diocese, 1894, p. 62; Journal of the 120th Annual Conference of the Protestant Episcopal Church, South Carolina Diocese, 1910, p. 52.

11. Letter under the seal of Episcopal Bishop John Gravatt, circa 1951. Heathwood Hall Archive.

12. Information in this paragraph drawn largely from Thomas, 736-738.

13. Heathwood Trustees Report to the Upper Diocese of South Carolina, circa 1951. Files of Heyward Robinson.

14. Committee Report by John LeMaster Jr., 1951. Heathwood Hall Archive.

15. National Real Estate Clearing House, 42 East 53rd Street, New York, Listing No. 42817, 6/49. Heathwood Hall Archive. This listing was for the mansion and 9 acres—presumably including land later subdivided into separate lots.

16. Thomas, p. 736-738; Heathwood Trustees Report to the Upper Diocese of South Carolina, circa 1951 (Files of Heyward Robinson). The governance structures of Episcopal schools vary. Parish schools serve as extensions of individual parishes, and are governed by a parish's vestry. Diocesan schools operate under the aegis of the bishop. Heathwood Hall was incorporated as an independent entity (Certificate of Incorporation, State of South Carolina, March 13, 1951, Heathwood Hall Archive), and its initial governance structure featured a board of trustees including both clergy and laypeople, who articulated an ecumenical openness to students of diverse religious affiliations. Yet there was frequent confusion about Heathwood Hall's relationship to the church, which has changed from time to time. A 1960 Diocesan Convention stipulated that Heathwood Hall was "an institution of this diocese" to be governed by a board whose trustees were to be nominated by the bishop. Yet that was a debatable claim in light of the school's

incorporation documents, and subsequent reorganizations expanded the number of trustees, diluting the influence of the clergy.

17. "New Era Starts at Heathwood," *The State*, April 1, 1951, p. 54.

18. "Upper SC Diocese to Found School," *The State*, March 18, 1951, p. 1.

19. "Alterations and additions to Heathwood Hall" and "Report of Committee by John LeMaster," 1951, Heathwood Hall Archive.

20. The snakes were "for the most part in containers," recalled Susu Ravenel, the daughter of founding principal Susan Woodward. "Mother didn't know what the hell to do with those snakes ... but I was terrified."

21. "Good Shepherd Parish School to be Merged with Heathwood Hall," *The State*, April 15, 1951, p. 8.

22. "Heathwood Hall Episcopal School Opens for the First Time," *The State*, September 11, p. 2.

23. Dewey, p. 77-80.

24. Author interview with Susu Ravenel, daughter of Susan Gibbes Woodward.

25. Susan Gibbes Woodward Robinson obituary, *Charleston Post and Courier*, Mar. 20, 2012.

26. St. Catherine's School website. www.st.catherines.org/about/history

27. "Heathwood Hall Episcopal School Opens for the First Time," *The State*, Sept. 11, 1951, p. 2.

28. For example see "Heathwood Hall School Accepting Applications," *Columbia Record*, June 11, 1951, p. 9.

29. Annual Report, Apr. 17, 1952. Files of Heyward Robinson.

30. Annual Report, May 11, 1953. Heathwood Hall Archive.

31. Eleven of these were for whites, and five for Blacks; Columbia had three such schools for whites and one for Blacks. (Edgar 1992, p. 128.)

32. "Miss Louly's Kindergarten Moves to Heathwood," *The State*, Sep. 12, 1954, p. 68.

33. 1954 Annual Report, Heathwood Hall Archive.

34. Page Steinert did not fully retire until age 85, after more than four decades teaching kindergarten at Heathwood Hall. ("Page Lane Steinert obituary," *The State*, Jan. 24, 2006, p. B-4.)

35. This remained the case until the public library ended the arrangement in 1970. (Board Meeting Minutes, Dec. 3, 1970. Heathwood Hall Archive.)

36. Reminiscence of Elsie Lamar, circa 1991. Heathwood Hall Archive.

37. "Religious Education Program at School," circa 1950s, Heathwood Hall Archive.

38. Reminiscence of Elsie Lamar, circa 1991. Heathwood Hall Archive.

39. "Traditional Egg Hunt to be Resumed," *The State*, Apr. 13, 1952, p. 49.

40. "Many Children Attend Heathwood Egg Hunt," *The State*, Apr. 18, 1952, p. 14.

41. "Obituary of Elsie Lamar," *The State*, Dec. 3, 2002, p. B4.

42. Trustees letter to Mary Anderson, March 29, 1960. Heathwood Hall Archive.

43. Letter from Elsie Lamar to Trustees, April 2, 1960. Heathwood Hall Archive.

44. Reminiscence of Elsie Lamar, circa 1991. Heathwood Hall Archive.

45. Author interview with Raven Tarpley; 2003 Yearbook, p. 233; among other sources.

46. Prioleau was not the only student who viewed Lamar in these terms. "She raised all of us," recalled his contemporary Mary Gilkerson.

47. Board Meeting Minutes, June 1, 1960. Heathwood Hall Archive.

48. The use of fractional parts to represent religious faith would seem to underscore that the quality being measured had less to do with theology than genealogy. (Annual Report, April 1961, Heathwood Hall Archive.)

49. "Income of Persons and Families in the United States: 1961," US Department of Commerce, Bureau of the Census, Series P-60, No. 39.

50. Reminiscence of Elsie Lamar, circa 1991. Heathwood Hall Archive.

Two: AN OPEN SCHOOL

1. "Racial Barriers At Day School Here Dropped," *Columbia Record*, Feb. 23, 1965, p. 3

2. Code of Laws of South Carolina 1952, p. 327.

3. Article III, Section 33, South Carolina Constitution (as of 1952). It should go without saying that, as a matter of biology, human blood has no bearing whatsoever on socially constructed racial categories.

4. "Red Carpet Out for Gov. Byrnes: Carolina Klan Has Had Warning," *Washington Post*, Jan. 14, 1951, p. 21.

5. Speech by James Byrnes to the South Carolina Education Association, March 16, 1951 (cited in Ball, p. 140). Byrnes was in the vanguard of the "Massive Resistance" movement by which Southern states opposed school integration for roughly a decade after *Brown v. Board of Education*. Their guiding principles were codified in the 1956 "Southern Manifesto," signed by 19 US senators and 82 Congressional representatives from Southern states.

6. "South Carolina Voters Back Byrnes School Clause," *Christian Science Monitor*, Nov. 6, 1952, p. 17.

7. Quint, p. 16.

8. McNeill, p. 12.

9. Cohodas, p. 177.

10. Quint, p. 114.

11. Giordano, p. 147.

12. Quint, p. 114.

13. Quint, p. 48.

14. Sass, Herbert Ravenel. "Mixed Schools and Mixed Blood," *The Atlantic Monthly*, November 1956, p. 45-49.

15. *Plessy v. Ferguson*, 163 U.S. 537 (1896)

16. Steeley, p. 71-89.

17. *McCollum v. Board of Education*, 33 U.S. 203 (1948)

18. Zimmerman, p. 138-150.

19. Zimmerman, p. 150.

20. "Trustees Plan for Opening of Elementary Church School," *The State*, Apr. 1, 1951, p. 54.

21. Board Meeting Minutes, Aug. 26, 1958. Heathwood Hall Archive.

22. Board Meeting Minutes, Sep. 16, 1958. Underlining the school's financial precarity was the rejection of a $150/month bid for lawn maintenance as "obviously prohibitive." Heathwood Hall Archive.

23. Board Meeting Minutes, Oct. 14, 1958. Heathwood Hall Archive.

24. Board Meeting Minutes, Dec. 5, 1958. Heathwood Hall Archive.

25. Board Meeting Minutes, Dec. 15, 1958. Heathwood Hall Archive.

26. Heathwood Hall Foundation certificate of incorporation, Feb. 1959. Heathwood Hall Archive.

27. Board Meeting Minutes, Mar. 12, 1959.

28. No Board meeting minutes survive from the period between June 1 (which contained no mention of this matter) and October 31, 1960.

29. Board Meeting Minutes, Oct. 31, 1960. Heathwood Hall Archive.

30. Letter from Roberts, Jennings, Thomas & Lumpkin, Feb. 14, 1961. Heathwood Hall Archive.

31. Letter under the seal of Episcopal Bishop John Gravatt, circa 1951. Heathwood Hall Archive.

32. Board Meeting Minutes, Mar. 16, 1961. Heathwood Hall Archive.

33. Board Meeting Minutes, Apr. 12, 1961. Heathwood Hall Archive.

34. Board Meeting Minutes, May 23, 1961. Heathwood Hall Archive.

35. Correspondence dated Oct. 31 and Nov. 2, 1961. Heathwood Hall Archive.

36. Heathwood Hall Episcopal School Bylaws, circa 1961. Heathwood Hall Archive.

37. Letter, circa 1962. Heathwood Hall Archive.

38. Board Meeting Minutes, Mar. 8, 1962. Heathwood Hall Archive.

39. Board Meeting Minutes, Oct. 2, 1962. Heathwood Hall Archive.

40. Board Meeting Minutes, Oct. 2, 1962. Heathwood Hall Archive.

41. Board Meeting Minutes, Mar. 26, 1963. Heathwood Hall Archive.

42. Appointment card, Nov. 1, 1963. Heathwood Hall Archive.

43. Letter from Elsie Lamar, October 6, 1964. Heathwood Hall Archive.

44. As attested in a second letter, from Lamar to Faulk, on October 6, 1964.

45. Purdy, p. 77-78.

46. *Journal of the General Convention of the Protestant Episcopal Church*, 1958, p. 319-320.

47. This nullification appears to have resulted in the expungement of the January 22, 1965 meeting minutes.

48. A letter announcing the Jan. 22 meeting suggests that it was attended by a slightly different subset of trustees than the Jan. 27 meeting—where the Rev. William Gatling, Jr. dissented repeatedly from resolutions that passed with a majority vote.

49. The resolution passed by a 94 to 43 vote. "Resolution States Voluntary Race Difference Recognition," *The Living Church*, May 6, 1956, p. 13.

50. "Agony, Tension, and Heresy," *The Living Church*, May 6, 1956, p. 10.

51. *Journal of the General Convention of the Protestant Episcopal Church*, 1958, p. 317.

52. *Journal of the General Convention of the Protestant Episcopal Church*, 1958, p. 319.

53. *Journal of the General Convention of the Protestant Episcopal Church*, 1964, p. 978.

54. "Highlights of 42nd Convention's Opening Day," *The State*, Jan. 29, 1964, p. 24.

55. Pinckney acknowledged opposition to National Council "mandates" on racial matters by professing to find them "disturbing"—but reaffirmed his basic commitment to integration by expressing hope "that individuals as well as parishes and missions who have taken the way of non-support or partial support to the Church's Program will seriously consider changing their thinking and action and support [it] in full." (*Journal of the Forty-Second Annual Convention of the Episcopal Diocese of Upper South Carolina*, 1964, p. 46.)

56. Among others, student Mary Bentz Gilkerson and teacher Patsy Malanuk would credit Stirling as an adamant proponent of integration within Trinity Cathedral and Heathwood Hall.

57. Cardinal Newman was a Catholic school in Columbia. In 1961, the Catholic diocese of South Carolina had announced that Catholic schools would desegregate no later than public schools. In the summer of 1963, the diocese announced its policy to desegregate all 37 of its schools by fall of 1964. (McNeil, p. 29.)

58. Letter from John A. Pinckney, Jan. 6, 1965. Heathwood Hall Archive.

59. Reminder card, January 8, 1965. Heathwood Hall Archive.

60. According to some second-hand reports, it was a highly charged, contentious meeting that split the parent body into two camps, as reflected in the ultimate departure of some families from Heathwood.

61. No school handbook for 1965-66 or 1966-67 could be found in the Heathwood Hall Archive. There is no indication that the single teacher not present in 1967-68 resigned for reasons related to integration. In fact, a higher natural rate of faculty attrition might have been expected, considering the frequency of turnover due to childbearing among a predominantly female faculty.

62. There is no documented reaction of the Heathwood Hall Foundation, which seems have dissolved at some point in the mid-1960s. In early 1968, however, Hammond Academy

announced that its capital fundraising drive would be chaired by Tucker Weston, who had apparently shifted his allegiance in the meantime. ("Weston Heads Hammond Fund Drive," *Star Reporter*, Jan. 11, p. 4A.) The 1959-chartered Heathwood Hall Foundation is not to be confused with the Foundation for Heathwood Hall, an unrelated entity established in the early 1970s to hold property titles for the South Beltline campus.

63. The records of these meetings are extraordinary; the Heathwood Hall Archive contains no documentation whatsoever for such meetings about white children, much less at this level of detail.

64. Crumlin's daughter also eventually got a spot in kindergarten. (Letter of April 22, Heathwood Hall Archive.)

65. Letters from Elsie Lamar, 1965. Heathwood Hall Archive.

66. A.C. Flora is a public high school in Columbia.

67. Founded in 1865 as the Tappan School, named after the New York abolitionist Lewis Tappan, the Avery Normal Institute was a private secondary school that trained multiple generations of Black professionals and leaders in Charleston before becoming a public school in 1947 and closing in 1954. In 1985, alumni established a successor organization, the Avery Research Center for African American History and Culture, as an affiliate of College of Charleston. ("History of the Avery Research Center," avery.cofc.edu)

68. Fredrina Tolbert's 2016 album *Recital* includes songs in English, German, French, and Italian.

69. This accelerated promotion was reflected in the 1972 and 1973 Yearbooks. Heathwood Hall Archive.

70. Noble Cooper was a member of the first Heathwood varsity boys basketball team to play against Hammond—albeit in an unofficial capacity, since Hammond's administration refused to sanction a game. See Chapter Five.

71. Hawkins, p. 239.

72. In 1973 the Heathwood Hall Board of Trustees was expanded from 12 to 25 members, of whom four were to be Episcopal clergy. This reorganization, conducted in accordance with a Diocesan Convention of February 1973, mandated that Episcopalians comprise the majority of the Board, rather than its entirety as had previously been the case. ("Heathwood Hall Newsletter," circa February 1973. Heathwood Hall Archive.)

Three: **BIRTH OF THE HIGHLANDERS**

1. Letter of January 13, 1969. Heathwood Hall Archive.

2. Speech by Richard Nevius circa 1969, Heathwood Hall Archive.

3. Speech by Richard Nevius circa 1969, Heathwood Hall Archive.

4. The inclusive ethos of the NAIS stood in contrast to the South Carolina

Independent Schools Association, which supported schools with racially exclusionary policies at that time.

5. 1970-71 Yearbook. This T-shaped modular structure would later be moved, in the manner of a mobile home, to the new campus, where it would become the dining commons with its attached classrooms.

6. There was "considerable discussion," in the run-up to the property conveyance, "concerning the future residential development of the area." (Board Meeting Minutes, Mar. 19, 1973, Heathwood Hall Archive.) In 1999, the Manning family nearly consummated a sweeping deal that would have been the basis for a $1 billion mixed-used development. But the plans foundered for reasons largely stemming from the low-lying land's susceptibility to flooding. ("Burwell Manning obituary," *The State*, Feb. 6, 2005, p. B4.) The Manning property was one of several considered as a new site for Heathwood Hall. Others included a 60-acre parcel near Caughmans Pond (about 5 miles east of the Veterans Affairs Hospital on Garners Ferry Road), offered as a swap for the Heath Mansion property; a second parcel in the Veterans Hospital vicinity (see Works Progress Administration, p. 374) that had been the original site of the Epworth Children's Home, offered for sale; and a parcel referred to as the "Moore-Bostick-Hampton property." (Board Meeting Minutes, Feb. 1, 1973. Heathwood Hall Archive.)

7. This entity, which was created in conjunction with the acquisition of the new campus, is unrelated to the Heathwood Hall Foundation of the late 1950s and early 1960s.

8. Deed registered in Richland County Deed Book D-393, page 811. Heathwood Hall Archive. In 1981 the agreement was revised to give the trustees sole possession of a part of the property, for the purposes of obtaining a mortgage. By 1996, Heathwood Hall had fee simple ownership of approximately 122 acres, which is the extent of the current campus due to relinquishment of a parcel containing dikes along the river. ("Summary of transactions affecting real property owned/occupied by Heathwood Hall," circa 1998, Heathwood Hall Archive.) Heathwood Hall's original campus was sold in 1975 for $225,000. (Board Meeting Minutes, May 8, 1975; Heathwood Hall Archive.)

9. "Captain Devanny kept breaking me down in rank because I did not get my hair cut short enough," recalled Class of 1958 Howe cadet Dick French, "and, finally, he threatened to take me to the barber himself." (*Howe Military School Class of 1958 Memory Book*, p. 95.) At Heathwood, Devanny enforced a requirement that boys' hair be cut "above the collar." Girls were permitted, after some discussion, to wear slacks in 1974. (Board Meeting Minutes, Oct. 8, 1974. Heathwood Hall Archive.)

10. Enacted by the trustees on Nov. 9, 1972. "Actions of the Board of Trustees, 1972-1982," Heathwood Hall Archive.

11. Devanny did, however, explore the possibility of establishing an ROTC unit at Heathwood Hall. (Board Meeting Minutes, Mar. 14, 1974. Heathwood Hall

Archive.) He also brought Gen. William Westmoreland, former commander of US forces during the Vietnam War, as the commencement speaker for 1974, the year Westmoreland unsuccessfully ran for South Carolina governor as a Republican. (Board Meeting Minutes, Apr. 18, 1974. Heathwood Hall Archive.)

12. Such a curriculum, it elaborated, should be determined with the assistance of "professional people, not salesmen."

13. "A Statement of Principle by the Faculty," May 3, 1971. Heathwood Hall Archive.

14. Which, to complete the joke, was for Gasque's purposes synonymous with "the North."

15. To a reader sniffing merry mischief made at Q's expense, the author pleads *nolo contendere*—but hastens to add: Tally the adverbs in this footnote and the paragraph that spawned it, and take note of the beloved teacher's preferred allotment.

16. 1972 Yearbook, p. 7. Heathwood Hall Archive.

17. Reminiscence for 40th anniversary celebration, circa 1991. Heathwood Hall Archive.

18. Reminiscence of Nancy Boyle circa 1991, Heathwood Hall Archive. A Midlands farmer or stickler for detail might dispute her use of the term "red mud," but not the fact that mud of one variety or another predominated on the new campus.

Four: OUTWARD BOUND

1. Many weren't, but would be placed the following year. (1976 Yearbook, Heathwood Hall Archive.)

2. Board Meeting Minutes, Feb. 17, 1976. Heathwood Hall Archive.

3. Reminiscence for 40th Anniversary celebration, circa 1991. Heathwood Hall Archive.

4. It weighed more heavily on the average Black Southern family, for whom tuition represented 10.2 percent of median income as opposed to 8.7 percent in 1967. ("Consumer Income," US Department of Commerce, Series P-60, No. 118, March 1979, p. 60-62; "Consumer Income," US Department of Commerce, Series P-60, No. 55, Aug. 5, 1968, p. 5. Tuition rates courtesy of Heathwood Hall Archive.)

5. The US inflation rate in 1975 was 9.1 percent. One wonders how the polled students would have responded to a glimpse of 1980, when it hit 13.5 percent.

6. Teachers almost invariably experienced this day as the hottest of the year.

7. The thirst for this kind of engagement had been evident since at least 1974, during Heathwood's final spring semester in the mansion. Apparently attempting to up the ante for the school's athletic banquet that year, Devanny sought a "nationally known athlete" as a keynote speaker—expressing optimism to the Board that Heathwood would be able to book recent NFL MVP Award winner O.J. Simpson. This at a time when the school ended at ninth grade and had no football program. In the end they settled for Digger Phelps, then the head basketball coach at University of Notre

Dame. For Phelps it must have been a curious engagement: an athletic banquet gig at a school that did not yet have its own indoor basketball court. (Board Meeting Minutes, Feb. 14 and Apr. 18, 1974. Heathwood Hall Archive.)

8. The enrollment certificates, modeled after a program at Christ Church Episcopal School in Greenville, SC, was "in essence, the borrowing of capital from parents." (Board Meeting Minutes, Nov. 13, 1975. Heathwood Hall Archive.)

9. See Vitalis, chapter 3.

10. "Metal Prices in the United States Through 2010," US Department of the Interior, Scientific Investigations Report 2012-5188.

11. Board Meeting Minutes, Jan. 6, 1976. Heathwood Hall Archive.

12. Board Meeting Minutes, Feb. 11, 1988. Heathwood Hall Archive.

13. Reminiscence of Jim Gasque, circa 1991. Heathwood Hall Archive.

14. Board Meeting Minutes, Aug. 8, 1974. Heathwood Hall Archive.

15. Reminiscence of Nancy Boyle, circa 1991. Heathwood Hall Archive.

16. Walker remembers a smaller number of students at detention—"maybe 55," in his recollection, "but I'm sure she saw it as a ridiculously large number."

17. 1975 Yearbook. Heathwood Hall Archive.

18. Trustee Julian Hennig, for example, had requested a flooding report on the new campus property in 1973. (Board Meeting Minutes, July 13, 1973. Heathwood Hall Archive.)

19. NOAA, p. 18.

20. Board Meeting Minutes, Oct. 13, 1976. Heathwood Hall Archive.

Five: **PROGRESSIVE PIVOT**

1. "Headmaster Search: Student input," Oct. 27, 1977. Heathwood Hall Archive.

2. Frank, who distinguished himself at MAIS via efforts to expand African American involvement in Southern private schools (Wilson, chapters 1-6), would continue working with Heathwood on strategic planning into the 1980s.

3. Board Meeting Minutes, Oct. 13, 1983. Heathwood Hall Archive.

4. In interviews and conversations with the author, Shirley repeatedly invoked the famous declaration of William Faulkner's character Quentin Compson at the end of *Absalom, Absalom!* "Why do you hate the South?" asks the Canadian Shreve McCannon in a final query for his Mississippian college roommate. "'I dont hate it,' Quentin said quickly, at once, immediately; 'I dont hate it,' he said. *I dont hate it* he thought, panting in the cold air, the iron New England dark; *I dont I dont! I dont hate it! I dont hate it!*"

5. See for instance: Du Bois, W.E.B. *Black Reconstruction in America*, 1935 (first publication); Hackney, S. "*Origins of the New South* in Retrospect," *Journal of Southern History*,

Vol. 8, No. 2, May 1972, p. 191-216; Parfait, C. "Reconstruction Reconsidered: A Historiography of Reconstruction, from the late 19th Century to the 1960s," *Etudes Anglaises*, 2009/4, Vol. 62, p. 440-454; among many others.

6.   Wilson, p. 108.

7.   Board Meeting Minutes, June 23, 1977. Heathwood Hall Archive. The numbers Devanny cited do not match class rosters as depicted in yearbooks with exactitude, but yearbooks show that there were approximately 35 Black students in 1975-76 (when the school only went up to eleventh grade) and fewer than 15 in 1977-78.

8.   1980 Yearbook, Heathwood Hall Archive.

9.   Heathwood's 1984-85 Upper School English curriculum listed roughly 55 titles as supplementary reading. Despite an impressive breadth of authors, which ranged from Homer and Plato to Kurt Vonnegut and Albert Camus, the list included zero non-white writers. ("Curriculum 1984-85," Heathwood Hall Archive.)

10. Zimmerman, chapter 2.

11. Intra-squad scrimmages at UNC left Cooper with an indelible impression of Michael Jordan—and "a better understanding that I needed to become a dentist."

12. Szakacsi, who amassed 605 basketball victories and 206 baseball wins, became one of very few coaches to win state titles in four sports. Named the National Coach of the Year in 1986, he was later honored by South Carolina Governor Carrol Campbell, who declared February 2, 1988 "Cy Szakacsi Day." The annals of Heathwood sports history contain no instance of greater hilarity than the commemorative ceremony where athletic director Sal Anacito was to introduce Campbell to mark the occasion. "It is my honor to introduce the governor of South Carolina—" Anacito began, before stopping short. "The governor of South Carolina … the governor of South Carolina," he repeated, before turning to Szakacsi and blurting, within range of the hot microphone, "What's the governor's name?!" Whereupon it emerged that Cy wasn't sure, either. ("South Carolina great, Midlands coaching legend Szakacsi dies," *The State*, Nov. 9, 2019, B-2; oral histories, Heathwood Hall Archive.)

13. Shirley, p. 112.

14. Between 1977 and 1980, Heathwood's median SAT math scores lagged those of NAIS peers by 50 to 100 points. Heathwood's median SAT verbal scores typically exceeded those of peers by slightly smaller margins. ("A Blueprint for the Decade Ahead," May 6, 1982. Heathwood Hall Archive.)

15. These Upper School teachers were part of what Shirley regarded as a core group of "battle-tested veterans" who played a critical role in sustaining Heathwood through the flood and Earl Devanny's death. Others included Jimmy Walker (who became Upper School principal and associate headmaster), Middle School principal Al Newell, and Lower School principal Polly Nettles.

16. A 1977 Board resolution, passed unanimously, prohibited "fire arms of any kind" on campus "without specific permission." (Board Meeting Minutes, Sep. 8, 1977. Heathwood Hall Archive.) But in the 1980s and 1990s, permission was either freely granted or the prohibition was not enforced. For many students, it was regular practice on Fridays during hunting season to bring rifles and ammunition to school, even aboard school buses, ahead of a weekend spent hunting. There is no record of any accident or tragedy having arisen from this practice, perhaps on account of how seriously young South Carolina hunters were trained in the safety, maintenance, and storage of firearms.

17. "Land of Opportunity," *Wichita State University Alumni Magazine*, Summer 2005.

18. The bread-swapping baking enthusiast evinced considerably more interest in saluki dog breeding, for example, than in Gamecock football or the pennant race.

19. Backwards, in the dark, in a 1955 Chevrolet. "You had to watch all the tombstones, because the tombstones were right close to road. We had girls against boys, and we were determined that the boys were *not* going to win. So every week we would go out to the cemetery and practice. And then we had one big playoff. And the girls beat the boys, because we had so much time practicing and the boys didn't practice, because they were into football and things like that. So that's what we did for about an hour and a half on Friday nights … We kept waiting to see if somebody was going to come out of the graves to tell us to get out of there. But we never knocked down a tombstone." (Author interview with Sister Canice Adams, aka Margaret Adams.)

20. Gayle Averyt, who had been a driving force behind Heathwood's relocation to the Congaree campus, would continue to be an especially influential supporter of the school, both as a philanthropist and advisor.

21. Most often in mathematics, for which cognitive-developmental readiness is particularly variable among children.

22. One was the author of this book. The other knows who he is.

23. Author interview with Jennifer Coggiola Morgan.

24. Robin McLeod, incidentally, was a daughter of Nancy Boyle.

25. *"Caroline: I knew when I met you in Mrs. Heard's class last year that you would become a good friend. And you have! It's been a wonderful year together. Love, Mrs. Ashley."* Ashley's influence would stretch over the better part of two decades. For Class of 1994 alumna Jennifer Coggiola Morgan, her art room above the gym was a "place of solitude and comfort. I lived up there," Morgan said, "crying with her, laughing with her." A quarter-century later, she declared, "I can still smell the wax."

26. They were closely rivaled by Bill Cherry, who in addition to teaching computer programming across the age spectrum, coached soccer, golf, and (even after his formal retirement) bowling.

27. 1985 Yearbook, Heathwood Hall Archive.

28. The track, which was catalyzed by Susan Gibbes Robinson's philanthropy, was named in honor of her first husband. (Board Meeting Minutes, Sep. 17. 1987. Heathwood Hall Archive.)

29. This was dismantled in the late 1980s to make way for the Woodward track.

30. This rendition follows an (only slightly more straight-faced) account offered by Jim Gasque in a 1991 reminiscence. Heathwood Hall Archive.

31. 1987 Yearbook, p. 38. Heathwood Hall Archive.

32. Board Meeting Minutes, July 28, 1983. Heathwood Hall Archive.

33. Lipman, p. 17.

34. "Proposal for Computer Education," 1982. Heathwood Hall Archive.

35. Shirley, p. 108.

36. Disclosure: The author is their oldest child.

37. Not to be confused with Yancey McLeod III, the son of Robin and Yancey McLeod Jr. The elder McLeod was a trustee and land conservationist who enjoyed substantial local renown as a water-skier. His daughter, Margaret McLeod Willcox, would become Board chair in 2019.

38. Board Meeting Minutes, Apr. 23, 1986. Heathwood Hall Archive. It is also curious to note that the Board meeting of Nov. 8, 1984, where the Popps first introduced the idea of the auction, was the first whose minutes were produced on a dot-matrix printer. Although the auction emerged as one of the most successful fundraising events, it was not the only one. Another initiative was the Booster Club's "Heathwood 100," which combined a steak dinner with a raffle. As Tate Horton recalled, it was a lucrative and easy-to-run event—while it lasted. "One of my jobs, as treasurer of the booster club, was to mail out the invitations. It worked fine, for several years. Then, a few weeks after I'd mailed out the invitations for our next Heathwood 100, I received an official-looking envelope in the mail. It was a cease and desist letter from a postal inspector that cited a section of the US Code putting me on notice that using the mail to sell lottery tickets was punishable by fine or by imprisonment for not more than two years, or both. The Heathwood Booster Club immediately went back into the business of operating the concession stand at football games." (Author correspondence with Tate Horton.)

39. Cherry later gave this program, which cleverly withheld information in a manner that encouraged anxious bidding leaders to outbid themselves, to the Columbia Art Museum—which was one of many local institutions to adopt charity auctions in the wake of Heathwood's success.

40. NBRS Awardee Database, portal.nationalblueribbonschools.ed.gov/schools/history

41. "Education Department Honors Exemplary Schools," *Education Week*, Aug. 22, 1985.

42. Tuition at that level represented some 21.7 percent of the median income for Black families in the South. ("Money Income of Households, Families, and Persons in the

United States, 1987," US Department of Commerce, Series P-60, No. 162. Feb 1989)

43. Board Meeting Minutes, Dec. 17, 1987, Heathwood Hall Archive. Between 1976 and 1982, for example, Heathwood's expense per student had exceeded the annual tuition rate by as much as $365, or 25 percent. ("Blueprint for the Decade Ahead," May 6, 1982. Heathwood Hall Archive.)

44. Board Meeting Minutes, Dec. 7, 1987. Heathwood Hall Archive.

45. Board Meeting Minutes, March 26, 1987. In the coming years, Hammond's tuition would gradually gain parity with Heathwood's.

46. "Residential Finance," US Department of Commerce, 1990 Census of Housing, 1990-CH-4-1, p. 2-139.

47. In its 1982 "Blueprint for the Decade Ahead," Heathwood identified the Economic Recovery Act of 1981's sweeping tax reductions for upper-income earners as an expected driver of enrollment demand and tuition inflation. The rising number of two-earner families was noted as another contributor to this trend. ("Blueprint for the Decade Ahead," May 6, 1982, Heathwood Hall Archive.)

48. Board Meeting Minutes, Nov. 13, 1986 and Sept. 17, 1987.

49. Coalition of Essential Schools "Common Principles." essentialschools.org/common-principles/

Six: AN ESSENTIAL SCHOOL

1. School Profile 1986-87, Files of Heyward Robinson. "First semester grades may appear depressed as a result of adjusting to the new evaluation system," this document warned.

2. Coalition of Essential Schools "Common Principles." essentialschools.org/common-principles/

3. "Margaret Woods Meriwether obituary," *The State*, Apr. 13, 2013, A-7.

4. Venables freely dubbed his "Danny Madison Band" recordings for students who provided blank cassette tapes—as long as they were Dolby hi-bias cassettes and not ordinary consumer-grade ones. Years later, Class of 1996 alumnus and guitarist Van Anderson would occasionally cap a day of lawyering by playing gigs with Venables.

5. "Bob Shirley came up to me after about five years," Haarlow recalled, "and said, 'You're not really interested in pedagogy, are you? And I said, 'Bob, I'm really not. Give me a teacher who likes the kids and is somewhat intelligent, and he is going to help those kids learn. [For me] it's not about a particular structure.' And he said, 'What would you think about becoming head of the Middle School, where the pedagogy is not as important?'" Several years later, the two men essentially rehashed the same conversation—which led to Haarlow's redeployment as head of a counseling program. "I didn't quite fit the mold of what he was after as a Middle or Upper School head," Haarlow

said. "Most headmasters that I have known would simply release that person and get in a person more suitable to what he wanted to accomplish. But not Bob ... He valued me as a person." Haarlow saw the same pattern play out for a number of coaches and administrators. "He certainly released some people, but the ones he thought had value to the school, he molded something new for them," Haarlow said about Shirley. "To me, that is the way a leader should lead."

6.   1984 Yearbook. Heathwood Hall Archive.

7.   1987 Yearbook. Heathwood Hall Archive.

8.   1992 Yearbook. Heathwood Hall Archive.

9.   Board Meeting Minutes, Apr. 14, 1988. Heathwood Hall Archive.

10.   The COVID-19 pandemic forced a pause in 2020 and 2021.

11.   "State playoff," *The State*, Apr. 13, 1989, p. 100.

12.   Heathwood's home floor advantage had a second source: the thin carpet that covered the court. A generation of Highlanders wore carpet burns as badges of honor, especially during tryouts. A generation of opponents watched their bounce passes skid into their teammates' knees.

13.   Danforth also left, in the locked networking room where he carried out the crime, "an index card containing detailed instructions showing exactly how to fix it." Bob Shirley, who sniffed out the perpetrator, never forgot Danforth's response to his demand for the purloined room key. "Dr. Shirley," Danforth replied—in the headmaster's telling—"these keys have been passed down for years from one generation of students to the next. Are you seriously going to make *me* be the one who breaks the chain?"

14.   The son of a biomedical researcher, Terracio leveraged laboratory access into science fair posters that likely intimidated his teachers almost as much as his classmates.

15.   Board Meeting Minutes, Dec. 9, 1993. Heathwood Hall Archive.

16.   "Heathwood dominates, honors players," *Columbia Star*, Feb. 14, 2014.

17.   Wood recalled, almost as vividly, the team's visit to a Shoney's restaurant on the trip back to Columbia. There was a TV in the corner, and not everyone had seen the game tape yet. "We asked if we could put the VHS tape in the tape player. And as soon as the shot went in, everybody in the room jumped up and yelled like it was the end of the game again."

18.   "Heathwood Hall Queen of PAC Hill," *The State*, Mar. 3, 1994, p. 91.

19.   "Heathwood Hall's O'Gorman is Moving Forward," *The State*, Dec. 4, 1997, p. 61.

20.   The transition began with football, basketball, volleyball, soccer, and softball, which would be played within SCISA; meanwhile baseball, cross-country, track, and golf would be played within CISAA. (Board Meeting Minutes, Sep. 26, 1996. Heathwood Hall Archive.)

21.   "Private Schools Take Varied Paths with Similar Goals," *The State*, Mar. 9, 1995, p, 75. One of the advantages of CISAA, in Bob Shirley's view, was exposing Heathwood's

parent body to peer institutions in Charlotte, which were both "more progressive" and possessed superior campus facilities than peer institutions in South Carolina. "Heathwood can belong to the South Carolina league and never see a crane on any campus," Shirley observed to the trustees in 1996. (Board Meeting Minutes, Sep. 26, 1996. Heathwood Hall Archive.)

22. 1979 Yearbook. Heathwood Hall Archive.

23. Board Meeting Minutes, Apr. 13, 1989.

24. Board Meeting Minutes, Feb. 20, 1992. Heathwood Hall Archive.

25. Board Meeting Minutes, Mar. 20, 1997 and Jan. 8, 1998; 1998-99 Budget Notes. Heathwood Hall Archive.

26. Upper School tuition was higher than in the lower grades. Heathwood Hall financial records provided by assistant head of school Liz Summers, director of finance and operations.

27. The 1999 tuition represented 17.6 percent of the median annual income of white families in the South, and 27.6 percent of the median income of Black ones. (Historical Income Tables: Families, 1967-2019. US Census Bureau.)

28. Financial Aid Report, September 1999. Heathwood Hall Archive.

29. Compared to NAIS averages, Heathwood at this time aided a greater percentage of its minority students but offered them somewhat smaller amounts. Roughly half of Heathwood's minority students received some need-based aid in 1999, compared to 34.3 percent of NAIS minority students overall. But while 41.6 percent of NAIS aid dollars went to students of color, minority students received 28 percent of Heathwood's aid budget.

30. See, for instance, "Music Aids Causes, Fun, Activism: Students Protest Amid Jazz Festival," *The State*, May 28, 1990, p. 1B; "Club Membership Not Progress for Blacks," *The State*, Jan.10, 1991, p. 8A.

31. "The only thing we got was slavery and a little bit of Martin Luther King," she said. Apart from some books that Lark Palma recommended outside the classroom, Hurst failed to recall reading any book-length work by an African American writer at Heathwood.

32. In 2000 the South Carolina Senate voted to transfer the flag from the dome to a memorial to fallen Confederate soldiers on the State House grounds. In 2015, less than one month after the mass shooting of African American worshippers in Charleston's Emanuel African Methodist Episcopal Church by a white supremacist, Gov. Nikki Haley ordered the flag to be removed from the State House grounds entirely.

33. Shirley, Romero said, "always had my back"—and also pleaded with him to soften his stubborn refusal to utter the words "Yes, ma'am" and "No sir" to teachers. This etiquette was required of all students. But as a child who felt his dignity was under assault, Romero—who took no issue with addressing his elders as Mr. or Mrs.—recoiled from the use of terms that smacked of racial servitude. In time he overcame his

"immaturity" and adopted the deferential Southern custom. "I earned my way out of that reputation in seventh grade," he said.

34. Romero and Bakir both suffered falling grades during their relationship, and though each one conceded that youthful romance is a classic distractor, both were convinced that they were graded and policed more harshly once they began dating. Yet they also were quick to name Heathwood adults who became supporters and mentors. Daniel Venables, Bakir said, "was beyond nice to me." Romero would recall Sal Anacito's encouragement, Stan Wood's tough love, and Bob Shirley's moral support as central elements of his Heathwood experience.

35. He also found a new yardstick to measure his Heathwood education. Placed in AP classes in Spring Valley, he was stunned to be assigned textbooks he had already encountered years before at Heathwood.

36. "The head of a school is the first among equals," Shirley said. "That's a Greek idea. He has to be a leader among leaders."

37. Board Meeting Minutes, Dec. 7, 1989 and Feb. 7 1991. Heathwood Hall Archive.

38. Board Meeting Minutes, Sep. 24, 1992. Heathwood Hall Archive.

39. Mueller, p. 778.

40. The following year Cherry would oversee the completion of a "fiberoptic backbone" throughout campus. In September 1995 he used it to demonstrate the World Wide Web to trustees. (Board Meeting Minutes, Sep. 21, 1995. Heathwood Hall Archive.)

41. 1999 Yearbook. Heathwood Hall Archive. DuBose was not, however, the only bagpiper to grace Heathwood's campus over the years.

42. He left to become a lawyer. "Physically, mentally, emotionally," he reflected, "I've never had a harder job than teaching."

43. 1995 Yearbook. Heathwood Hall Archive.

44. Princeton University, for instance, which had accepted 25 percent of applicants in 1968, admitted 16.9 percent in 1988 and 13.1 percent in 1998. The trend would intensify for students who were entering Lower School in the late 1990s; Princeton admitted less than 7 percent of applicants in 2015. The sheer size of the Millennial generation, whose members applied to college in greater proportions than previous cohorts, drove similar trends at colleges across the country. ("Report of the Undergraduate Admission Study Group," Princeton University, Oct. 5, 1998; "Comparing Princeton '64 with Princeton '92," *New York Times*, June 7, 1989, p. B-6.)

45. The template for high school curricula and course sequencing was originally codified in 1892 by the National Educational Association's "Committee of Ten."

46. An internal 1998-99 study of ten peer institutions found that Heathwood was the lone school using an integrated math curriculum. (Report of the Education Committee, 1999-2000. Heathwood Hall Archive.)

47. Education Committee Report, 1999-2000. Heathwood Hall Archive.

48. Daniel Venables was the single greatest classroom teacher this author ever encountered. Nate Terracio's analogy described it best: "He would crack open a closet door, and you would see a piece of what was inside. And if you were like, 'Can we open the door further?', he was like, 'Sure!' Because the problem with math is that the door is infinite. You can just keep opening that door! And he didn't feel obligated to close it just because we were on a schedule and there were rules about what we were and weren't supposed to cover. All of us in that class, we would go off on tangents and he could bring us back home, so that we didn't totally go down a rabbit hole. But 30 minutes out of the 45 minutes could be spent on something that wasn't part of the lesson plan, and then he would tie it all back together."

49. One rather modest example was Shirley's 1994 decision to do away with the Order of the Tartan, a longstanding selective student society (see Chapter Four) whose vague entry criteria and elitist overtones conflicted with Shirley's egalitarian bent.

50. Such as through a $500,000 state grant longtime Heathwood supporter and advisor Gayle Averyt helped him obtain in the 1990s.

Seven: CAMPUS RENAISSANCE

1. This requirement could often be satisfied by courses in subjects like ethics or mythology, rather than explicitly Christian content.

2. Board Meeting Minutes, Sep. 12, 2002. Heathwood Hall Archive.

3. Students could also opt for a different holy text, such as a Jewish prayer book or the Koran, in consultation with chaplain Raven Tarpley. Often non-Christian students chose to receive a Bible nevertheless, having developed a spiritual or literary appreciation for it through Upper School courses in the New and/or Old Testament. (Author interview with Raven Tarpley.)

4. "Obituary of Elsie Lamar," *The State*, Dec. 3, 2002, p. B4.

5. Jacobsen, p. 343.

6. No teacher suffered relocation to the "trailer park" more reluctantly than Jim Gasque. After prying the room number off the door of his longtime pod classroom and affixing it to his trailer, he arranged for Pulliam Morris Interiors, one of Columbia's premiere interior decorating firms, to gussy up his new Room 17 with Roman shades and a custom paint job. Some years later he managed to reclaim his original classroom—moving the numeral 17 once again to restore the room-numbering system he had disrupted.

7. Board Meeting Minutes, May 17, 2001. Heathwood Hall Archive.

8. Ultimately the school retired $3 million of the bonds early to make up for a fundraising total that fell a bit short of the ambitious original goal. (Author correspondence with Liz Summers, director of Heathwood Hall finance and operations.)

9. "Trends in Family Wealth, 1989-2013." Congressional Budget Office, August 2016.

10. While the seventh grade continued to undertake a traditional camping trip in North Carolina, Lower Schoolers had the opportunity to pitch tents in the lawn between the Robinson Center and the ECLC.

11. "Burwell Manning obituary," *The State*, Feb. 6, 2005, p. B4.

12. Author interview with Lynn Manning Cooper.

13. Sharon Shirley, who was named the 2001 SCISA Lower School Teacher of the Year, was unrelated to Bob Shirley.

14. Melville's titular character is impressed by the Royal Navy from a merchant ship whose name provides one of the novella's most famous lines. As the smaller ship sails off, Billy Budd cries out: "And good-bye to you too, old *Rights-of-Man*."

15. All Kinds of Minds website: allkindsofminds.org

16. In broad strokes, regulatory enthusiasm has fallen most readily on girls' bodies and boys' hair. Heathwood permitted girls to wear slacks as an alternative to dresses in 1974, but banned jeans along with halter tops (Board Meeting Minutes, Oct. 8, 1974). By the early 1980s, to judge from yearbooks, Heathwood girls were doing more than their fair share to keep the denim industry solvent. Then jeans were banned across the board during the Hickman era. As of 2021, Upper School girls were prohibited from wearing skinny jeans, low-rise pants, and any type of dress, skirt, or shorts whose fabric ended more than 3 inches above the knee (Upper School Dress Code, 2021).

    Boys' hair attracted administrative and trustee attention at least as far back as the early 1970s, when Earl Devanny required it to be cut above the collar (Board Meeting Minutes, Oct. 8, 1974). But male locks began flowing more freely by that decade's end. The innovations of youth often put the school on the defensive, as in 1991: "Because some unusual haircuts have shown up on campus recently," Bob Shirley observed at the Nov. 14 Board Meeting that year, "the Upper School is working on a hairstyle policy." Yet to judge from yearbook pictures, boys with shoulder-length hair escaped that episode unshorn.

    Students occasionally took pains to make their voices heard. At a 1988 Board meeting, Josh Lieb, representing student council president Molly Curry, conveyed unspecified student objections to dress code enforcement, leading to a "compromise." (Board Meeting Minutes, Sep. 22, 1988.) The Heathwood Hall Archive also contains a thick stack of remarkably impassioned parent complaints about dress code policies and proposals. A full history of Heathwood's clothing and hair regulations could fill a companion volume to this general history.

17. Later Robertson found a garbage bag full of "wild" three-piece suits his father had acquired in the 1970s, and began wearing those to school, figuring that they complied with the code as it was then written. "It was my low-level, low-risk protest," he recalled. In 2021, as he prepared to move from Amazon's Alexa New Initiatives division to become a digital archivist for the South Carolina Department of Archives and History, his natural beard had reached New Testament dimensions. "Or maybe even Old Testament," he allowed.

18. Board Meeting Minutes, Nov. 16, 2000. Heathwood Hall Archive.

19. Board Meeting Minutes, Apr. 27, 2007. Heathwood Hall Archive.

20. AC Flora implemented an IB program in 2000; Lexington High School in 2006. International Baccalaureate, IBO.org.

21. Board Meeting Minutes, Sept. 21, 2006. Heathwood Hall Archive.

22. Board Meeting Minutes, Sept. 21, 2006. Heathwood Hall Archive.

23. Ben Lippen began high school operations in northwest Columbia in 1988, expanded into lower grades during the 1990s, and opened a second campus in 2006. The school requires families to be active members of an evangelical congregation and to affirm the school's doctrinal "Statement of Faith." (Ben Lippen website: www. benlippen.com/admissions/day-student)

24. 2004 Yearbook, p. 71. Heathwood Hall Archive.

25. 2001 Yearbook, p. 67. Heathwood Hall Archive.

26. 2002 Yearbook, p. 50; 2008 Yearbook, p. 54. Heathwood Hall Archive.

27. 2002 Yearbook. Heathwood Hall Archive.

28. "Heathwood wins state math meet for second straight year," *Columbia Star*, Feb. 6, 2009. Wee claimed the meet's top individual prize in both years.

29. "Crescent City school briefs," *New Orleans Advocate (Nola.com)*, Nov. 10, 2015.

30. 2008 Yearbook. Heathwood Hall Archive.

31. As evidenced by their disappearance from yearbooks, and the recollections of students and faculty.

32. 2008 Yearbook, p. 52. Heathwood Hall Archive.

33. 2009 Yearbook. Heathwood Hall Archive.

34. "Election Results 2008, *New York Times* (web), Dec. 9, 2008.

35. Opening day enrollment figures and financial aid information courtesy Liz Summers, Heathwood director of finance and operations. In the 2007-08 school year, Heathwood distributed $1.18 million in financial aid in addition to $426,000 in tuition remission for the children of faculty and staff.

36. Diversity figures courtesy Willis Ware, Heathwood director of diversity, equity, and inclusion.

37. "Heathwood Hall's Coach Daye to Retire," *Columbia Star*, Aug. 31, 2007.

38. Board Meeting Minutes, Mar. 15, 2001. Heathwood Hall Archive.

39. The boys and girls varsity basketball teams typically traveled together and played back-to-back games.

40. Wilson, to be fair, was not only surrounded by stronger teammates, but often sat out for long stretches in the second halves of blowout games.

41. In interviews for this book, Black students from the 20th century almost invariably reflected, without prompting and often at great length, on the ways that their racial identities made their experiences of Heathwood different from those of white peers.

Black graduates from roughly 2005 and later were much likelier to say that their racial identities mattered less than how long they had attended the school.

Eight: **ADVERSITY**

1. Board Meeting Minutes, Mar. 19, 2009. Heathwood Hall Archive.
2. Head of School Report: Admissions, Mar. 19, 2009. Heathwood Hall Archive.
3. The 2009-2010 tuition represented fully one-quarter of the median family income of white families in the South, and 38 percent of the median Black family's annual earnings. (Historical Income Tables: Families, 1967-2019. US Census Bureau.)
4. *NAIS Trendbook 2020-2021*, National Association of Independent Schools.
5. Liz Summers was emblematic of this trend. Having begun her banking career in Columbia in the 1980s with Bankers Trust of South Carolina, she "survived four mergers" to end up as an employee of Bank of America, a multinational headquartered in Charlotte, before she shifted to the education sector by joining Heathwood's staff in 2001.
6. "Kline Iron & Steel Company History and Reflections," University of South Carolina Libraries: Department of Oral History.
7. Improving South Carolina's public schools had been an abiding interest of former headmaster Bob Shirley, who in the 1990s pursued initiatives to grow the Coalition of Essential Schools network within the state's public education sector.
8. "And that's a very real fear," Jones said, "at every school that I've been to that attempted anything beyond sort of marking an edge to the map of LD services."
9. An outside audit of the athletics program eventually resulted in a passing grade. But leaders within the athletics department felt targeted, while some faculty members were vexed by what they saw as overattention to sports at the expense of academic issues.
10. Board Meeting Minutes, Mar. 18, 2010. Heathwood Hall Archive.
11. Faculty members widely echoed this view in interviews with the author. Some also acknowledged that Jones had faced faculty opposition during the selection process. Jones' entry was complicated by many teachers' longstanding affection for Anne Weston, who had been an internal candidate for the permanent head of school position.
12. After a pause for prudence's sake, the capital campaign for this building was largely completed during Chuck Jones' tenure.
13. Head of School Report, August 2014. Heathwood Hall Archive.
14. In a 2021 interview, Heath expressed joy about his coming transition back to full-time classroom teaching after several years as a mid-level administrator at the Christchurch School in Virginia.
15. Cameron's population has since declined, modestly, to 424 as of the 2010 Census.
16. Sasnett was also the 2008 SCISA Middle School Teacher of the Year.

17. South Carolina Wildlife Federation Board of Directors bio. (www.scwf.org/scwf-board)

18. *Brachydanio rerio*, better known as zebrafish, are a model organism for genetic research. Metzger and Prioleau earned an invitation to the America Junior Academy of Science meeting the following year in Vancouver, as did sophomore Maddie Norris, whose psychology paper won the Winthrop University Behavioral Science Award. Apologies to Highlanders who advanced to the AJAS in other years, who are too numerous to list here. (Heathwood Hall Honors Science Program website, archived page. www.heathwood.us/ourprogram/SCJAS11.html)

19. "Heathwood wins green neighborhood community group award," heathwood.org, Dec. 11, 2015: www.heathwood.org/heathwood-wins-green-neighborhoodcommunity-group-award-keep-midlands-beautiful; "Garden Profile: Thematic Gardens of Heathwood Hall," Heathwood Hall Archive.

20. 2013 Yearbook, Heathwood Hall Archive.

21. 2012 Yearbook, Heathwood Hall Archive.

22. 2014 Yearbook, Heathwood Hall Archive.

23. House Resolution 5139 of the South Carolina General Assembly, 120th Session, 2013-2014.

24. By the end of Wilson's second-grade year, she stood taller than her teacher Katherine Juk Draffin, a Class of 1994 alumna and former varsity basketball player who joined the Lower School faculty in 2002.

25. MaxPreps statistics (maxpreps.com) and "A'ja Wilson is on top of her game," *Carolina News and Reporter*, Sep. 30, 2020.

26. Game recap drawn from video highlights: "A'ja Wilson drops 37 and hits buzzer beater to win state championship," YouTube, www.youtube.com/watch?v=GOszTjqmR4I

27. At the beginning of the 2014-15 school year, the S&P 500 had nearly tripled from its 2009 low point.

28. "Trends in Family Wealth, 1989-2013," Congressional Budget Office, August 2016; "The Distribution of Household Income, 2015," Congressional Budget Office, November 2018.

29. In an interview with the author, Heath declined to explain the reasoning for his decision.

30. Gasque died on Nov. 1, 2014. "Heathwood teacher remembered for his love of literature, language," *The State*, Nov. 4, 2014, p. A-7.

31. American Crossword Puzzle Tournament standings, 2015. www.crosswordtournament.com/2015

32. Board Meeting Minutes, Apr. 23, 2015.

Nine: REVIVAL

1. Hinchey eventually took these questions and reflections to history teacher Sara Burrows, who built on them to create a Winterim program on Columbia's urban history.

2. In an instance of serendipity, Hinchey's path to Heathwood ran through Lark Palma. After interviewing Hinchey for a position at Catlin Gabel that eventually went to an internal candidate, Palma encouraged him to apply for an opening at Heathwood under Michael Heath.

3. "Flood of 2015 was a record-setter in SC," *The State*, Oct. 22, 2015, web edition.

4. "Father takes kids out of school in Confederate flag battle," *The State*, Oct. 7, 2017, p. A-1.

5. Willcox, who chaired the Board during the COVID-19 pandemic, faced her fair share of challenges.

6. "Heathwood's Rebel Flag Drama: Another side to the story," FITSnews, Oct. 5. 2017: https://tinyurl.com/5n7uu7je

7. Rox Pollard was not a Heathwood alumnus.

8. Clemson University Annual Reports: 1979-80 and 1989-90; Clemson Common Data Set, 2011 (https://tinyurl.com/cctn98x7); Clemson 2020 Freshman Profile (https://tinyurl.com/5n863yzc)

9. *NAIS Trendbook 2019-2020*, National Association of Independent Schools.

10. LEAP: Learning, Engagement, Action, Possibilities.

11. Heathwood Hall website: www.heathwood.org/ leap-week-offers-enhanced-opportunities-experiential-learning

12. 2018 Yearbook, p. 68. Heathwood Hall Archive.

13. 2017 Yearbook. Heathwood Hall Archive.

14. *Bouie v. City of Columbia*, 378 US 347 (1964).

15. "Middle School Launches Club Day," Sep. 24, 2019. Heathwood.org.

16. 2020 Yearbook, Heathwood Hall Archive.

17. Kids might be given a prompt like "Two students have been saying mean things to each other on Instagram Messenger. Do you think the school should get involved?" After selecting one of four possible answers, the class-wide results pop up on a screen to form the basis of an open-ended discussion. (Example courtesy Brice Spires.)

18. 2018 Senior Exhibitions program, Heathwood Hall Archive.

19. Guo also cited an excellent lunch in the Dining Commons during her exploratory visit to campus.

20. As a practical matter, this club was perhaps more Chinese than truly international, as a simple function of where most international students came from.

21. 2016-17 Annual Report. Heathwood Hall Archive.

22. 2018 Yearbook, Heathwood Hall Archive; "Heathwood Students Launch

Expanded Sally Salamander Tour of Columbia," heathwood.org; "Steel Drums on Main Mark Launch of Public Art Project," *Post and Courier* Web edition, Sep. 17, 2014.

23. "South Carolina Students Rise to the Top of NPR's Student Podcast Challenge," NPR.org, June 7, 2021. https://tinyurl.com/mryxxc7j

24. "Heathwood Hall Upper School Profile," Heathwood Hall Archive.

25. 2018 Yearbook, Heathwood Hall Archive.

26. "Heathwood Artists Display Work at Still Hopes," Apr. 11, 2019. Heathwood.org.

27. Summer Camp listing, 2021. Heathwood.org.

28. 2019 Yearbook. Heathwood Hall Archive.

29. 2015 Yearbook. Heathwood Hall Archive.

30. "Heathwood Students Earn Adopt-a-Stream Certification," Aug. 19, 2019. Heathwood.org.

31. Heathwood Hall mission statement, circa 2020. Heathwood.org.

32. "State of the School" address, Chris Hinchey, February 2021. Heathwood Hall Archive.

33. "Report and Recommendations of the Education Committee For Heathwood Hall High School," circa 1972-73. Heathwood Hall Archive.

34. "A Blueprint for the Decade Ahead," May 6-7, 1982. Heathwood Hall Archive.

Epilogue: PANDEMIC CODA

1. "Pneumonia of unknown cause—China," World Health Organization, Jan. 5., 2020.

2. "Trump says he trusts China's Xi on coronavirus and the US has it 'totally under control'", CNBC.com, Jan. 22, 2020: https://tinyurl.com/29hfy76u

3. Huang et al, "Clinical features of patients infected with 2019 novel coronavirus in Wuhan, China," *Lancet*, Jan. 24, 2020.

4. "China confirms human-to-human transmission of 2019-nCoV, infection of medical staff," *Xinhua News Agency*, Jan. 20, 2020.

5. "China coronavirus: Lockdown measures rise across Hubei province," BBC News (bbc.com), Jan. 23, 2020; "Public Transport In Wuhan Suspended Due to Coronavirus Concerns," NPR (npr.org), Jan. 22, 2020.

6. "1st U.S. Case of Coronavirus Confirmed in Washington State," NPR (npr.org), Jan. 22, 2020.

7. New York City experienced a particularly intense wave of COVID-19 cases, hospitalizations, and deaths in March and April of 2020. During the period between March 11 and April 27, the city recorded some 20,900 more deaths than would have been typically expected, the overwhelming majority of which were attributed

to COVID-19. "N.Y.C Deaths Reach 6 Times the Normal Level, Far More Than Coronavirus Count Suggests," *New York Times* (web), Apr. 27, 2020.

8. Executive Order 2020-09, Mar. 15, 2020, South Carolina Office of the Governor.

9. 2021 Yearbook, p. 24. Heathwood Hall Archive.

10. 2021 Yearbook, p. 31. Heathwood Hall Archive.

11. 2021 Yearbook, p. 32-33. Heathwood Hall Archive.

12. 2021 Yearbook, p. 28. Heathwood Hall Archive.

13. 2021 Yearbook, p. 34-39. Heathwood Hall Archive.

14. Author interview with Liz Summers.

15. Author interview with Liz Summers.

16. Quarantine length depended on the circumstances, but typically lasted 10 days. (Fall 2020 Reopening Notes and COVID-19 Protocol flow chart, Heathwood Hall Archive.)

17. 2021 Yearbook, p. 40-41. Heathwood Hall Archive.

18. "Richland One students start classroom returns on Oct. 12," *Post and Courier*, Oct. 7, 2020, Web edition.

19. "Richland schools will move entirely to online instruction following winter break," *Post and Courier*, Dec. 14, 2020, Web edition.

20. "Richland school districts preparing for five-day returns in March," *Post and Courier*, Mar. 3, p. A-9.

21. "Tracking Coronavirus in Richland County, SC," *New York Times* Web edition: www.nytimes.com/interactive/2021/us/richland-south-carolina-covid-cases.html

22. The national contest garnered 9,000 entries; Class of 2021 alumna Charlotte Hughes was named one of 130 finalists. "The Winners of our 2nd Annual Personal Narrative Contest," *New York Times* Web edition, Jan. 20, 2021.

SOURCES

BOOKS AND SCHOLARSHIP

Ball, Howard. *A Defiant Life: Thurgood Marshall and the Persistence of Racism in America.* New York: Crown Publishers, 1998.

Blum, John Morton. *Years of Discord: American Politics and Society, 1961–1974.* W.W. Norton, 1991.

Cohodas, Nadine. *Strom Thurmond & the Politics of Southern Change.* Simon & Schuster, 1993.

Dewey, J. "My pedagogic creed." *The School Journal,* 54 (1897).

Edgar, Walter. *South Carolina: A History.* University of South Carolina Press, 1999.

Edgar, Walter. *South Carolina in the Modern Age.* University of South Carolina Press, 1992.

Egerton, John. *Shades of Gray: Dispatches from the Modern South.* LSU Press, 1991.

Giordano, Ralph. *Pop Goes the Decade: The Fifties.* Greenwood Press, 2017.

Hawkins, J. Russell. "Religion, Race, and Resistance: White Evangelicals and the Dilemma of Integration in South Carolina, 1950-1975." Ph. D. diss., Rice University, 2009.

Howe Military School Class of 1958 Memory Book. No publisher, 2008.

Jacobsen, Annie. *Surprise, Kill, Vanish: The Secret History of CIA Paramilitary Armies, Operators, and Assassins.* Little, Brown, 2019.

Lipman, Matthew. *Harry Stottlemeier's Discovery.* Institute for the Advancement of Philosophy for Children, Montclair State College, 1974.

Lucas, Marion B. *Sherman and the Burning of Columbia,* University of South Carolina Press, 2000.

Maxwell, Angie and Shields, Todd. *The Long Southern Strategy: How Chasing White Voters in the South Changed American Politics.* Oxford University Press, 2019.

McNeill, Paul Wesley. "School Desegregation in South Carolina, 1963-1970." EdD diss., University of Kentucky, 1979.

Mueller, Scott. *Upgrading and Repairing PCs.* 14th Edition, Que Publishing, 2003.

National Association of Independent Schools: *Trendbook 2019-2020* and *Trendbook 2020-21*.

National Oceanic and Atmospheric Administration (NOAA). *Climatological Data: National Summary,* vol 27, no 10, October 1976.

Protestant Episcopal Church of South Carolina. *Report of the Committee on the Destruction of Churches in the Diocese of South Carolina During the Late War.* Charleston: Joseph Walker Stationer and Printer, 1868.

Purdy, Michelle. *Transforming the Elite: Black Students and the Desegregation of Private Schools.* University of North Carolina Press, 2018.

Quint, Howard H. *Profile in Black and White: A Frank Portrait of South Carolina.* Washington D.C.: Public Affairs Press, 1958.

Robertson, David. *Sly and Able: A Political Biography of James F. Byrnes.* New York: W. W. Norton & Company, 1994.

Shattuck, Gardiner. *Episcopalians and Race: Civil War to Civil Rights.* University of Kentucky Press, 2003.

Shirley, James Robert. *An Independent Voice: A Life of Lessons Learned in Schools.* Independently published (Amazon), 2020.

State of South Carolina. *Code of Laws of South Carolina 1952, Volume 7.* The Lawyers Co-Operative Publishing Co., 1952.

Steeley, Robert Joseph. "A History of Independent Education in South Carolina," PhD diss., University of South Carolina, 1979.

Thomas, Albert S. *A Historical Account of the Protestant Episcopal Church in South Carolina, 1820-1957,* R.L. Bryan Co., 1957.

Vitalis, Robert. *Oilcraft: The Myths of Scarcity and Security That Haunt US Energy Policy.* Stanford University Press, 2020.

Wilson, Zebulon Vance. *They Took Their Stand: The Integration of Southern Private Schools.* Mid-South Association of Independent Schools, 1983.

Works Progress Administration (Writers' Program). *South Carolina: A Guide to the Palmetto State.* Oxford University Press, 1941

Zimmerman, Jonathan. *Whose America? Culture Wars in the Public Schools.* Harvard University Press, 2002.

PERIODICALS

The Atlantic Monthly

BBC

Carolina News and Reporter

The Charlotte Observer (North Carolina)

The Christian Science Monitor

CNBC

The Columbia Record (Columbia, SC)

The Columbia Star (Columbia, SC)

Education Week

Etudes Anglaises

The Index Journal (Greenwood, SC)

Journal of Southern History

The Lancet

The Living Church (Milwaukee, Wisconsin)

The Los Angeles Times

The Montgomery Advertiser (Alabama)

National Public Radio

The New York Times

Post and Courier (Charleston, SC)

The Shreveport Times (Louisiana)

The State (Columbia, SC)

Time Magazine

Wichita State University Alumni Magazine

Xinhua News Agency (China)

ARCHIVES

Congressional Budget Office

Gallup Organization

Heathwood Hall Archive

Protestant Episcopal Church, Diocese of South Carolina

Richard M. Nixon Presidential Library: White House Central Files, Staff Member and
Office Files

South Carolina Election Commission: Supplemental Report of the Secretary of State to the General Assembly of South Carolina, Election November 5, 1968.

South Carolina Encyclopedia (scencyclopedia.org), University of South Carolina, Institute for Southern Studies

US Department of Commerce, Bureau of the Census

University of South Carolina Libraries: Department of Oral History

Walker Local and Family History Center, Richland County Public Library Digital Collection: Oral Histories from Richland Library

AUTHOR INTERVIEWS

Unless otherwise noted, all statements quoted in the text derive from the following interviews.

Sister Canice Adams (aka Margaret Adams), Mar. 16, 2021

Rhodes Amaker, July 1, 2021

Terrance Bannister, Apr, 17, 2021

Clinch Belser Jr., Mar. 1, 2021

Duncan Belser, Mar. 23, 2021

Freeman Belser, June 15, 2021

Mary Belser, Mar. 23, 2021

Rip Blackstone, Apr. 5, 2021

Davis Buchanan, June 29, 2021

Bill Cherry, Mar. 30, 2021

Lynn Manning Cooper, Mar. 24, 2021

Noble Cooper Jr., Feb. 6, 2021

Norrie Cooper, Feb. 26, 2021

Gayle Darby, Feb. 17, 2021

Jonathan Danforth, Apr. 9, 2021

Kevin Dickey, Feb. 23, 2021

Katherine Juk Draffin, June 29, 2021

Bernie Dunlap, Feb. 12, 2021

Walter Edgar, Mar. 19, 2021

Frank R. Ellerbe III, June 10, 2021

William Ellerbe, July 1, 2021

Amanda Finney, June 10, 2021

Betty Gasque, Mar. 12, 2021

Mary Bentz Gilkerson, Oct. 25, 2021

Kexin "Cassie" Guo, June 18, 2021

Ted Graf, Mar. 19, 2021

Bob Haarlow, Mar. 9, 2021

Scott Harriford, July 1, 2021

Leslie Haynsworth, Mar. 10, 2021

Michael Heath, June 16, 2021

Jay Hennig, June 29, 2021

Steve Hickman, Apr. 10 and June 21, 2021

Chris Hinchey, Apr. 14, 2021

Tate Horton, Apr. 26, 2021

Eveleigh Horton Huey, Apr. 27, 2021

Charlice Hurst, Jan. 19, 2021

Marshall James, Apr. 2, 2021

Chuck Jones, June 16, 2021

Yana Johnson, Apr. 16, 2021

Laurel Seibels Justice, Apr. 30, 2021

Nadege Vaultier Keller, Apr. 16, 2021

Jaelen King, June 4, 2021

Steven Larkin, Feb. 22, 2021

Josh Lieb, Apr. 29, 2021

Patsy Malanuk, Mar. 15, 2021

Timothy McKnight, June 18, 2021

Jennifer Coggiola Morgan, May 5, 2021

Suzanne Jackson Nagy, Apr. 16, 2021

Dan Palma, Apr. 30, 2021

Lark Palma, Apr. 6 and Apr. 30, 2021

Christian Pearson, Apr. 15, 2021

Michael Perry, Feb. 3, 2021

Sally Plowden, June 11, 2021

Will Prioleau, Feb. 19, 2021

Anna Ponder, Feb. 23, 2021

Joseph Pope, Apr. 13, 2021

John W. Popp Jr., Apr. 16, 2021

Carol Popp, Apr. 16, 2021

John Pulford, Mar. 31, 2021

Marsie Pulford, Mar. 31, 2021

Susan "Susu" Gibbes Woodward Ravenel, Feb. 15, 2021

Elizabeth Rice, Feb. 7, 2021

Joseph Rice, Feb. 7, 2021

Joseph Rice Jr., May 25, 2021

Grant Robertson, July 23, 2021

Stefan Romero, Apr. 27, 2021

Tyna Bakir Romero, May 19, 2021

Sarah Roth, Apr. 15, 2021

Robert Royall, Mar. 23, 2021

George Scouten, Apr. 14 and June 15, 2021

Robert Shirley, multiple interviews, 2020 and 2021

Elisha Sircy, June 7, 2021

Brice Spires, June 2, 2021

Liz Summers, Apr. 14, 2021

Raven Tarpley, June 3, 2021

Nate Terracio, May 2, 2021

Caroline Tinch, Apr. 13, 2021

Eliza Nixon Thorne, June 11, 2021

Charles Tolbert, June 28, 2021

Susan Milliken Umbach, Feb. 19, 2021

Daniel Venables, Mar. 18, 2021

Jimmy Walker, Feb. 10, 2021 and Apr. 7, 2021

Julian Walker, Apr. 11-24, 2021

Tong "Ray" Wang, June 18, 2021

Willis Ware, Apr. 16, 2021

Anne Weston, May 2, 2021

Jeff Whalen, June 3, 2021

Margaret McLeod Willcox, Mar. 24, 2021

Stan Wood, Mar. 30, 2021

Brionna Dickerson Zimmerman, Apr. 14 and June 4, 2021

THIRD-PARTY INTERVIEWS

Claudia Barton with Jimmy Walker, 2020

Scott Devanny with Jimmy Walker, 2020

Bernie Dunlap with Bob Shirley, 2020

Frank Ellerbe with Bob Shirley, 2020

Jay Hennig with Jimmy Walker, 2020

August Krickel with Jimmy Walker, 2020

Leighton Lord and Caroline Averyt Lord with Bob Shirley, 2020

Wade Mullins with Jimmy Walker, 2020

Rox Pollard with Bob Shirley, 2020

Robert Royall with Margaret Clarkson, 2020

Dick Stanland with Jimmy Walker, 2021

Jim Smith with Bob Shirley, 2020

Sarah Sturtevant with Jimmy Walker, 2020

Julian Walker with Bob Shirley, 2020

Anne Weston with Jimmy Walker, 2021

Margaret McLeod Willcox with Bob Shirley, 2020

ACKNOWLEDGEMENTS

Writing is a solitary and often lonesome labor. Especially writing a book. But the year I spent working on this project overflowed with help and guidance from an exceptional collection of people.

It started in May 2020 with a phone call from Bob Shirley. Having encountered a magazine article I'd written about the education and emotional development of adolescent boys, Bob got my number from my mother and called me out of the blue. It had been at least 20 years since we had last spoken. We talked for more than an hour. Penned up in our homes during the first wave of the pandemic, we carried on like two conversation-starved men enchanted by a sudden and boundless buffet. From observations about contemporary American boyhood and updates on one another's lives, we moved along to US politics and the lure of modern tribalism; 19th-century Russian novelists and Aristotle's notions about the good life; the concept of non-religious tithing and the mental world of medieval man; Faulkner and Baldwin and Vonnegut and the Stoics; and, inevitably, the evolution of progressive education. Then we hung up, waited three weeks, and did it all over again, picking up where we left off.

By and by Bob coaxed me into joining a biweekly virtual meeting of a committee that had formed to explore and develop an institutional history of Heathwood Hall. Why I agreed, despite a burgeoning allergy to video conference calls, only became clear to me later: I had unwittingly joined a sprawling network of men and women linked by a semi-conscious willingness, even eagerness, to do anything for Bob Shirley.

But what a pleasure it was to join that committee. It brought the satisfaction of reconnecting with old acquaintances: Bill Cherry, Stan Wood, Jimmy Walker, Margaret McLeod Willcox—all of whom would share time and insights whose value to this project is hard to overstate. And it introduced me to lovely new ones. Margaret Clarkson, a Heathwood parent and trustee whose knowledge of the school's early community reflects an intimate connection that stretches back to kindergarten at the mansion, shared it with a free-flowing generosity. Marshall James and Eliza Nixon Thorne proved to be exquisitely thoughtful alumni from before and after my own time, and I look forward to the day our paths cross in the real world.

Leslie Haynsworth merits far more than a single paragraph of acknowledgement—so I am happy to attest that her sharp editorial eye has refined and improved countless passages in this book. And beyond facilitating a rich research trip to campus in April 2021, she was a constant source of remote assistance in too many ways to count. She is a testament to Heathwood's ability to attract top-drawer talent across the entire staffing spectrum. So are Beth McMahan, Julie Benoit, Sarah Hughes, and most especially Nicole Morris, who not only found and scanned decades' worth of Board meeting minutes for my benefit, but has the sunniest voice and demeanor I have ever encountered when dialing an organization's front office.

How could I do justice to the heroic efforts of Brice Spires to advance this project? Copious references to the "Heathwood Hall Archive"—a term that conjures catalogued cabinets of neatly organized files—are surely the most misleading thing about this volume. In reality, Brice wrestled this "archive" out of an almost hopeless chaos of cardboard banker boxes crammed with an indiscriminate mishmash of vital documents and random clutter. Using a single-page scanner to share hundreds of images of the good stuff, he went beyond the call of duty again and again, undeterred by dead ends. During my research trip to campus, raising dust clouds from a caged file box graveyard in a room known as the Dungeon, I noticed a giant black safe whose door was locked behind a spinning dial. My queries surfaced a consensus among staff that the last possessor of the combination had died several years before. This hulking lockbox, which looked like something train robbers might blast open in a silent movie from the 1920s, was big enough to hold almost anything. I had to get into it. After I left for the day in defeat, word traveled to Brice, who fetched a crowbar and pried the door off its hinges. Alas, it did not contain the missing Board meeting minutes of 1965-70, but there could have been no more fitting display of the dedication and sinew that characterized his commitment to this endeavor.

Caroline Tinch was a Heathwood Hall junior when she volunteered to be my on-campus student assistant. She worked through the summer as a rising senior, mining more than three decades' worth of yearbooks with a perceptive sense of historical relevancy that was all the more impressive considering that her main academic interests lie elsewhere. I suspect that Heathwood cannot claim all the credit for her poise, but the school should take pride in whatever it has done to hone her proficiency.

This volume is better for the keen questioning and sustaining enthusiasm of John Cooper and Lynne Bowman. I am beyond lucky to be able to count one as a spiritual and literal fellow traveler, the other as my mother-in-law, and both of them as friends. I am indebted to Walter Edgar and Margaret Cooper Dunlap for their research assistance, and to Jason Popp for proofreading. I also benefited from Heathwood's institutional attitude toward this project, which combined broad cooperation with a grant of virtually unlimited scholarly autonomy. (To my knowledge the only records deliberately withheld from me were Board Meeting Minutes from after 2015, to preserve the confidentiality of trustee discussions that remain relevant to present-day school governance.) Suffering neither censorship nor interference, I was free to follow the facts wherever they might lead. The shortcomings in these pages are mine alone.

I interviewed 90 people on the record, and at length, for this project. Still more sat for interviews by Bob Shirley and Jimmy Walker. (A complete list can be found in the Sources section.) I cannot express sufficient gratitude to all of these former students, teachers, administrators, and trustees for the candor and nuance that marked so many of their reflections. Although spatial limitations kept me from doing any of these conversations full justice, I profited immensely even from interviewees whose quotations ended up on the cutting room floor. I beg their understanding, and hope that all of them find some value in the end result.

The most frustrating thing about trying to distill 70 years of history and dozens of distinct perspectives into a single coherent volume is the impossibility of giving every teacher his or her due. It will surprise few readers that certain figures came up again and again in interviews: Ms. Page, Jim Gasque, John and Marsie Pulford, Bob Shirley, Anne Weston, Bill Cherry. These and other names are strewn like confetti over the pages of this book. But a complete list of the teachers and coaches cited by former students would run much deeper.

If this were a book about my own personal experience of Heathwood Hall, it would have more to say about Amy Railsback Graf, who exposed me to authors, styles, and ways of thinking about writing in a manner that stretched my mind in directions no one else quite reached for. I would have revisited the day John Pulford coaxed me into an epiphany about fascist regimes that struck my brain like a lightning bolt I had called down upon myself—the subtlest trick of a teacher in total control of the intellectual voltage. I would have expounded at length about Rip Blackstone, who cemented a love of basketball that 30 years, half a dozen orthopedic injuries, two surgeries, and an ever-lengthening three-point line have yet to dent. And those are just three examples. I keep coming back to something my classmate and friend Nate Terracio told me. When asked to name an adult who made a difference to him at Heathwood, he replied: "The short list would be the adults that *didn't* make a difference." While working on this book I occasionally wondered what my teachers remember most vividly about me: intellectual curiosity, airy egoism, or blithe entitlement. I don't know. But I do know this: a great many of them helped the former trait vanquish the latter two—even if it took another decade to complete the conquest. But some work needs constant renewal, and I am grateful to those who tried to set my rudder straight when I did not always welcome another hand upon the wheel.

I undertook this project as one person among three who spent a full year working or studying full-time under the same roof. Exiled from my office just as Philadelphia children were sent home from their classrooms to endure the tribulations of Zoom schooling, I relied heavily on the patience and good humor of my two sons. Noah and Miles came to an illuminating realization about just how straightforward my profession is. Half of it consists of dialing up strangers and asking, "May I have your permission to record our conversation?" The other half is typing. That sounds a little irritating from the perspective of a fourth- and seventh-grader trying to stay tuned to whatever their teacher is doing inside a three-by-four-inch box on a computer screen. But I could hardly have wished for more companionable and good-natured home-office mates. I was also absolutely inspired by their resilience in a challenging year. They were fun to be with at the board game table, in the kitchen, on the basketball court, and out on a ramble. They continue to teach me so much: about generosity, open-heartedness, the art of enthusiasm, and other wisdoms of youth that are too often hidden by the blinders of middle age. Thanks for being patient with me, guys—and thanks for breathing some fun into the off hours.

Liz, when I try to consider all the ways you have made my writing, my thinking, my whole life better than I ever really imagined it could be, words fail me in a manner that you never have. Thank you for walking this road with me over the past year. I am excited to round the next bend together and greet a fresh view. Shall we stick by each other as long as we live?

Few observations are more trite than, "But for my parents, I wouldn't be here at all." Yet it is doubly true as far as this book is concerned. My search for a fulfilling life has been buttressed by their moral support for as long as I can remember. And it is to them, of course, that I owe my formal education, starting with the 13 years I spent at Heathwood Hall. In a life governed largely by outrageous good fortune, the smallest fraction of which I have done anything to deserve, that education has proven to be a cornerstone impervious to erosion. Thank you, Mom and Dad, for that and so much else.

ABOUT THE AUTHOR

Trey Popp is a 1993 graduate of Heathwood Hall. He lives with his family in Philadelphia, where he is a journalist and writer. He is also the author of *Black Mountain, Blue Field: A Journey Through Montenegro*.

CPSIA information can be obtained
at www.ICGtesting.com
Printed in the USA
LVHW111925080422
715714LV00020B/915/J

9 780578 339597